Praise for

The War That Made the Roman Empire

"Actium was one of the most important battles in history, and Barry Strauss brings this stunning maritime collision vividly to life."
—Admiral James Stavridis, USN (Ret), 16th Supreme Allied Commander at NATO and author of *Sea Power: The History and Geopolitics of the World's Oceans*

"The victory at Actium, Mr. Strauss argues in this splendid book, allowed Augustus to build an empire that lasted for nearly 500 years. The price was the destruction of the man who dared to oppose him, along with the woman for whom he had risked everything."
—Arthur Herman, *The Wall Street Journal*

"Barry Strauss has the rare ability of being able to bring ancient history to life in a way that is both profoundly learned and highly readable. . . . [Although] most readers will know the outcome of one of history's most famous battles, Strauss somehow manages to maintain the suspense and tension until its end. . . . Superbly recounted."
—Andrew Roberts, *National Review*

"[Strauss] is both a first-rate scholar who knows and understands his subject thoroughly and a fluent communicator. . . . A splendid account of those dramatic events and people who may not have been all that nice but were certainly never dull."
—Adrian Goldsworthy, *The New Criterion*

ALSO BY BARRY STRAUSS

Ten Caesars: Roman Emperors from Augustus to Constantine

The Death of Caesar: The Story of History's Most Famous Assassination

*Masters of Command: Alexander, Hannibal, Caesar,
and the Genius of Leadership*

The Spartacus War

The Trojan War: A New History

*The Battle of Salamis: The Naval Encounter That Saved Greece—
and Western Civilization*

*What If?: The World's Foremost Military Historians
Imagine What Might Have Been* (contributor)

Western Civilization: The Continuing Experiment
(with Thomas F. X. Noble and others)

*War and Democracy: A Comparative Study of the Korean War
and the Peloponnesian War* (with David McCann, coeditor)

Rowing Against the Current: Learning to Scull at Forty

*Fathers and Sons in Athens: Ideology and Society
in the Era of the Peloponnesian War*

Hegemonic Rivalry: From Thucydides to the Nuclear Age
(with Richard Ned Lebow, coeditor)

*The Anatomy of Error: Ancient Military Disasters and Their
Lessons for Modern Strategists* (with Josiah Ober)

*Athens After the Peloponnesian War:
Class, Faction and Policy, 403–386 B.C.*

The WAR That MADE the ROMAN EMPIRE

Antony, Cleopatra, and Octavian at Actium

BARRY STRAUSS

Simon & Schuster Paperbacks

NEW YORK   LONDON   TORONTO
SYDNEY   NEW DELHI

Simon & Schuster Paperbacks
An Imprint of Simon & Schuster, Inc.
1230 Avenue of the Americas
New York, NY 10020

First Simon & Schuster trade paperback edition March 2023

SIMON & SCHUSTER PAPERBACKS and colophon are registered trademarks
of Simon & Schuster, Inc.

For information about special discounts for bulk purchases, please contact Simon &
Schuster Special Sales at 1-866-506-1949 or business@simonandschuster.com.

The Simon & Schuster Speakers Bureau can bring authors to your live event.
For more information or to book an event, contact the Simon & Schuster Speakers
Bureau at 1-866-248-3049 or visit our website at www.simonspeakers.com.

Interior design by Paul Dippolito

Manufactured in the United States of America

1   3   5   7   9   10   8   6   4   2

The Library of Congress has cataloged the hardcover edition as follows:

Names: Strauss, Barry S., author.
Title: The war that made the Roman Empire : Antony, Cleopatra,
and Octavian at Actium / by Barry Strauss.
Other titles: Antony, Cleopatra, and Octavian at Actium
Description: First Simon & Schuster hardcover edition. | New York :
Simon & Schuster, 2021. | Includes bibliographical references and index.
Identifiers: LCCN 2021007113 | ISBN 9781982116675 (hardcover) | ISBN
9781982116682 (trade paperback) | ISBN 9781982116699 (ebook)
Subjects: LCSH: Actium, Battle of, 31 B.C. | Rome—History—Civil War,
43–31 B.C. | Cleopatra, Queen of Egypt, –30 B.C. | Antonius, Marcus,
83 B.C.?–30 B.C. | Augustus, Emperor of Rome, 63 B.C.–14 A.D.
Classification: LCC DG268 .S77 2021 | DDC 937/.05—dc23
LC record available at https://lccn.loc.gov/2021007113

ISBN 978-1-9821-1667-5
ISBN 978-1-9821-1668-2 (pbk)
ISBN 978-1-9821-1669-9 (ebook)

In memory of my parents

Contents

Maps

Author's Note

Ancient names are, with a few exceptions, spelled following the style of the standard reference work *The Oxford Classical Dictionary*, 4th ed. (Oxford: Oxford University Press, 2012).

Chronology

March 15, 44 BC	Caesar assassinated.
November 27, 43 BC	Second triumvirate established.
October 42 BC	Battles of Philippi.
41 to 40 BC	Perusine War.
41 BC	Antony and Cleopatra meet at Tarsus.
40 BC	Treaty of Brundisium; Antony and Octavia marry.
39 BC	Treaty of Misenum.
37 BC	Treaty of Tarentum; triumvirate renewed.
Spring to summer 36 BC	Antony's failed invasion of Media Atropatene.
September 3, 36 BC	Battle of Naulochus.
35 to 33 BC	Illyrian War.
Summer 34 BC	Antony conquers Armenia.
Autumn 34 BC	Donations of Alexandria.
December 31, 33 BC	Triumvirate expires.
March 32 BC	Antony and Cleopatra rally forces in Ephesus.
May to June 32 BC	Antony divorces Octavia.

Probably late summer 32 BC	Octavian declares war on Cleopatra.
About August 32 BC	Antony's forces gather on west coast of Greece.
Winter 32 to 31 BC	Antony and Cleopatra winter in Patrae.
March 31 BC	Agrippa captures Methone and kills King Bogud.
April 31 BC	Octavian crosses Adriatic Sea and encamps near Actium.
Summer 31 BC	Agrippa inflicts multiple defeats on enemy navy.
Late August 31 BC	Antony and Cleopatra decide to leave Actium.
September 2, 31 BC	Battle of Actium.
Late September 31 to July 30 BC	Antony and Cleopatra in Alexandria.
August 1, 30 BC	Antony commits suicide; Octavian enters Alexandria.
August 8, 30 BC	Octavian meets Cleopatra.
August 10, 30 BC	Cleopatra commits suicide.
Late August 30 BC	Caesarion is murdered.
August 29, 30 BC	Octavian annexes Egypt.
About 29 BC	Dedication of Actium Victory Monument.
August 13 to 15, 29 BC	Octavian celebrates triple triumph in Rome.
January 16, 27 BC	Octavian receives name Augustus.
August 19, AD 14	Death of Augustus.

The Eastern Mediterranean

| 0 | MILES | 400 |
| 0 | KM | 400 |

(BLACK) SEA

CASPIAN SEA

PONTUS

ARMENIA

Artaxata

CAPPADOCIA

COMMAGENE

Tarsus

Carrhae

PARTHIA

Phraaspa

Antioch

SYRIA

Euphrates

ASSYRIA

Ecbatana

Ptolemais

MESOPOTAMIA

Damascus

Tigris

JUDEA

Jerusalem

Masada

NABATAEAN
KINGDOM

PERSIAN GULF

RED SEA

Prologue:
A Forgotten Monument

Nicopolis, Greece

High on a hill astride a peninsula lying between the sea and a wide and marshy gulf, in a seldom-visited corner of western Greece, stand the ruins of one of history's most important but least acknowledged war memorials. Its few remaining blocks only hint at the monument's original grandeur. Just decades ago, these stones lay in an overgrown, Ozymandian jumble, but today, after years of excavation and study of the site, they reveal something of their original craftsmanship.

Today's visitor sees regular blocks of limestone, marble, and travertine lining a terrace on a hillside. It is easy to make out remaining parts of the original Latin inscription, its letters carved with classical precision. Behind those inscribed blocks stands a wall marked at regular intervals by mysterious recesses. They are sockets for inserting the butt ends of the bronze rams of galleys captured in the fight. The rams protruded from the walls at 90 degrees, thirty-five rams in all. It was a massive display, the largest known monument of captured rams in the ancient Mediterranean. It was a trophy in all its barbaric splendor, adorned with weapons taken by force.

Yet, as any Roman knew, victory lay in the hands of the gods, and they were not forgotten here. Behind the two walls, higher up on the hillside, stood a huge open-air sanctuary consecrated to the war god Mars and the sea god Neptune. There was also an open-air shrine to Apollo, the lord of light. A sculpted frieze commemorated the triumphal procession in Rome that had celebrated the victory. The massive complex covered about three-quarters of an acre.

The monument might be considered the cornerstone of the Roman Empire. And it was entirely appropriate that it was laid here in Greece rather than in Italy, six hundred miles from Rome. This monument recalled a battle that took place in the waters below: the Battle of Actium. It was a struggle for the heart of the Roman Empire—over whether its center of gravity would lie in the East or the West. Since Europe was the child of the Imperial Rome that emerged from this battle, the struggle was indeed a hinge of history.

The battle also represented two ways of war, the eternal choice in strategy between the conventional and the unorthodox. One side embodied what seemed to be a sure thing: big battalions, the latest equipment, and ample moneybags. The other side lacked funds and faced resistance at home, but it had experience, imagination, and audacity. One side counted on waiting for the enemy, while the other risked everything on an attack. One side sought a head-on battle, while the other chose an indirect approach. Even today these issues remain central to strategic debate.

On a September day more than two thousand years ago, the crews of six hundred warships—nearly two hundred thousand people—fought and died for the mastery of an empire that stretched from the English Channel to the Euphrates River, and would eventually reach even farther, from what is today Edinburgh, Scotland, to the Persian Gulf. One woman and two male rivals held the fate of the Mediterranean world in their hands. That woman, accompanied by her maidservants, was one of the most famous queens in history: Cleopatra.

Cleopatra was not simply the queen of hearts and the icon of glamor immortalized by William Shakespeare, but also one of the most brilliant and resourceful women in the history of statecraft. She was one of history's greatest what-ifs. She was at least part Macedonian, part Persian, and plausibly part Egyptian. Few women in history have played as big a role in the strategy and tactics of a world-defining war as did Cleopatra.

Her lover Mark Antony—he of Shakespeare's "Friends, Romans, countrymen," and the man who was Julius Caesar's eulogist in the Forum after the Ides of March and Caesar's avenger on the battlefield, at Philippi—was there fighting beside her. In the opposing camp stood Octavian Caesar, the future Emperor Augustus, and possibly the greatest imperial founder the Western world has ever known. Beside him was his right-hand man and indispensable admiral, Marcus Vipsanius Agrippa. Although often overlooked, Agrippa was the real architect of victory. He and Octavian were one of history's great leadership teams. Not present at Actium but there in spirit (she was in Rome) was Cleopatra's rival for Antony's affection: Octavian's sister and Antony's recently divorced wife, Octavia. Although usually thought of as deferential and long-suffering, Octavia was, in fact, a skilled intelligence operative, based in the bedroom of her brother's chief rival, no less. As often happens in history, seemingly minor players were major influencers.

Actium was the decisive event, and its consequences were enormous. If Antony and Cleopatra had won, the center of gravity of the Roman Empire would have shifted eastward. Alexandria, Egypt, would have vied with Rome as a capital. An eastward-looking empire would have been more like the later Byzantines, with even more emphasis on Greek, Egyptian, Jewish, and other eastern Mediterranean cultures than in the Latin-speaking elite of Imperial Rome. That empire might never have added Britain to its realm, might never have clashed with Germany, and might never have left the deep imprint that it did on western Europe. But it was Octavian who won.

About two years after the battle, around 29 BC, he dedicated the monument on the site of his headquarters and had it inscribed thus:

The Victorious General [*Imperator*] Caesar, son of a God, victor in the war he waged on behalf of the Republic in this region, when he was consul for the fifth time and proclaimed victorious general for the seventh time, after peace had been secured

on land and sea, consecrated to Mars and Neptune the camp
from which he set forth to battle, adorned with naval spoils.

The monument commands a panorama. To the south and east lies
the Gulf of Actium (today's Gulf of Ambracia); to the southwest, the
island of Leucas (today, Lefkada); to the west, the Ionian Sea; to
the northwest, the islands of Paxos and Antipaxos; to the north, the
mountains of Epirus. Anyone looking up, from land or sea, would
catch sight of the victory monument above.

In the plain below the monument, the victor established a new city,
as antiquity's great conquerors were wont to do. He called it Victory
City, or, in Greek, Nicopolis. It thrived during the following centuries
as a port city and provincial capital as well as a tourist destination for
a quadrennial athletic festival, the Actian Games.

Victory City: no sooner had the warriors departed than the myth-
makers descended. Was Actium a great victory? If acres of marble,
legions of administrators, and quadrennial sweating athletes and
cheering spectators said so, it must be true. The history books agreed,
but the victors wrote those books. Octavian, or Augustus, as he would
soon be known, would no doubt have approved of British prime min-
ister Winston Churchill's later dictum: the great Englishman said that
he was confident of the judgment of history because "I propose to
write that history myself." At Nicopolis, Augustus wrote it in stone.

He also wrote it in ink, in *Memoirs* that were famous in antiquity.
Although they influenced a few later surviving ancient works, the
memoirs themselves disappeared long ago. Those surviving works
offer only a sketchy picture of Actium, and they contradict each other
on important points. Nor do we have Antony's or Cleopatra's version,
although those too have left a few traces in the extant sources. The
real story is hard to recover.

Actium was a great battle, but it did not stand alone. It was the
climax of a six-month campaign of engagements on land and sea. A

brief but decisive campaign in Egypt followed a year later. Nor were all of the operations military. The war between Antony and Octavian involved diplomacy, information warfare—from propaganda to what we now call fake news—economic and financial competition, as well as of all the human emotions: love, hate, and jealousy not least among them.

Like so much of what we think we know about Actium, the city and the monument that loomed above it are part of a myth. It's a myth that's all the more insidious for being invisible. Actium has generated a rich heritage of scholarship. Scholars know that the real story of Actium is far from the official version, and even they have disagreed over time. In the 1920s a leading school of thought pronounced that Actium was a minor battle because it opened and closed so quickly, and only Octavian's propaganda made it seem significant. This school has since been supplanted, thanks to more recently discovered archae-ological evidence and reinterpreted literary sources. The new mate-rial transforms the war that killed Antony and Cleopatra and made Octavian into Augustus, Rome's first emperor, into an ever more in-triguing conflict.

Not only is the lore of Cleopatra among the richest in history, but she herself invested the contest with mythic meaning from the start, as did both Octavian and Antony. Octavian professed to be the cham-pion of the god of reason—Apollo—against the forces of brute and intoxicated irrationality. He claimed that the war was a battle of East versus West, of decency versus immorality, and of manliness versus a virago. Moderns tend to turn these categories around and see his propaganda as racism, orientalism, and misogyny.

What Antony or Cleopatra thought is harder to reconstruct, but the sources offer clues. Cleopatra asserted that she was the leader of the resistance against Rome, the champion of the entire eastern Med-iterranean rising in armed and righteous anger against the arrogant invader from the West. More than that, she claimed to be a savior, the earthly embodiment of a goddess, Isis, whose victory would usher in a golden age. Antony, proud to be her consort, claimed to be inspired by the god who had conquered Asia, Dionysus, and he saw Octavian as not merely jealous but impious. (That Dionysus was also the god of alcohol gave Octavian's propagandists an opportunity to moralize.) On a more mundane note, Antony considered himself the defender of the Roman nobility and the Roman Senate against a tyrannical up-start of low birth. Cleopatra felt that she was protecting the three-hundred-year-old House of the Ptolemies. And they both knew that they had to stop Octavian's challenge or risk losing everything they had built for themselves and their children.

This book re-creates the Battle of Actium in detail. It also offers the first reconstruction of the turning point of the war: surprisingly, an engagement that took place about six months before Actium. It offers a reconstruction of the operational details of Agrippa's dar-ing amphibious assault on Antony's rear that shocked the enemy and upended his expectations. Pitched battle captures the world's imag-ination, but often in the history of war, it is unconventional tactics, executed in surprise, that make a difference. In the case of the Ac-tium War, for instance, a key role was played by the deposed king of ancient Mauretania, fighting at a place called Methone, in an obscure corner of southern Greece. Antony, Cleopatra, and Octavian were nowhere to be seen.

Yet, as important as Agrippa's amphibious attack was, it needs to be put in the context of a nonmilitary struggle that was more than a year old when it took place. The real war was an integrated campaign involving not only armed violence but also diplomacy, political ma-neuvering, information warfare, economic pressure—and sex.

Antony emerges from recent biography as a more impressive fig-ure than previously believed. Source criticism, for example, has led to a new understanding of Antony's "Parthian Disaster" of 36 to 34 BC, a military campaign that was only indirectly aimed at the kingdom of Parthia and that, if not a success, was hardly a disaster. In fact, the diplomatic aftermath allowed Antony to regain much of what he had lost. Yet that success makes his failure at Actium puzzling.

There is a mystery to be solved. The Actium War ended in the new city on the plain and in the gleaming monument of bronze and stone on a hill beside the sea. But the conflict that gave rise to it began a dozen years earlier in Rome.

Part 1

THE SEEDS OF WAR

44 to 32 BC

Chapter 1

The Road to Philippi

Rome-Philippi, 44 to 42 BC

THE BATTLE OF ACTIUM IN 31 BC IS ROOTED IN events going back decades. But it grew in particular out of a war that started in 49 BC when Julius Caesar crossed the Rubicon River into Italy. By taking his legionaries and fording that small river, which marked the boundary between the military zone of Gaul and the civilian area of Italy, Caesar began a civil war that went on for four years. Caesar defeated all his enemies, and, in the end, he was proclaimed Rome's first-ever dictator in perpetuity. That created so much hostility among the old elite that a group of senators stabbed him to death in a meeting of the Senate in Rome on March 15, 44 BC. The infamous Ides of March.

The assassins thought that they were restoring the republic. Instead, they stirred up a coalition that eventually united Caesar's fractious followers. It took more than a year for those followers to come together, and then only after a period of armed conflict that left a legacy of distrust. In April 44 BC, however, their paths briefly crossed. It was the month after Caesar's murder, in a season of rain showers and blossoms but overshadowed by death.

April 44 BC found all the leading players of the next decade and a half in and around the city of Rome. They were the protagonists of the history not just of Rome but also of the Mediterranean. Mark Antony was one of two consuls, Rome's highest public officials; the other consul was a man of much less authority. Cleopatra was queen of Egypt, ruler of the wealthiest independent kingdom left in the Roman sphere. Octavian had just been named Caesar's son by posthumous adoption and heir to most of the dictator's enormous fortune. His older sister, Octavia, was married at the time to an important Roman politician and ex-consul, but that would change in the not-distant future. Finally, there was Agrippa, Octavian's boyhood friend and trusted companion, later to become his indispensable admiral. These men and women were about to scatter across the Roman world, but they would all meet again, most of them in battle at Actium, thirteen years later.

Cleopatra left Rome first. A combination of business and pleasure had brought the young queen to the city the year before. She was twenty-five years old. It was not unusual for foreign rulers to visit Rome on diplomatic matters, but Cleopatra was also Caesar's mistress. After their affair in Egypt, she gave birth to a son in 47 BC. Named Ptolemy called Caesar, he is better known by his nickname, Caesarion. Cleopatra claimed that Caesar was the father. The dictator himself neither acknowledged nor denied it. Perhaps she had brought the boy with her to Rome. In any case, it appears that she had just conceived another child by Caesar but suffered a miscarriage.

Cleopatra did not depart Rome quickly after the Ides of March. She wasn't just a grieving mistress but also a queen, and, for Egypt's sake, she needed to ensure the continued friendship of Rome's new rulers—whoever they would be. She had met many prominent people during her time in Rome, including Mark Antony.

One of Caesar's best generals, Antony was the scion of a leading but louche noble family. At thirty-nine, he was the old man of this company. A warrior at heart, he was also a gifted orator. He was no revolutionary and had more respect for the republic's traditional institutions than some, but he was hardly a principled conservative.

Aged eighteen, Octavian was a prodigy. On his father's side, he came from the Italian upper middle classes, but his mother's mother belonged to one of Rome's great noble houses, the Caesars. Julius Caesar was his great-uncle, and he took the boy under his wing after Octavian lost his father at the age of four. In autumn 45 BC, six months before his death, Caesar changed his will to Octavian's benefit. Caesar then sent the eighteen-year-old across the Adriatic Sea to take part in the organization of a new military campaign in the East planned for later 44 BC. At the news of Caesar's assassination, Octavian returned to Italy and, moving cautiously, eventually made his way to Rome, accompanied by an entourage including Agrippa. Now Octavian, undaunted by his youth, aimed for great power. Antony resented the young man's claim to have leapfrogged to the top because of Caesar's will, and he had every intention of thwarting Octavian.

Already in that Roman spring of 44 BC, these five men and women must have suspected that their ambitions would bring them together and apart. They could never have guessed, however, just how much drama lay ahead.

The Rise of Antony

In April 44 BC Caesar's assassins made their way out of Rome and Italy to the various provinces. Some commanded armies, some governed provinces, some raised money, some recruited allies—but all prepared for a coming struggle with the supporters of the late dictator. In Rome, politics coalesced around Antony and Octavian.

It isn't easy to tell Antony's side of the story. Most works produced after Actium championed the victor, Octavian, not the defeated Antony. With the exception of the coins issued in his name—indicators of his communications strategy—and a few quotations from his letters, Antony's own works are lost. What does survive is Plutarch's *Life of Antony*, the single most important literary source. A masterly writer, Plutarch (Lucius Mestrius Plutarchus, who died sometime after the year 120) is at his best in *Antony*, the most memorable of his fifty biographies known collectively as *Parallel Lives* or *Plutarch's Lives*. Shakespeare used the *Life* as the basis for his play *Antony and Cleopatra* in 1607. But Plutarch must be read cautiously. To begin with, he wrote more than a century after Antony's death. Although he consulted earlier sources from both sides, Plutarch tends to give the official, Augustan point of view. Besides, Plutarch has his own literary and philosophical agenda to advance, and he is not above creative invention from time to time. In the ninth volume of *Lives,* Plutarch paired Antony with Demetrius the Besieger (337 to 283 BC), famous as a great but failed Macedonian king and general.

Even more problematic is *Philippics*, consisting of fourteen speeches against Antony written in 43 BC by Marcus Tullius Cicero—a very hostile source. Various histories written in the Imperial era preserved information about Antony, and the most important are works by two Roman citizens from the Greek East: Appian of Alexandria (who died sometime around AD 165) and Cassius Dio of Bithynia (today's northwestern Turkey) (died about AD 235).

Reading between the lines will help to reconstruct Antony's version of history, but it can never provide as much detail as there is about his victorious rival, Octavian—soon to become Augustus, Rome's first emperor. Even two thousand years later, we study Augustus for lessons in everything from the rules of power to life hacks. Nobody looks to Antony for lessons except negative ones.

Antony was born on January 14, around 83 BC, into a noble Roman family. The Antonii were successful but scandalous, and Antony ran true to form. His paternal grandfather, Marcus Antonius, a distinguished orator and lawyer, served in the two high offices of consul and censor. Yet he was murdered in 87 BC during the civil wars between two Roman generals: Gaius Marius and Sulla (Lucius Cornelius Sulla Felix). It was said that his hiding place was betrayed by his weakness for wine. The old man's severed head was nailed to the speakers' platform in the Forum along with those of other prominent victims, including Antony's maternal grandfather and uncle.

Young Antony grew up in the shadow of their deaths and of his father's failure when given command of a campaign against pirates based in Crete. The father, also named Marcus Antonius, performed so poorly that people stuck him with the catty nickname Creticus, implying he was the "Conqueror of Crete." He died shortly afterward.

Antony's mother, Julia, remarried a patrician who was expelled from the Senate for immorality a year after serving as consul. In 63 BC he joined in what became known as the Catiline Conspiracy, a violent movement in aid of debtors and political renegades. Betrayed and arrested, he was executed without trial on the order of Cicero, who was consul. Antony loathed Cicero from then on.

Handsome young Antony was vigorous, athletic, charming, and charismatic. At various periods of life, he wore a beard in imitation of Hercules, the demigod claimed by his family as an ancestor. Yet Antony was no model youth. He grew notorious in Rome for drinking, womanizing, racking up debts, and keeping bad company before settling down some by his midtwenties. He studied rhetoric in Greece and excelled as a cavalry commander in the East between 58 and 55 BC. In his earliest armed encounter, he was the first man on the wall during a siege, thereby demonstrating great physical courage. Other military engagements followed. As an officer, he endeared himself to his soldiers by eating with them.

Antony served Caesar well in Gaul. Among other things, he was Caesar's quaestor—both paymaster and quartermaster—and he worked closely with his commander, to whom he then owed a lifelong obligation of loyalty (*fides*). Back in Rome in 50 BC, Antony held elective office as one of the ten people's tribunes, elected each year to represent ordinary citizens' interests. Antony tried to stop the Senate from replacing Caesar as governor of Gaul and ordering his arrest, but he was rebuffed and fled Rome for Caesar's camp.

Antony then emerged as a fine general and political operative during the civil war (49 to 45 BC) that followed Caesar's crossing the Rubicon. He received such important assignments as organizing the defense of Italy, bringing Caesar's legions across an enemy-infested

Adriatic Sea, and linking up with Caesar in Roman Macedonia. Antony rendered his greatest service at the Battle of Pharsalus in central Greece on August 9, 48 BC, where he commanded Caesar's left flank in that decisive battle against his rival, Gnaeus Pompeius Magnus (106 to 48 BC), known as Pompey the Great. When Caesar's veterans broke Pompey's ranks, Antony's cavalry chased the fleeing enemy.

Yet for all his success in the field, Antony was never the man in charge. In politics, he displayed less than a deft touch. He went back to Rome on Caesar's orders after Pharsalus, while Caesar spent the next year in the East. In Rome, Antony served as master of the horse (*magister equitum*), as a dictator's second in command was called. Antony now resumed with abandon his debauched lifestyle. The sources speak of wild nights, public hangovers, vomiting in the Forum, and chariots pulled by lions. It was hard to miss his affair with an actress and ex-slave who went by the stage name of Cytheris, "Venus's Girl," since she and Antony traveled together in public in a litter.

Both civil and military order in Rome slipped away from Antony's control. When proponents of debt relief and rent control turned violent, he sent troops into the Forum, and blood flowed—they killed eight hundred. Meanwhile, some of Caesar's veteran legions, now back in Italy, mutinied for pay and demobilization. Caesar returned to Rome in the fall. He put down the mutiny and agreed to reduce rents, although he refused to cancel debts. As for Antony, Caesar condemned him in the Senate but soon forgave him.

Antony now settled down once more by marrying again after a divorce, this time choosing a twice-widowed noblewoman, Fulvia. Of all the powerful Roman women of the era, Fulvia is in a class of her own. She recruited an army. Hostile propaganda claimed that she once even wore a sword and harangued the troops, but she did most of her fighting with words. A supporter of the common people through and through, Fulvia married three politicians in turn: first, the street-fighting demagogue Publius Clodius Pulcher; then, Gaius Scribonius Curio, a people's tribune who supported Caesar; and, finally, and most fatefully, Antony. His enemies claimed that Fulvia controlled Antony, which is not true. But this strong woman probably stiffened his spine, and she almost certainly shared with Antony the political skills learned from her two previous husbands. Antony benefitted from this partnership.

Antony played key roles in the events of the fatal year of 44 BC. At the festival of the Lupercalia in Rome on February 15, it was Antony who offered Caesar the crown, thereby shocking a crowd in the Roman Forum. Caesar refused ostentatiously—twice.

At a Senate meeting on the Ides of March, March 15, a group of assassins, led by Marcus Brutus, Gaius Cassius Longinus, and Decimus Brutus, struck down Caesar. Had Antony been sitting beside his colleague in the Senate House, he might have helped fight off the killers long enough to allow friendly senators in the room to come to Caesar's aid and save his life. But Antony was outside the building, where one of the conspirators had purposefully detained him, thereby leaving Caesar alone on the podium when the assassins surrounded him and struck.

Antony fled after the murder, supposedly having disguised himself by changing his toga for a slave's tunic—but that is surely slander. In the following week, he played a key role. He talked armed and angry supporters of Caesar out of attacking the assassins, who had taken refuge on the Capitoline Hill. He steered the Senate into a compromise, offering amnesty for the killers while maintaining all of the measures that Caesar had put into effect as dictator. He moved successfully that the Senate abolish the hated title of dictator. Then, he turned around and presided over a funeral for Caesar so emotional that it devolved into a riot, after which a mob murdered one supposed assassin (it was the wrong man) and intimidated the others, who soon fled Rome.

Antony was in the prime of life and ready to don Caesar's mantle as heir. But in his will, Caesar left his name and most of his fortune to Octavian. Antony no doubt burned about this. Octavian was kin to Caesar, but so was Antony—although only a distant cousin. Time and again Antony had risked his life for Caesar on the battlefield and sealed the great man's victories; Octavian had yet to draw first blood.

The Rise of Octavian

He was born on September 23, 63 BC. Or, rather, we might ask: *Who* was born then? Even Octavian's name is a matter of public relations. He was born Gaius Octavius. After accepting the offer of posthumous adoption in Caesar's will, Octavius became known as Gaius Julius Caesar Octavianus. Or, rather, he *should* have been called that, according to standard Roman naming practices. But he rejected the name Octavianus and insisted on being called Caesar. Most historians today call him Octavian, but only until he reached the age of thirty-five in 27 BC. From then on, he took the title by which he is best known today: Augustus. It is complicated, but so was the man behind the names.

His father, also Gaius Octavius, was wealthy and ambitious but not a Roman noble, and he came not from the capital but from a small town to its south. His ticket upward was his marriage to Julius Caesar's niece Atia Balbus, but he died suddenly when Octavian was four years old. Although Atia remarried soon, she entrusted Octavian to her mother, Julia, who raised the boy during his formative years. Julia's brother was in the process of conquering Gaul and becoming the first man in Rome.

While Octavian grew up, Caesar was revolutionizing Rome, which functioned as a self-governing republic. The people and the elites shared power through institutions such as assemblies, courts, elected officials, and the Senate. In theory, at any rate: in practice, the republic could not prevail against a conquering general like Caesar and his tens of thousands of loyal soldiers.

Rome, it seems, was caught in a maze of political, military, social, economic, cultural, and administrative impossibilities. Only someone who could tame Rome and its empire could bring lasting peace. Caesar was not that man. He was a conqueror, not a builder. But if Caesar couldn't do it, who could?

Caesar had no legitimate son of his own, although, as mentioned, he probably had sired Caesarion. Technically, Cleopatra might well have held Roman citizenship, as her father had, but what mattered in the public eye was that she was queen of Egypt. Instead of Caesarion, Caesar chose Octavian as his heir.

Burning with ambition, Octavian was a natural politician: intelligent, charming, and careful in his choice of words. He was bright eyed and handsome, with slightly curly blond hair. Short and somewhat frail, he was not imposing in his looks, but he made up for it by the force of his character. Although not a born soldier, he was tenacious, cunning, and brave, with an iron will. And he had his mother, Atia, who surely sang his praises to Caesar at every opportunity.

A prominent boy such as Octavian had many friends, one of whom turned out to be his lifelong right-hand man, Marcus Agrippa. Like Octavian, he came from a prosperous Italian family, although without any connection to the Roman nobility. What Agrippa had in abundance was practical genius. He was courageous, assertive, and, above all, loyal. To be sure, Octavian had a gift for making men follow him. In Agrippa's case, Octavian went to Caesar and got Agrippa's brother freed from imprisonment even though he had fought against Caesar. Agrippa was grateful.

Young Octavian had many mentors in developing guile: his mother, who talked her way into a hiding place with the vestal virgins when the Senate wanted to take her hostage; his sister, Octavia, who might have had something to do with her first husband Gaius Claudius Marcellus's surprising conversion from staunch enemy of her family to docile friend; his stepfather, an ex-consul who survived a civil war without taking sides; his great-grandmother and grandmother, who together gave detailed evidence in court of a female in-law's adultery, thereby sparing the man of the family, Caesar, from having to dirty his hands in public in order to get a divorce. And last but not least, there was Julius Caesar, one of history's masters of deceit. An hour at the feet of Caesar was worth more than a term of lectures by a professor. And Octavian spent many hours there.

First, Caesar favored young Octavian with a series of public responsibilities. The seventeen-year-old even marched in Caesar's triumphal parades in Rome in 46 BC, an honor usually reserved for a victorious general's son. The next year, Octavian made his way to his great-uncle's military campaign in Hispania. Caesar was sufficiently impressed by the maturing youth to change his will in Octavian's favor. The document was deposited with the vestal virgins in Rome and, as far as we know, kept secret.

Caesar planned a three-year war of conquest in the East. He aimed to conquer Dacia (modern Romania) and to avenge an earlier Roman defeat at the hands of the Parthians, who ruled much of southwest Asia and represented the only state strong enough to challenge Rome in the Near East. Caesar named Octavian, at the age of eighteen, his master of the horse, a position that offered visibility and networking opportunities. The expedition was scheduled to begin in March 44 BC. Around December 45 BC, Octavian left Rome at Caesar's command and, along with Agrippa, crossed the Adriatic to Caesar's military headquarters in what is today Albania. There Octavian made very useful contacts with legionary commanders.

But the Ides of March changed everything. In the aftermath of Caesar's assassination, Octavian returned cautiously to Rome, escorted by some of Caesar's partisans and soldiers.

After a slight hesitation, and against his mother's and stepfather's advice, Gaius Octavius accepted Caesar's adoption. He insisted from then on that he be addressed as Caesar. His mother was the first to do so.

Though only eighteen, Octavian aimed high. After an apprenticeship under Julius Caesar, he was ready to take the Forum by storm. It was as if by some sudden shock all the springs of an immobile Roman catapult had been set in motion.

Obstacles, however, abounded. Antony was consul and wanted to brush Octavian aside in order to claim Caesar's mantle. Conservative republicans, for their part, had no use for Caesar's adopted son, because they wanted to rid themselves of the dictator's legacy for good. Meanwhile, a throng of ambitious people wanted to use Octavian to advance their own agendas.

Caesar had been an extremely wealthy man. Octavian would have been one too, had he gotten his hands on that three-quarters of Caesar's estate that was promised to him in the will. He never saw it. Antony took control of most of the funds and refused to release them, claiming the need to investigate what part belonged to Caesar and what part belonged to the Roman people. Instead, Octavian got his money from several other sources: (1) Caesar's treasury in Apollonia (in today's Albania) to subsidize the Parthian War—or at least some of the funds, since Octavian claimed to have turned some or all of this over to the Roman state; (2) loans from Caesar's supporters, including bankers and wealthy freedmen; (3) money borrowed from his mother and stepfather; (4) the proceeds from selling or mortgaging his own property and that portion of Caesar's property that he was able to take over; and (5) the one-fourth of Caesar's estate that the dictator had left to Octavian's cousins. Not bad, but not in a league with the funds that Antony would later haul in from the East.

Octavian was a crafty young politician on the make, possessed of plenty of glowing prospects. He faced potential ruin or supreme possibilities, could he but master the situation. Master it he did. Octavian wasn't just a Roman, but a Caesar. Antony once dismissed him as a boy who owed everything to his name, but Antony missed the point. As far as Octavian was concerned, what mattered wasn't the name but the heritage it represented.

Octavian was motivated by a sense of honor, and that played well with the Roman public, who set high store on a person's reputation. In the Forum in November 44 BC, eight months after Caesar's assassination, he gave a speech while stretching out his right hand to a statue of

Julius Caesar and swearing by the hopes of attaining all his adoptive father's offices and honors. It was no small claim for a nineteen-year-old to aspire to the status of Rome's first dictator for life.

Around the same time, young Octavian succeeded in convincing two hardened Roman legions to defect to him from Antony. Octavian's agents mingled with the troops and exploited their anger at Antony's stinginess and harsh discipline. It was a lesson in how to leverage military from political power, and it was a skill that Octavian would hone to perfection over the years ahead. It was also a demonstration of Octavian's lack of interest in republican traditions. He had no legal authority to raise troops. His was, in effect, a private army.

But that did not prevent the last lion of the Roman Senate, Cicero, from supporting Octavian. The great statesman and orator had abhorred Caesar's dictatorship and supported his assassins. Cicero had little reason to trust Caesar's heir. But Octavian appealed both to Cicero's hatred of Antony, a personal and political enemy, and to the old man's vanity. With Cicero's endorsement, the Senate empowered Octavian and his private army to join the two consuls in a war against Antony.

In April 43 BC the two sides fought two battles outside of the city of Mutina (now Modena) in northern Italy. It was Octavian's first test by fire, and Antony claimed that his much younger foe failed and turned coward. But, if no natural warrior, Octavian was capable of courage. At the second battle in 43 BC, for instance, he picked up the eagle when his legion's eagle bearer (*aquilifer*) was wounded. In wars, as in all else, Octavian displayed self-control, down to and including moderate drinking, even in the rowdy company of soldiers.

As it happened, the two consuls died shortly after being wounded in these battles. Octavian now became commander of the Senate's armies. No surprise that suspicion has fallen on him for poisoning the consuls.

Antony withdrew, with his surviving troops in good order, and went over the Alps to Gaul, where he built up wide support among

Roman commanders. At this point, Octavian decided to switch sides, dropping his support for Cicero and the Senate as quickly as he had offered it a year earlier.

Octavian had concluded that the Senate was getting ready to turn on him now that he had defeated Antony and driven him north across the Alps. The Senate, in fact, preferred to support Caesar's assassins. Antony, for his part, made an alliance in Gaul with Marcus Lepidus, another of Caesar's former generals. This gave him control of nearly twenty legions—about as many as Octavian had. Knowing that Marcus Brutus and Gaius Cassius, two of Caesar's assassins, were raising an army in the East to fight Caesar's partisans, Antony and Octavian concluded that they were better off joining forces.

In autumn 43 they agreed to govern Rome jointly, along with Lepidus, and to divide control of legions and provinces. Their government was known as the triumvirate. A law was formally passed in Rome instituting it for five years on November 27, 43 BC. Rome still had a Senate and the various other instruments of government, but in practice, the triumvirs ruled.

Brutus and Cassius plotted to reconquer Rome and restore the old republic, with rule by the Senate and the traditional nobility. Fighting them would take money, which the triumvirate planned to raise through taxation as well as extortion. They published lists of political opponents and personal enemies—men whose property was to be confiscated and whose lives were forfeit; each had a price on his head. These were by and large supporters of the republic. Many fled, but in the end, more than two thousand of the wealthiest Romans died: three hundred senators and two thousand equestrians, or Roman Knights, the class just below the senators in wealth and honors. Because the lists were called written public notices, or *proscriptiones* in Latin, these attacks are known as the proscriptions. They lasted about a year and a half. Cicero was the most famous casualty. Antony wanted his archenemy dead. Octavian said later he tried to save Cicero, but, if so, he didn't try very hard.

During the triumviral era, Romans who wanted to survive raised the practice of hedging their bets to an art form. It was prudent to make multiple contributions to rival politicians, to be friendly to everyone, and to maintain a cautious ambiguity about one's opinions. Some withdrew from public life; a few had the resources and talent to turn to writing. Sometimes, of course, principle or ambition required boldness, and one had to take a stand, but not necessarily for long.

Rarely in history have so many powerful people changed sides so often—and with such good reason. There were three triumvirs, but only Antony and Octavian mattered. Every day, the balance shifted between them; today one up, tomorrow the other. Marcus Lepidus never had the power or the ambition of the other two. A "slight, unmeritable man," Shakespeare's Antony calls Lepidus, and history tends to bear this out. Octavian eventually fired him and sent him into internal exile south of Rome for the rest of his life.

Triumviral Rome was an age of traitors and turncoats, defectors and double agents. Most of the major actors themselves switched loyalties at one point or another, often more than once. It was the rare person such as Marcus Agrippa who throughout his career remained faithful to one leader: Octavian. Or Gaius Asinius Pollio, the general, statesman, and historian who refused Octavian's offer to betray Antony and join him. Few other Romans could match Pollio's stubbornness or his success as a survivor, come what may.

Philippi

The showdown with Brutus and Cassius came in 42 BC outside the city of Philippi in northern Greece along a great Roman road, the Via Egnatia. Antony and Octavian were cocommanders. Philippi had many of the elements of the great battles of the era. It was a Roman civil war. It pitted east against west. It was a land battle but would also be shaped by sea power. One side at Philippi was rich in money and supplies, the other rich in initiative. What made Philippi unique, however, was a cause. Every army of the civil wars claimed to be fighting in the name of the republic, but, with Brutus at its head, the eastern army at Philippi might actually have meant it. Brutus was not just a politician but an orator and philosopher who took his principles seriously.

As the great clash approached, Brutus wrote with courage and acceptance to Titus Pomponius Atticus, a close friend of Cicero's and a shrewd observer of politics. Either they would free the Roman people, Brutus wrote, or they would die and be freed from slavery. Everything was safe and secure, he added, except the outcome.

Before Philippi, Brutus and Cassius paid their troops with a coin commemorating the assassination. The obverse (head) depicts Brutus or perhaps an ancestor; the reverse (tail) shows two daggers, like the ones used to kill Caesar, as well as the "freedom cap" worn by former slaves. The legend says, "Ides of March." The symbolism is clear: the assassination of Caesar freed Rome. Rare and prized, it may be the most famous coin of the ancient world. Most of the surviving examples are silver. One of the few gold versions sold in 2020 for nearly $4.2 million, setting a record as the most valuable ancient coin ever sold.

Brutus's cause—and that of Cassius and the other men who had killed Caesar—was not free of tarnish. They called themselves Liberators, but they were oligarchs. Although they assassinated Caesar in the name of liberty, they meant the liberty of a few elite families to hold the reins of power over fifty million people. Caesar might have been a dictator, but he was also a champion of popular causes who chose Italian commoners and elites of the conquered provinces as his close advisors. Caesar cared little for elections or constitutional precedents. He rode roughshod over the institutions of the Roman Republic, but those institutions enshrined a narrow-minded ruling class. The future demanded change, and Caesar knew it. He was unable to usher it in, however, without haughtiness, violence, and dictatorship. The result was civil war. The decision to kill Caesar was selfish and shortsighted, but not without idealism. In a sense, Brutus really was the noblest Roman of them all, as Shakespeare's Antony proclaims.

The odds were good for Brutus and Cassius at Philippi. Their numbers were strong, and they had an excellent position on the high ground straddling the Roman road. Mountains protected their northern flank, and a marsh protected their southern flank. In Cassius, they had a very good commander, with Brutus by his side. They controlled the sea and stationed their fleet nearby on an island from which it could bring supplies to a port not far from their camp. Octavian and Antony, by contrast, had a difficult time shipping their troops across the Adriatic. One lucky break came courtesy of Cleopatra.

She had returned to Egypt in 44 BC. There she had to contend with the growing power in the East of the men who had killed Caesar. Despite pressure from Cassius and his forces, the Egyptian queen managed to avoid giving him the financial help that he wanted. She distrusted him both as one of Caesar's assassins and also as someone who was considering supporting the claims to Egypt's throne of her exiled sister, Arsinoe. As Antony and Octavian marched on Philippi, Cleopatra put together a small fleet and sailed to their aid. It sustained damage in a storm, and Cleopatra got sick—perhaps seasick—and had to return to Egypt. But the fleet had helped Octavian and Antony by drawing away the republicans' ships from Italy, thereby giving the two men the opportunity to transport some of their troops safely across the Adriatic. Cleopatra made plans to build a new fleet, but events outstripped her.

Once Antony and Octavian reached Philippi, they were short of food. They had twenty-two legions, many of them veterans, but the pressure was on them, while a well-supplied Brutus and Cassius could sit back and let the enemy starve. Brutus and Cassius were able to receive provisions from their nearby naval base. To nullify that advantage, Antony demonstrated audacity and resourcefulness. He began to build a causeway across a marsh, along with fortifications, in the hope of outflanking the enemy and threatening its supply route. At first Antony used the tall reeds of the marsh to hide his project, but eventually the secret was out, and Cassius began to construct a wall of his own to cut off Antony's project. On or about October 3 Antony attacked Cassius's wall and broke through into Cassius's camp, starting a major battle. Meanwhile, on another part of the field, Brutus was victorious and took Octavian's camp. Octavian, it seems, was sitting out the battle and, fortunately for him, had already fled. Later accused of cowardice, Octavian explained that he was ill at the time and had experienced a vision warning him of danger, and so he was able to leave before it was too late. Illness is plausible, since Octavian faced recurrent medical challenges.

Unfortunately, Cassius mistook the confused scene and thought that Brutus had been defeated, so he committed suicide. Cassius's death turned a battle that was a draw into a strategic disaster, as Brutus had insufficient operational experience.

Brutus distrusted the loyalty of Cassius's men, and he suffered at least one notable defection among his eastern allies. The general who represented the kingdom of Galatia in central Asia Minor (modern Turkey) switched to Antony. That general's overlord was Deiotarus, the elderly king of Galatia, who had changed sides twice before in Rome's civil wars. One wonders if, with his usual ruthlessness, Deiotarus had ordered his commander to pick the likely winner at Philippi.

Brutus let himself be talked into a lethal blunder. He could slowly have starved out Antony and Octavian while revictualling his forces by sea. Instead, about three weeks after the first battle, on October 23, Brutus attacked rashly and was defeated. In the aftermath, he committed suicide. Octavian, who had recovered from his illness, issued the bloodthirsty command to cut off Brutus's head and send it to Rome to place at the foot of a statue of Julius Caesar as revenge.

Antony was the architect of victory at Philippi—a thorough, decisive success. When he and Octavian divided the empire, it is no surprise that Antony got the richer part. He took the East and made his base in Athens, while Octavian ruled the West from Rome. Gaul, however, remained in Antony's hands. Lepidus, the least powerful of the three triumvirs, held only Roman Africa (roughly, modern-day Tunisia).

It certainly looked as if Antony had gotten the best deal. With its agriculture, artisanship, trade, and cities, the East offered an incomparable tax base. However, much of the East had been conquered by Rome only recently, which left Antony both diplomatic and administrative challenges—as well as an opportunity to extract "gifts" from local authorities in exchange for his support. Then there was the chance of completing Caesar's legacy and winning military glory and political power by waging war on Parthia. In addition to all that, as mentioned, Antony also maintained a base in the West in Gaul.

Octavian, rooted in the West, had limited funds. Yet his position in Italy allowed him to keep a deft hand on Roman politics. Besides, he had an incomparable asset: Italian manpower. Roman generals preferred overwhelmingly to recruit legionaries in Italy. His control of Italy left Octavian in a position to bargain. He could offer legionaries in exchange for wealth or the weapons that wealth could buy—above all, ships. First, however, Octavian had to master the situation in Italy, which was teeming with land-hungry veterans.

What lay ahead would test the skills of the wiliest political veteran. Octavian would have to rise to the challenge at the young age of twenty-two.

Chapter 2

The Commander and the Queen

Ephesus-Tarsus-Alexandria-Perusia, 42 to 40 BC

AFTER PHILIPPI, ANTONY WENT SOUTH TO ATHENS, where he spent the winter of 42–41 BC. In the spring, he crossed the Aegean Sea to Ephesus (in what is now western Turkey), a great port and religious center. He had two legions with him. His goals were to install his followers in power, raise money, and shore up support for the military campaign he had in mind. Before his assassination, Caesar had planned to wage war on the Parthians. Antony wanted to resume that conflict. Victory would give him both the material resources and the prestige to dominate Roman politics. But the war required careful planning, preparation, and fund-raising, and that would take time.

Antony proceeded to tour the wealthy cities of the East. He put loyalists in power and punished those who had made deals with Brutus and Cassius by demanding ten years' back taxes to be paid in just two years. Continuing eastward, he arranged the affairs of states in central Asia Minor to his liking. In one kingdom, Cappadocia, he had an affair with the royal courtesan Glaphyra, at least according to verses that Octavian wrote later. Glaphyra already had a son by her royal companion, and, upon the man's death, Antony appointed the lad as king.

Antony paid attention to his public image, peccadillos aside. He was probably already cultivating a reputation as the new Dionysus when the people of Ephesus hailed him with that title upon his entrance into town. Dionysus was a favorite god of kings and conquerors in the last centuries BC, and with good reason. Although nowadays Dionysus is associated with alcohol and revelry, to the Greeks, he was the god not only of wine but also of liberation and conquest. Myth said that Dionysus had conquered Asia, and Alexander the Great was thought to be following in the god's footsteps by invading the Persian Empire. More recently, King Mithradates VI of the kingdom of Pontus (who reigned from 120 to 63 BC), an enemy of Rome, identified himself with Dionysus. So did King Ptolemy XII of Egypt (reigned from approximately 80 to 51 BC), also known as Auletes—that is, "Flute Player"—nicknamed apparently for his performances in festivals. He was a friend of Rome, and Cleopatra's father.

Dionysus was preeminently a god of the East. Traditional Roman severity looked down on his wild rites and unfettered worshippers, yet, even in Rome, the god had his followers. Gnaeus Pompey (Gnaeus Pompeius Magnus, that is, "Pompey the Great"), for example, modeled his African triumph of 79 BC on Dionysus's mythical Indian triumph. Julius Caesar may have set up a shrine to Dionysus in his villa across the Tiber River from Rome. In a revealing link to the East, Antony also associated himself with Hercules, the demigod often connected with Alexander the Great.

Tarsus

From Cappadocia, Antony made his way south to the Mediterranean coast of Asia Minor. He made his headquarters in Tarsus, an ancient port on the route from Syria to the Euxine (Black) Sea. It was to Tarsus that he summoned Cleopatra. Egypt was a wealthy country, and it could offer the money and material support needed for a war against the Parthians. Besides, Antony wanted to call Cleopatra to account for the alleged support that she had provided to the cause of Brutus and Cassius during the Philippi campaign; she was, in fact, innocent. The queen came, but she took her time about it. When she did arrive in Tarsus, Cleopatra made one of history's most memorable entrances.

Upon her arrival, the queen switched from a seagoing vessel to a river boat for the row up the city's river. The Ptolemies had a tradition of traveling in splendid royal barges. Shakespeare's description in *Antony and Cleopatra* cannot be improved on:

> *The barge she sat in, like a burnish'd throne,*
> *Burn'd on the water: the poop was beaten gold;*
> *Purple the sails, and so perfumed that*
> *The winds were love-sick with them; the oars were silver,*
> *Which to the tune of flutes kept stroke, and made*
> *The water which they beat to follow faster,*
> *As amorous of their strokes. For her own person,*
> *It beggar'd all description: she did lie*
> *In her pavilion—cloth-of-gold of tissue—*
> *O'er-picturing that Venus where we see*
> *The fancy outwork nature: on each side her*
> *Stood pretty dimpled boys, like smiling Cupids,*
> *With divers-colour'd fans, whose wind did seem*
> *To glow the delicate cheeks which they did cool,*
> *And what they undid did.*

Shakespeare was following, in turn, the account in Plutarch's *Antony*, which compared Cleopatra to Aphrodite in a painting, with Erotes, or Cupids, standing on either side and fanning her, while her serving maids, dressed like sea deities, or the Three Graces, manned the rudders and the ropes.

It was an audition, and Cleopatra knew it, but the show was not merely theatrical. According to Plutarch, the people of Tarsus abandoned Antony on his tribunal in the forum and streamed to witness the arrival of Cleopatra's barge. Plutarch adds that a rumor spread: "Aphrodite had come to make merry with Dionysus for the good of Asia."

Cleopatra identified herself with Aphrodite—the Roman Venus—the goddess of love, as well as with Isis, Egypt's supreme female deity and a mother goddess who was popular around the Mediterranean. Her Egyptian subjects treated Cleopatra as Isis's earthly incarnation. Egyptians considered the god Osiris to be the equivalent of Dionysus, and Isis's consort.

By her grand entrance into Tarsus, Cleopatra was saying to Antony, in effect: "Propaganda is a force multiplier, my dear general. Join me in the role of my consort, Osiris-Dionysus, and the two of us can achieve great things." She then turned down Antony's dinner invitation, to insist that he come to her. Or so legend has it; it suited both players to keep the magnificent symbol of the barge on center stage.

Antony had surely met the queen before, either during his visit to Egypt in 55 BC or one of her stays in Rome between 46 and 44 BC. He was nevertheless impressed.

Cleopatra passed her audition. Antony followed Cleopatra back to Alexandria to spend the winter. Before their departure from Tarsus, the queen's troublesome sister was murdered in Ephesus's Temple of Artemis, where she lived in exile; whether she was killed at Cleopatra's behest or Antony's is debatable. In any case, Antony and Cleopatra became lovers and strategic partners. The result, which would shake the Mediterranean world, was a tribute to one woman's strategic genius.

Cleopatra

Cleopatra could ride a horse and hunt; she knew how to dignify a throne or go slumming at night in the poorer parts of town; organize a fishing party or build a battle fleet. She could charm a general or confound a philosopher, and she could do it in at least seven languages. She could mix poison like an alchemist or dole out tax breaks like a skillful politician. She stood over her children like a lioness and was devoted to her late father. She was the goddess of love and the goddess of motherhood in the eyes of millions, and both avenger and savior in the eyes of millions more. She reclined beside one lover in a round of banquets in the palace and felt the night air of the river on a cruise down the Nile with another. An hour in her presence, and a man would dream of cities and kingdoms. Generals and statesmen and rebel slaves had failed to defeat Rome, but she came closer than they. Her statue would stand in Egypt long after her death, but it also stood in Rome. Cleopatra fascinated even those who feared her, and she still rivets our attention.

Now twenty-eight, she had claimed Egypt's throne since the age of eighteen in 51 BC, ruling continuously except for a year or so of forced exile when her brother and coruler, Ptolemy XIII, along with their sister, drove her out. However, Cleopatra soon turned the tables: she raised an army that defeated her brother in a naval battle in which he drowned; we know what happened to her sister, Arsinoe. She is suspected of having arranged the poisoning of another brother with whom Cleopatra briefly had to share the throne. That left the devious queen to share her throne with her son, a toddler, which meant that, in effect, she ruled alone.

Cleopatra came from one of the proudest families in the ancient world. The Ptolemies descended from one of Alexander's marshals, and they had ruled Egypt for three hundred years. Their ranks included a number of strong women, of whom Cleopatra was the greatest. During the centuries they ruled, the Ptolemies were the worst of kings and the best. They were greedy, brutal, incestuous voluptuaries whose courts luxuriated in wealth as a sign of power. Among the Ptolemies, there were roly-poly kings and hard-drinking womanizers attended by eunuchs. Yet the Ptolemies were also astute politicians, careful administrators, and bold strategists. They were builders and visionaries. The Ptolemies presided over one of the most creative eras in the annals of ancient Greek culture. The dynasty built a capital city whose very name bespoke magic. Its lighthouse was accounted one of the Seven Wonders of the World, its library was unparalleled, and its pleasures were envied. Marbled, multicultural, teeming, and resplendent, Alexandria was the greatest metropolis of the Mediterranean, far outstripping in its grandeur, if not its population, a still rather provincial Rome.

The Romans had won an empire without building an imperial capital. They would correct that deficiency, thanks in no small part to the influence of Alexandria, but in Cleopatra's lifetime, they hadn't yet made Rome a splendid city. The forest of marble that, even in ruins, still impresses a visitor to Rome today did not exist in 41 BC. But Roman military power and diplomatic reach were at their zenith. So was a combination of arrogance, greed, and fear that, along with a political system that prized imperial expansion, made it hard for the Romans to resist new conquests.

Although Rome had left Egypt independent, its commanders had meddled in the country for more than a century, mercilessly squeezing Egypt's financial resources and humiliating its rulers with gusto. But the Senate didn't like it when an individual Roman enjoyed the prestige of conquering a rich new province, the way Caesar had when he triumphed over Gaul. And Egypt was the richest country in the Mediterranean. The senators preferred to let Egypt remain nominally free but serve in practice as a Roman bank account. It was a far cry from the grandeur that had been.

Who Was Cleopatra?

One cannot write about Cleopatra with ease. The literary sources are thin and scattered, and most of them reflect a hostile tradition laid down after Octavian became the emperor Augustus. The evidence of art and archaeology is copious and intriguing but about as straightforward as a sphinx. Of Cleopatra it may be said, as much as of anyone, that the real story never made it into the history books.

What, for example, did Cleopatra look like? Shakespeare imagined her as someone whom Antony could never leave because "Age

cannot wither her nor custom stale / Her infinite variety." But what
was her real appearance?

If only we knew. We have no bones to analyze. What we do have,
though, are images, carefully cultivated by Cleopatra, to put her in a
good light, or by her enemies, to do the opposite. She presented herself now as Greek, now as Egyptian, now as a feminine beauty, now
as an almost masculine woman, depending on the audience and the
purpose. Had Cleopatra succeeded, we would compare her to a grand
strategist like England's Queen Elizabeth I or to an empire builder
like Russia's Catherine II the Great. Instead, our Cleopatra is sexy
when we should be looking for majesty.

Literary sources, when not downright hostile, make clear that the
combination of Cleopatra's voice, appearance, and character proved
charming. They disagree, however, about whether she was incom-
parably beautiful or merely good-looking. She was apparently petite
enough for one man to carry her in bedding from a boat to a room in
the palace. She was robust and healthy enough to give birth to four
children.

Coins offer an intriguing but inconsistent set of images. Cleopatra minted bronze and silver coins throughout her twenty-one-year
reign. Those from the first dozen or so years (51 to 38 BC) show a
youthful and striking-looking woman in profile. She has high cheekbones, a long and pronounced nose, and a jutting chin. Her neck is
bare above the outline of a dress; on one coin of this era, a necklace
is visible, as are the folds of her dress. Cleopatra's hair is luxuriant
and pulled back into a chignon. It is carefully coiffed in the "melon"
style, with tight braids divided into sections like the skin of a melon.
She wears a broad diadem—that is, a ribbon that denoted royalty in
ancient Greek monarchies. On some coins, she has rolls of fat on her
neck, so-called Venus rings, a traditional feature of portraits of Ptolemaic queens, and which might speak more to Cleopatra's claim to
distinguished ancestry than to her real appearance. This Cleopatra is
generally attractive, but, what matters more, she is imposing. She is,

after all, a queen, and the reverse of the coin illustrates an eagle, for centuries the symbol of her dynasty.

A different image emerges from the coins issued in the second half of Cleopatra's reign (37 to 30 BC). These were years with Antony, and the coins, appropriately, show his face on the reverse side. These coins were meant to project the queen's power. Compared to the image on the earlier issues, this Cleopatra appears massive, stiff, and older. She has a thick neck, with an incongruous Adam's apple, and she wears a cloak normally worn only by men. This portrait of Cleopatra matches the equally massive image of Antony on the reverse. An inscription names her as "Cleopatra Thea [Goddess]," associating her with an ancestor who ruled both Egypt and Syria. Antony is named "Imperator [Victorious General] for the Third Time and Triumvir." In short, the coins present caricatures of power: a manly woman (Cleopatra) and a colossus of a man (Antony), and not an accurate portrait of either person.

About a dozen sculptures or engravings in the Greco-Roman style resemble the attractive if sharp-edged Cleopatra of the earlier coins. Only one or two are generally accepted by most scholars as really Cleopatra, while the rest occasion disagreement. A wall painting in Pompeii, Italy, depicting a queen and an infant might well be Cleopatra with the infant Caesarion, and it might be based on the most generally accepted bust of her.

There are also about a half dozen statues of a royal woman in the Egyptian style that some identify as Cleopatra. The subject of these statues wears an elaborate wig and a stylized cobra headband symbolizing sovereignty and divine authority. The facial features are those of generic images of Egyptian royalty. A wall relief on an Egyptian temple shows Cleopatra and Caesarion making offering to the gods. These stylized portraits look like something out of the pharaonic past and provide no information about Cleopatra's real appearance.

We are left with the impression of an image master. Cleopatra might not have minded the thought that she is still keeping us guessing.

Through her father, Cleopatra was at least partly of Macedonian descent. Neither of Cleopatra's grandmothers is known. Her paternal grandmother was probably not a member of the Ptolemaic dynasty because her children were considered illegitimate. She might have been Egyptian, Macedonian, or any one of several other nationalities. Cleopatra's maternal grandmother and grandfather are also unknown. Her ancestors included at least one part-Persian woman. There is good reason to think Cleopatra's mother was half Egyptian. The woman, otherwise unknown, seems to have come from a prominent family of Egyptian priests that had married into the Ptolemies. That might help explain why Cleopatra, alone of the Ptolemaic rulers, spoke Egyptian. Hence, although certainty eludes us, it is reasonable to conclude that Cleopatra was of mixed ethnicity and perhaps mixed race, too.

Regardless of Cleopatra's ethnicity, Octavian's propaganda treated her in a bigoted manner. When referring to the queen, he rolled out the various Greco-Roman stereotypes of eastern decadence: eunuchs, gilded couches, drunkenness, madness, and effeminacy. He accused her of corrupting Antony, who allegedly adopted such alien, barbaric, and effeminate customs as donning purple clothes, wearing a Persian short sword instead of the good Roman *gladius*, and even sleeping under mosquito netting. Octavian called her an Egyptian, while conveniently omitting her descent from one of Alexander the Great's Macedonian marshals.

Cleopatra certainly suffered from massive sexist bias. Octavian and his propagandists accused her of unmanning Antony. She enslaved him, bewitched him, softened him, corrupted him with sensual passions and with foreign customs, turned him against his fatherland and his friends, disgraced his navy by her feminine presence in the manly world of war, gave orders to his soldiers, and talked him into surrendering the Roman Empire to her.

Egyptians, however, saw her as a great queen. If one leaves aside the bigotry, the Greco-Roman sources show that Cleopatra was an able administrator and a brave and skillful politician. That tradition lives on in the work of medieval Arab historians, whose opinion of her is entirely positive. They also admire her as a patron of science who made her own contributions to knowledge: the "Virtuous Scholar" is how they sum up the queen. They claim that she was interested in medicines, cosmetics, and the science of measurement, and that she wrote about all three. The Greek sources certainly make clear Cleopatra's interests in drugs and poisons. A Greek tradition, too, records that she loved learning and literature.

There is no way to ascertain the degree of fluency that Cleopatra had in the minimum of seven languages that she is said to have spoken besides her native Greek, including Arabic, Hebrew, Syriac, and Persian. Although Latin is not mentioned, a linguist of Cleopatra's skill would surely have learned Latin, given all the time that she spent in Rome and with Romans.

Mastering the New World Disorder

Anyone wishing to survive on the throne of Egypt had to learn Roman politics. Cleopatra had begun her education as a teenager with her father, King Ptolemy XII. He had ensured his throne through obsequious support for Rome. Egypt became a virtual client state, which made the king so unpopular in Alexandria that he had to spend three years in exile in Rome. After sitting at her father's feet, Cleopatra then moved on to advanced studies with the most powerful man in the world: Julius Caesar, her ally and lover.

Caesar came to Egypt in 48 BC while fighting a civil war. He wanted money to finance his army. The ruling king was Cleopatra's brother, Ptolemy XIII. He denied Caesar's request, but Cleopatra, whom Ptolemy XIII had forced off the throne, gladly offered to pay in return for Caesar's supporting her claim to power.

She was smuggled into the palace in Alexandria, concealed, as one story has it, in bed linens that were then unrolled in front of Caesar. That would certainly have made an impression, but sound political reasoning rather than spectacle urged Caesar to prefer Cleopatra to Ptolemy XIII. Put simply, she was weaker. Her brother had strong popular support in Alexandria; Cleopatra needed Rome. Then too, she offered money. She would make a loyal client as ruler of Egypt.

Still, there was more than a little chemistry between the conquering general and the queen. It wasn't just the age difference between his fifty-two years and her twenty-one, or the glamor of her dynasty and its link to Alexander. Caesar and Cleopatra were two of the most brilliant individuals of their age. This was, one suspects, the rarest of things: the marriage of true minds. Within a month of their meeting, Cleopatra was pregnant.

Caesar had few troops with him, and they were hard pressed in urban combat in Alexandria. Thanks to his military and political skills, as well as to allies from Judea and Arabia, Caesar survived and won the day. Ptolemy XIII died in the fighting, leaving Cleopatra as queen.

When Caesar and Cleopatra were together, the parties often went on until first light. They cruised on the Nile on her state barge. Accompanied by more than four hundred ships and a large contingent of soldiers, they pushed south nearly all the way to Egypt's southern border, past majestic temples and exotic flora and fauna. The purpose of the journey was as much political, to demonstrate the muscle behind Cleopatra's rule, as it was sight-seeing and romance.

In summer 47 BC, after Caesar's departure from Egypt, Cleopatra gave birth to Caesarion. It cannot be proven that Caesar was the baby's father, but there is no good reason to doubt it. Caesar allowed Cleopatra to give his name to the child. He welcomed Cleopatra to Rome, installed her in his villa across the Tiber, and erected a statue of her in the new Temple of Venus Genetrix—Venus the Ancestral Mother— which was the centerpiece of the new Julian Forum, or Forum of Caesar, that he built in the heart of Rome. He celebrated Venus as his putative ancestor, the founder of the Julian line, and his personal link to divinity. There is reason to think that the statue showed Cleopatra holding her baby son, Caesarion. Possibly, the statue was meant to represent Cleopatra as the goddess Isis with her son Horus as well as, perhaps, Venus/Aphrodite. A statue of Cleopatra and Caesarion as part of Caesar's ambitious new temple precinct would clinch the argument that he acknowledged his paternity.

It used to be argued that Caesar could not have fathered Caesarion since he was no longer capable of impregnating a woman. The alleged evidence for this argument is that Caesar had no known birth child after his daughter, Julia, who was born probably around 76 BC. She died in childbirth in 54 BC. The emphasis, however, must be on *known*. We do not know if Caesar had illegitimate children through his many love affairs.

Caesar's very close colleague Gaius Oppius denied that Caesarion was the dictator's son and published a pamphlet to this effect after Caesar's death. Oppius, however, was a supporter of Octavian and surely had to follow the party line on this matter, which was that Octavian was the one and only Caesar. Plutarch expresses doubts about Oppius's reliability as a source. Other ancient writers also denied Caesar's paternity, but they too might well have been following the official story.

For his part, Antony got up before the Senate in Rome and affirmed Caesar's paternity, saying that Oppius, Gaius Matius (another intimate of Caesar's), and other friends all knew it. Strong words, if not proof positive, since Antony was hardly objective.

No doubt Caesar left his young mistress a wealth of knowledge. By the time Cleopatra began her affair with Antony, she might have been so conversant about Rome that she could have tutored him in the fine points of a praetor's edict (a praetor being a senior Roman official with judicial authority) or a marching camp's construction plan. Cleopatra was too good a strategist for Antony to ignore and too intelligent to bore him.

Stories of her wit are many, but here are two of the best. Cleopatra once took Antony fishing on the Nile. He had bad luck but didn't want to admit it, so he had his slaves dive into the water and secretly attach his hook to several fish that had already been caught. Cleopatra saw through it but played along while planning a prank for the following day. She invited her friends to witness the joke. After Antony let his hook down into the water, she had a slave swim below and attach to it a salted herring from the Euxine (Black) Sea. When Antony pulled up his line, everyone laughed at the sight; but before he could feel humiliated, Cleopatra said to him: "Imperator, hand over your fishing rod to the fishermen of Pharos and Canopus [both places in or near Alexandria]; your sport is the hunting of cities, realms, and continents." It was insidious flattery. Cleopatra claimed superiority in a mere workingman's art while conceding the stuff of kings to her man.

The second anecdote comes from the banquet hall of the royal palace. Knowing that Antony loved to feast, Cleopatra once bet him that she could put on the most expensive banquet ever, one that would cost ten million sesterces. That was ten times the price of a marble statue by the most celebrated sculptor of the day. When the day came, Cleopatra served an ordinary banquet to an unimpressed Antony. He laughed at its frugality. Then she ordered the second course. As arranged, her servants brought out a single glass filled with vinegar. Cleopatra took one of the pearl earrings that she was wearing—a stunning piece of jewelry. She dropped it in the vinegar, which dissolved the pearl. She then drank the bizarre cocktail. She was about to do the same with her other earring when one of Antony's generals and a bon vivant of the court stopped her and declared that Antony had been defeated. Modern experiments show that it would have taken about twenty-four hours for vinegar (acetic acid) to dissolve a pearl, but it would indeed have done the job. So, Cleopatra could not have won the bet on the spot, as an ancient writer claimed, but won it she would have.

Antony liked the good life, and he got plenty of it in Alexandria. Not that he spent a lot of time there before the Actium War: only three winters (41–40 BC, 36–35 BC, and 34–33 BC). Yet the sources make it seem as if he immersed himself in the great city. In part, this probably reflects Augustan bias, since Alexandria was synonymous in the Roman mind with decadence. Yet it is easy to imagine the glittering metropolis exerting a powerful impact on him.

Plutarch accuses Antony of squandering time there. He regales his readers with gossip that his grandfather got from a friend who was a physician in Alexandria to one of Antony's sons by Fulvia: tales of feasts of roasted wild boar and extravagant gifts of gold and silver beakers. Cleopatra supposedly kept Antony amused with a constant round of games and hunts and drinking parties, and sometimes by going slumming together in costume through the streets of town. The Alexandrians supposedly lapped it all up and said with glee that while Antony put on a tragic mask with the Romans, he sported a comic mask with them.

Antony and Cleopatra formed a "society of the Inimitable Livers"—that is, "a society of those with Incomparable Lives." Plutarch says they spent their time feasting each other at extravagant expense. The term *society,* however, often referred to a religious association, and it is possible that the Inimitable Livers was dedicated to worshipping Dionysus. No doubt alcohol was part of the ceremony.

An inscription dated December 28, 34 BC, refers to Antony as a Great Inimitable Lover, not Liver, or literally, "Great and Inimitable in the Things of Aphrodite." Since Cleopatra was identified with Aphrodite, the inscription adds to the evidence that the Inimitable Livers was a religious society.

Perusia

While Antony and Cleopatra enjoyed the pleasures of the East, Octavian fought a war in Italy.

He had faced a sensitive task after Philippi, one that was certain to stir up opposition. It was his job to confiscate massive amounts of civilians' land in Italy to give to military veterans, including a large number of Antony's warriors, as a reward for their service. Those slated to lose their land protested, as did senators who believed that they and not the triumvirs, who were still in power, should make such momentous decisions. The opposition found its champion in Antony's brother, Lucius Antonius, consul in 41 BC, and Antony's wife, Fulvia, who raised an army against Octavian. By helping to recruit troops, which was usually a man's prerogative, Fulvia made no small impression. Antony himself, in the East, stayed out of the struggle. He could hardly oppose the distribution of land to his veterans, and, besides, he gave Lucius's and Fulvia's raw recruits few hopes against Octavian's experienced legions.

The war that followed is known as the Perusine War (41 to 40 BC). It takes its name from the central Italian town of Perusia (known today as Perugia), a prosperous city in rich farm country, where most of the fighting took place. We will never know the full story of the war. The sources vilify Fulvia as rapacious and domineering—the opposite of the ideal Roman matron, who was supposed to be an obedient homebody. As for Antony, the record leaves his role murky.

What is clear is that Octavian drove his opponents out of Rome, and surrounded Fulvia and Lucius and their army in Perusia. At this battle, Fulvia received the backhanded compliment of having her name inscribed on her enemy's sling bullets along with rude references to her private parts. Fulvia wrote to Antony's generals in Gaul to ask them to hurry across the Alps to her aid, but to no avail. Octavian's forces won. If the report is true and not just propaganda, Octavian then massacred a large number of enemy leaders on the altar of the deified Julius *and* on the Ides of March. Octavian supposedly met every request for mercy with a cold "It's time to die." If so, it was out of character. Octavian seems usually to have been an old man's young man, all craft and deliberateness. His usual motto was "Make haste slowly."

Octavian might well have been suspicious of Antony's declaration of innocence for the armed uprising led by his brother and his wife. Yet Octavian needed peace with Antony, so he allowed Fulvia to escape, along with Antony's mother, Julia. He shipped Lucius off to govern a province in Hispania. The reason for this pacific turn was the rise of a new threat: Sextus Pompey, the only surviving son of Caesar's rival, Gnaeus Pompey. That threat now loomed over the relations between Octavian and Antony in the second half of the year 40 BC.

Three Treaties and a Marriage

Sicily-Brundisium-Rome-Misenum-Athens-Tarentum, 40 to 36 BC

IN THE SPACE OF FOUR YEARS, BETWEEN 44 AND 40 BC, Antony and Octavian quarreled over Caesar's inheritance, insulted each other in public, went to war and stood with swords drawn on opposite sides of bloody battlefields, and made peace by dividing the Roman Empire between themselves and a third, less-powerful partner—but only on the condition of ordering the judicial murder of thousands of prominent Romans. Octavian had to engage in two wars in and around Italy: one waged by Antony's brother and Antony's wife, the other, by Sextus Pompey. In both cases, Octavian was suspicious of Antony's role.

The Rise of Sextus Pompey

With his older brother, Gnaeus, Sextus Pompey had put together an army that nearly defeated Caesar at the Battle of Munda in Hispania in 45 BC. After their defeat and his brother's death, Sextus went into hiding, regrouped, and emerged as both a military and, especially, a naval commander. He was, in effect, a free agent, now graced by the republic with an extraordinary command, now proscribed and exiled, now back in favor, now fighting for his life again. In the violent era of the triumvirs, Sextus can fairly be called a warlord. Octavian vilified him as a pirate.

Sextus brought together an impressive assortment of tactics. In 40 BC he built a navy of about 250 ships that dominated the waters around Italy. He secured the island of Sicily as a base and made it a refuge for proscribed politicians, die-hard republicans, enemies of Octavian, and runaway slaves. He demonstrated the ability to cut off Rome's food supply at will. Yet he remained popular there—in part because of his support for the refugees from the proscriptions and in part because of Octavian's missteps. When it came to public opinion, Sextus held the moral high ground. Yet, for all his talk of restoring the republic, he was probably an opportunist who would gladly have accepted a part in the triumvirate had it been offered.

Sextus was eager for an alliance with Antony, who, in turn, encouraged him but without making a commitment. From his base in Athens in 40 BC, Antony chose the old republican Gaius Domitius Ahenobarbus, whose fleet now joined Antony. Judging by his coin image, Ahenobarbus was a hard man. His profile shows a lean, manly head, an aquiline nose, a receding hairline crowned by thick, curly hair, and a powerful neck. The most striking feature is a full beard pointing to family pride. Romans did not normally wear beards, but the family name, Ahenobarbus, means "red beard" or, literally, "bronze beard."

Together Antony and Ahenobarbus sailed to Italy with two hundred ships. They were joined by seventy ships from Sextus. Would they make war or peace with Octavian?

Antony had the stronger position, with a commanding military reputation, a navy, the adherence of the Senate, the eager courting by Sextus Pompey, and the secret support of one of Octavian's best generals, his friend Quintus Salvidienus Rufus. Salvidienus had risen from obscurity. After destroying a key city that had supported the rebels in the Perusine War, Salvidienus was rewarded with a command in Gaul. Yet now, for reasons unknown, he was ready to defect to Antony.

Antony wanted to land in the southern Italian port city of Brundisium, an important harbor on the Adriatic coast and the jumping-off point to Greece. But the town shut its gates to him and his forces. Antony assumed that Octavian was behind the move, so he laid siege to the city. He also landed troops farther up the coast, and they skirmished with Octavian's forces. Antony's men came out on top. The result might have been an all-out war, but the soldiers on both sides held back. They knew that there was neither booty nor glory to be had in a civil war.

Besides, Octavian, who had a reputation for playing dice, had recently rolled two winning throws. He ended his first marriage, to Fulvia's daughter Clodia, saying the marriage had never been consummated. Instead, he now married Sextus's sister-in-law, Scribonia, which raised the possibility of an alliance between the two men. Then, when the governor of Antony's province of Gaul died in the summer of 40 BC, Octavian crossed the Alps and took over the province's eleven legions—just as a matter of safekeeping for Antony, he claimed. Octavian had already taken away Nearer Hispania (eastern Spain) and Gallia Narbonensis (modern Provence, France) from Marcus Lepidus on the suspicion of negotiating with Sextus, leaving Lepidus only the Roman province of Africa. Octavian now dominated the Roman West.

Had Antony been tempted to cajole or bribe his men into fighting Octavian's troops, it was too late. Antony's legionaries mingled with their fellow Roman soldiers under Octavian, and both armies demanded peace. In the autumn of 40 BC, negotiators from the two sides hammered out the Treaty of Brundisium, which rearranged the division of the empire. Antony received strengthened authority in the East and the authority to wage war against Parthia, while Octavian gained in the West. Antony had to accept the loss of Gaul. Octavian also took Illyricum (the coast of the former Yugoslavia), although he had yet to conquer most of its freedom-loving inhabitants. The dividing line between the two men's territories was located at the city of

Scodra (now Shkodër, in northern Albania). Antony also gave up his understanding, such as it was, with Sextus. Octavian received authority to make war on Sextus, although the possibility of an agreement was left open. In principle, Antony could continue to recruit legionaries in Italy. In practice, however, Octavian now controlled military enrollment there.

It was a significant victory for Octavian, but not a strategic one. The East was by far the wealthier part of the empire, as mentioned, making it an advantageous base. Success against Parthia, should he achieve it, would raise Antony's reputation to new heights; Italy would be Octavian's only if he could solve the problem of Sextus Pompey.

Unfortunately for Salvidienus, he was expendable. Antony betrayed him to Octavian. The Senate declared Salvidienus a public enemy, and his death followed, although it is unclear whether he was executed or committed suicide.

The triumvirs made a treaty, but they decided to take out an insurance policy, as it were: a marriage to unite the two families.

The Union of Antony and Octavia

Octavian and Antony agreed at Brundisium that Antony would marry Octavia, Octavian's sister. Bride and groom were both recently widowed. Fulvia had died in exile in Greece, while Octavia's husband, Gaius Claudius Marcellus, died in Italy. The union offered advantages to each of the two rivals. For Antony, it meant the chance to produce a son and heir who might unite the power of both families. For Octavian, it meant a priceless source of information from a sister in the enemy camp, as well as the chance for Octavia to shape Antony's actions. It was standard procedure in the Roman nobility to marry the daughter of a rival house in order to patch up a political quarrel. Then, too, there is what we might now call the *Godfather* principle: keep your friends close and your enemies closer. Given their past record of recrimination, war, and partnership in pursuit of murder, Antony and Octavian's decision to become brothers-in-law has all the sincerity of a Hollywood kiss or a gangland embrace.

Custom dictated that men negotiate marriage; in the absence of a living father, it was appropriate for Octavian to do so. But Roman law required that both prospective bride and groom consent, so we can be sure that Octavian consulted Octavia, both because he loved and respected his older sister and because a woman of her intelligence and independence would demand respect.

Historians assume that the match was Octavian's or Antony's idea, but it might have been Octavia who thought of it, although the information that Antony was a widower probably reached Octavia later than it reached Antony and Octavian. But she might have thought of the match earlier in the year, after Marcellus died. She and Octavian might have discussed the possibility of Antony divorcing Fulvia (which turned out to be unnecessary when she, too, died). It's even possible that Octavian obtained his sister's approval in principle before he left home to meet Antony. But we don't know.

The news had probably reached Rome that Antony had followed Cleopatra back to Egypt for the winter and that they had become lovers. She became pregnant then and delivered twins at some point during autumn 40 BC: a boy, Alexander Helios, and a girl, Cleopatra Selene. Even if Octavia and her brother had been aware of the twins, that probably would not have deterred them. The marriage was an affair of state, not a matter of the heart.

Octavia had learned the rules of political marriage from the women of her family. From her mother, who had been forced to start over after losing her husband while raising young children, she gained survival skills. From her great-grandmother, Aurelia Cotta, and her grandmother, Julia, she might have learned about the heritage of the family of the Caesars. Then there was Caesar's wife, Calpurnia. Daughter of a consul, she knew Roman politics as well as any man. Calpurnia had a nose for trouble: witness her imploring Caesar to stay away from the Senate on the Ides of March, a warning that he ignored. Nor did she make a fuss about her husband's various mistresses or his illegitimate child. Calpurnia might have taught Octavia a thing or two.

At the time she married Antony, Octavia was already a veteran of political marriage. Around 55 BC, as a very young woman, Octavia wed Claudius Marcellus, a prominent Roman politician from a noble family. At the time, she was no more than fourteen years old, but Roman women were allowed to marry as young as twelve. Marcellus was allied with Gnaeus Pompey, Caesar's adversary, but this was just another example of the union of rivals. Indeed, at the time, Pompey was married to Caesar's daughter, Julia.

About a year after Octavia's marriage to Marcellus, Julia died. In order to safeguard his political alliance with Pompey, Caesar offered him Octavia. He was prepared to have her divorce Marcellus. What Octavia thought is not recorded. In any case, Pompey declined. The prospect could hardly have endeared Caesar to Marcellus. As consul in 50 BC, Marcellus emerged as one of the leaders among Caesar's opponents in the Roman Senate. When civil war began, at first Marcellus fled Rome to join Pompey, but then he hesitated. He stayed in his villa near Naples. After a few months, he changed sides.

We can only wonder whether Octavia played a role in his decision. But after choosing to support Caesar, Marcellus remained with his faction after the dictator's assassination in 44 BC, perhaps becoming an intimate of Octavian's. As for Octavia, she bore Marcellus a son and two daughters, but she was not simply a stay-at-home mother. She was swept up at least twice in the turbulent politics in the years after Caesar's assassination.

In summer 43 BC Octavia and her mother were in Rome when Octavian sent an ultimatum to the Senate. The two women had to hide from their enemies in the Temple of Vesta before Octavian and his legions arrived in Rome to liberate them. Soon afterward, his mother, Atia, died. In previous years, Octavian had received career advice from his mother. Now, with her gone, perhaps Octavia stepped in to fill Atia's role. She was about twenty-six; Octavian, twenty. It was said afterward that he was always excessively fond of his sister.

The proscriptions saw Octavia involved in two mediation efforts in Rome in 43 BC, or at least two that we know of: there might have been others. Three years later, in 40 BC, Marcellus died. By that date, war between Antony and Octavian was looming until Brundisium saved the day. New arrangements ensued, capped by the marriage of Octavia and Antony.

The written sources depict Octavia as a Roman matron of the old school: virtuous, modest, humble, and obedient to and supportive of her husband. But the sources are suspect. They all postdate her brother's rise to supreme power as Rome's first emperor. Although the authors of those works were able to read a few texts sympathetic to Antony, and even some by Antony himself, they tend to follow the party line of the imperial dynasty. Yet no one who spent her life navigating the shoals of Roman politics, as Octavia did, could have survived without cunning, courage, and a fingertip feel for power.

For all the blandness of the official story, the truth peeks out. Plutarch reflects received opinion when he says that many people felt that Octavia would be a good influence on the rogue Antony, bringing Rome salvation and harmony; at the same time, his falling in love with her would make him forget Cleopatra. We get another, less idealistic point of view in Tacitus. He writes that years later, after Antony's defeat, Octavian's enemies said that it had all been a great come-on by Octavian to hoodwink Antony, and that his sister was the bait. Their marriage was "a treacherous connection," some said, as Tacitus reports.

Octavia was certainly pretty, to judge by coin portraits and sculpture. Her image is one of dignity, seriousness, a delicate set of features, and modest good looks. She usually has a slender neck, distinct cheekbones, and a calm gaze—except in some coins that thicken her features, perhaps in order to suggest harmony with her heavyset husband. Although Octavia was praised for her naturally attractive hair, she left nothing to chance. The images show her hair in a carefully coiffed bun, fastened in place by braids, a style possible only for a woman who could afford to keep a ladies' maid or two.

A New Golden Age?

Public opinion in Italy welcomed the marriage because it meant reconciliation and peace. For example, to cite a chance survival, the city government of Casinum (modern-day Cassino), south of Rome, restored a statue of Concordia, the goddess of marital and societal harmony, in October 40 BC to celebrate the new era of goodwill.

Antony and Octavian both issued commemorative coins. Each man put his own head on the obverse and the other's head on the reverse, and they displayed other symbols of agreement, too, such as the caduceus—the two serpents on a herald's staff that symbolize collaboration—or clasped hands. What is really striking, however, is the gold coin that Antony issued with his head on the obverse and *Octavia*'s head on the reverse. Depicting living people on coins was a long-established custom in the Greek East, where kings and queens were often shown together, but it was new in Rome. Julius Caesar had been the first living Roman to have his portrait on a coin. Other men followed, and women soon after. Octavia was probably only the second woman other than a goddess to appear on a Roman coin. If the identification is correct, the first was Fulvia, Antony's previous wife. Now Octavia was the female face of the city that ruled the world.

Today the loudest echo of Romans' collective sigh of relief in that autumn may well be Virgil's celebrated "Fourth Eclogue"—if it was not written before the marriage; the date is uncertain. In it, he first thanks Gaius Asinius Pollio, one of the peacemakers and a supporter of Antony as well as one of the two consuls in 40 BC, for negotiating the pact of Brundisium. Then the poet proclaims the coming of a new golden age, to be brought on by the birth of a boy. Virgil writes, addressing the goddess of childbirth, Diana, also known as Lucina:

> *Only do thou, at the boy's birth in whom*
> *the iron shall cease, the golden race arise,*
> *befriend him, chaste Lucina; 'tis thine own*
> *Apollo reigns. And in thy consulate,*
> *this glorious age, O Pollio, shall begin.*

Although later centuries would see this as a prophecy of the coming of Jesus Christ, who was born about four decades later, Virgil was thinking of an Italian child. He doesn't name names, but it is possible to interpret the poem as hope for a child born to Antony and Octavia.

In November Antony and Octavian traveled to Rome for the wedding. In addition to the usual festivities, they received from the Senate the right to celebrate an ovation. This was the highest honor that could be awarded for a bloodless victory. From the Roman point of view, Brundisium was a victory. To the Romans, peace never just happened; it was the result of hard work and usually of violent action, earned by victory. Hence, its achievement was worth celebrating.

An ovation was not as prestigious as a triumph, which marked a major military success. That says something about Rome's hierarchy of values. "Blessed are the peacemakers," a Roman might have said, "but not as blessed as the conquerors." As ovators, the two men had the right to enter Rome on horseback—wearing special crimson-striped togas, their heads crowned with a myrtle wreath—to the sound of flutes. From there they were to proceed to the Temple of Capitoline Jupiter, the city's chief shrine, and perform a sacrifice. (A triumphator would have ridden in a chariot, wearing a toga dyed solid purple and a laurel wreath, accompanied by trumpets.)

The Senate also proved agreeable to bending the rules of matrimony. A widow or widower was forbidden to remarry during the

ten-month period of mourning for the deceased spouse, but the senators lifted the ban in this case. Perhaps it helped that Octavia was
already pregnant with Marcellus's child before she married Antony,
which removed any doubts about paternity (a presumed reason for
the ten-month rule).

It might have happened as follows. At the age of twenty-three,
Octavian would be giving away the twenty-nine-year-old bride. The
groom was forty-three. If it was a typical Roman wedding, Octavian
paid for it and held the ceremony in his townhouse, located on the exclusive Palatine Hill. It was, one imagines, a grand affair with a large
guest list.

We would expect a woman of Octavia's dignity to have worn traditional dress, from orange slippers on her feet, to a woolen tunic fastened by a girdle with a complicated knot for the groom to untie, to the
orange-red veil. We don't know if she was still pregnant or had given
birth already. Antony was no doubt well turned out. Both bride's and
groom's houses would be festooned with flowers and green branches,
and the bride's house might be illuminated with torches.

The entrails of animals were examined to find favorable omens,
and a sacrifice was made to the gods. Octavian presumably handed
Octavia over to Antony. Then the custom was for a married woman
to help the couple join their two right hands.

The marriage contract would have been negotiated in advance,
but it was often sealed at the wedding. The contract would include
the question of the dowry and its fate in the case of divorce.

After the giving of presents, Octavia would have been escorted to
her new home by a merry torchlight parade. At the entrance, her husband would offer her fire (via a torch) and water (in a jar), considered
by the Romans as the essence of home and hospitality. The marriage
would be consummated in the bedroom.

The next day, the groom held a dinner and drinking party, where
the bride made her first offering to the household gods. A round of
parties would follow on the days afterward.

The Treaty of Misenum and Its Aftermath

The bond between the two triumvirs was celebrated widely in Rome. However, the people quickly turned on the new brothers-in-law when Sextus Pompey's fleet squeezed the city's grain supply. There were stonings, overturned statues, and riots. In response, Antony and Octavian had to bow to the public's will. In summer 39 BC they met with Sextus at Misenum, north of Naples, where the three made peace.

They sealed their agreements with a series of dinners. Security was not neglected: the men all had guards and carried concealed daggers. The triumvirs hosted their banquets in tents on the pier, but Sextus held his dinner aboard his flagship. He made a bitter joke about the ship being the only home he had left, which was a dig at Antony, who had confiscated the house of his father, Pompey.

But an even more memorable remark came when one of Sextus's admirals took him aside and suggested that he murder his two enemies aboard ship, and so win the empire. Supposedly, Sextus pondered the thought and then replied at last that the man should have killed them without asking permission, but now that he had, it was too late: Sextus could not approve so dishonorable a deed. If the story is true, it was more likely cunning than honor that moved Sextus, on the grounds that it was better to work with the devils he knew than the ones who might emerge in the turbulent aftermath of their murders.

Sextus had persuaded the triumvirs to make a power-sharing agreement that confirmed his base in Sicily and the islands while also adding Achaea, the northernmost region of the Peloponnese Peninsula in southern Greece. In return, he had to give up his raids on the Italian mainland and his granting freedom to runaway slaves. He was not, however, able to enforce the agreement. Sea power might have allowed Sextus to survive as the lord of the islands, but only if the triumvirs were willing to tolerate it. As it turned out, the triumvirs—particularly Octavian—had no intention of keeping their word.

In 39 BC Octavian met the girl of his dreams. She was young, beautiful, brilliant, and a product of two of the most noble families in Roman history: the Livii and the Drusi. Her name was Livia Drusilla, and she was nineteen. But there were problems. She was married, she was a mother, and she was pregnant with her second child. On top of that, her husband had fought on the losing side at Perusia, sending the married pair and their young son fleeing afterward to Sicily and then Greece. But then, as now, to forgive was divine, especially when it enabled a union between Italy's most powerful man and its most aristocratic woman. Octavian was already married to Scribonia, who was pregnant, but that proved a minor inconvenience. The day Scribonia gave birth to a daughter, on January 14, 38 BC, Octavian divorced her. Livia's husband divorced her a day or two later, and she and Octavian wed on January 17. Since Scribonia was Sextus Pompey's aunt, the divorce was an insult that would probably trigger a renewal of war, but that prospect suited the restless Octavian.

Octavian's plan combined money and treachery. On the one hand, he ordered warships to be built in two Italian ports. On the other hand, he lured away one of Sextus's best admirals, who brought with him ships, legions, and control of the Mediterranean islands Sardinia and Corsica. It was the same admiral who had supposedly advised Sextus to murder Octavian the previous year. The admiral went on to lose a battle, after which his fleet was destroyed in a storm. He did, however, succeed in killing Sextus's other remaining admiral, which was a great coup.

Now Octavian turned to Agrippa. Octavian wasn't much of a general, but Agrippa had proven himself a first-class commander in Gaul. Octavian recalled him to win the war at sea. Given the ambition that burned in many Roman hearts, it seems remarkable that the talented Agrippa accepted his subordinate position, especially in the halcyon days of treachery that marked the triumviral era. Perhaps it was unthinkable that someone without noble blood could aim for supreme power in Rome, and, since Agrippa lacked nobility, that kept him in his place. Surely Octavian deserves a lot of credit for calculating carefully just how much honor to give his talented general.

Octavian deserves credit, too, for knowing his limitations. He was a bad general but solved that problem by getting a good general—actually, a great general—to work for him. Octavian did not lack self-esteem, but he never let it blind him to his weaknesses. He thereby demonstrated self-control and maturity. Success against a man of Sextus's caliber, however, would not come quickly.

City of the Violet Crown

Athens was famous in antiquity for its purple sunsets, leading to the epithet "violet crowned." It was in lovely Athens that Antony and Octavia spent their happiest time together.

Antony was preparing a great military expedition against Parthia. So, he headed east in the autumn of 39 BC and took his wife with him. They also brought their newborn daughter, Antonia, who arrived in August or September 39 BC. The much-hoped-for child was not the boy prophesied by Virgil, which, in a male-centered culture such as Rome, surely came as a disappointment. They passed the winter together in Athens. Appian says that Antony was very much in love with his wife then, although he adds with a sneer that Antony was "by nature excessively fond of women." Certainly the two of them had a physical relationship, for Octavia eventually gave birth to a second daughter, Antonia the Younger.

Greeks had never been shy about flattering Romans, and the Athenians now did their part by worshipping Antony as Dionysus and Octavia as Athena, goddess of wisdom. They were also honored as the beneficent gods. They might have taken part in the annual Dionysia, a large festival honoring Dionysus. The god of liberation was a beloved symbol in the Greek world, while Athena was the holy patron of Athens. One wonders whether Octavia enjoyed the chance to put her hair down or whether, like a severe Roman matron, she took a dim view of the whole business. Antony, for his part, is alleged to have abjured sentimentality in favor of the bottom line, charging the Athenians a small fortune as the "dowry" for his marriage, as Dionysus, to Athena, that is, to Octavia.

Antony was soon busy again with a thick agenda of war and diplomacy. In 40 BC Parthia invaded the Roman province of Syria. The force was led by the Parthian royal prince and a Roman general who had supported Pompey and went to Parthia after Caesar's assassination in order to stir up support for the Liberators. The Parthian invaders defeated Rome's armies and overturned Roman rule from Asia Minor to the borders of Arabia. It was a potential disaster until Antony intervened.

He organized an army under the command of his best general, Publius Ventidius Bassus. In 39 BC Ventidius reconquered Asia Minor and captured and executed the Pompeian general at its head. The next year, he defeated a force of Parthian mailed cavalry in Syria; the Parthian commander, a prince, fell in battle. The East was firmly back in Rome's hands. The sources claim that Antony was jealous of Ventidius and even humiliated his successful commander, but that might just be enemy propaganda. Ventidius returned to Rome and celebrated a triumph, which he shared with his commander, Antony, in absentia, for Antony stayed in the East. It would be 150 years before another Roman commander was entitled to a triumph over the Parthians.

The Treaty of Tarentum

In 38 BC Antony made a quick and frustrating trip to Italy, where a planned meeting with Octavian never came off, and then a more substantive visit there the following year.

There were several reasons for the two to meet, although neither man trusted the other. Octavian's war against Sextus Pompey in the waters off southern Italy and Sicily was going badly. He needed more ships and money. Antony needed Roman legionaries for his war on Parthia. Legally he was allowed to recruit them in Italy, but as a practical matter, he needed Octavian to enlist the men for him. Finally, there was a constitutional issue. The triumvirate had formally expired at the end of 38 BC and needed to be renewed—or the two men would have to face the consequences of letting it lapse.

Octavian sent one of his closest advisors to Athens for preliminary negotiations with Antony. Although big issues remained, the meeting went well enough for Antony to sail to Tarentum in southern Italy in spring 37 BC. He brought with him three hundred ships; Octavia accompanied him. She was a key member of the negotiating team, and, it seems, was in no way slowed down by being in the first trimester of a pregnancy.

Octavian approached Tarentum but put off his meeting with Antony. That's when his wife came to the rescue! According to one source, Octavia took the initiative of meeting with her brother and answering his complaints about Antony point by point. In another version, she won over Octavian's two closest advisors first before pleading with him not to go to war with her husband, because she would feel wretched, no matter the outcome. Her approach succeeded. We might speculate that she also made it clear that she was a shrewd woman and that an advantageous deal with Antony was in the offing.

Octavian now agreed to an informal meeting with Antony outside of Tarentum. In a scene so cinematic that one can only hope it is true, the two imperators each rowed a small boat out into the Taras River (modern Tara). Then they argued about who should disembark on the other's bank of the river. Apparently, Octavian blinked: one report says that he cited his desire to see his sister as reason to give in and visit Antony's camp before Antony visited his. As Octavian surely knew, this minor concession was a good way to soften up his enemy. Octavian supposedly traveled with Antony in Antony's chariot to his lodgings, where he spent the night without a guard. Antony followed suit the next day and visited Octavian's camp.

It was the start of long, hard bargaining. After a summer of negotiating, a deal was reached: Antony would leave 120 warships with Octavian, who would supply twenty thousand legionaries to Antony. The ships were available immediately, but the soldiers would come later. Octavia, the story goes, persuaded the two men to sweeten the deal: Antony gave Octavian an additional 10 cutters, while Octavian added a thousand picked troops—allegedly to serve as Octavia's bodyguard but surely able to fight for Antony. The bottom line was that Octavian got his ships immediately, whereas Antony had to settle for a future promise.

The two also assented to renew the triumvirate for another five-year term. In addition, they agreed to betroth Julia, Octavian's daughter by his former wife, Scribonia, to Antony's older son by Fulvia. The boy, Marcus Antonius, nicknamed Antyllus (possibly after the hero Anto, son of Antony's alleged ancestor Hercules), was then six; the girl, an infant.

Skeptical historians say that the sources exaggerate Octavia's role, and maybe so. Self-interest dictated that both men resolve their differences and focus on their respective military campaigns. But self-interest doesn't always prevail without skilled mediation, a role that elite women such as Octavia often played in this period of Roman history. Even if Octavia wasn't the brains behind the Treaty of Tarentum, she was certainly its public face.

Antony or his followers issued bronze coins around the time of Tarentum, all of which feature galleys or seahorses on the reverse. The obverse depicts either Antony and Octavia facing each other or twinned portraits of Antony and Octavian (with the latter in the background) facing Octavia. It's tempting to see this as evidence of the propaganda value of Octavia as the glue binding the two imperators.

It has been suggested that the Roman historian Livy (Titus Livius) modeled the episode of the Sabine women, who interceded to prevent a war between their husbands and their fathers, on Octavia's successful mediation at Tarentum. The account appears in the first book of his voluminous history of Rome, published just ten years later, in 27 BC. If so, this sounds like official history again, for Octavia was not quite an honest broker. If she stood in the middle at Tarentum, she tipped the scales toward her brother.

The Roman world celebrated the news that Octavia had hammered out a peace between Antony and Octavian, but that masked the real story. Octavia had deflected Antony from Italy and neutralized his support for Sextus Pompey. She had thereby saved her brother, and that was what really mattered.

Sister, ambassador, soldier, spy. Negotiator, supplicant, fixer, wife. Those were the roles that Octavia had to play as she shuttled back and forth between two powerful men. And from time to time, she was a goddess as well. And a mother, of course, always a mother.

After Tarentum, Antony left a pregnant Octavia and their young daughter with Octavian, who took them back to Rome while Antony sailed to Syria. A few months later, Octavia gave birth to Antonia the Younger, born on January 31, 36 BC. It was not out of the ordinary for Antony to send Octavia back to Rome and to her birth family. If anything, it was unusual for him to have brought her to Athens in the first place, since Roman governors usually left their wives at home. True enough, his position as triumvir was unprecedented, but Octavia's presence in Athens was far from the Roman norm.

Octavia's life would be even less normal in the following years. The status of her marriage would move to the center stage of Roman politics. Nor was her role as a diplomat over.

Chapter 4

Octavian's Victory, Antony's Defeat and Recovery

From Sicily to the Parthian Empire, 36 to 34 BC

THE MID-30s BC WITNESSED A PERIOD OF RENEWED war, with fighting on land and sea, as close to Rome as the waters off Sicily and as far away as the frontier with the Parthian Empire. There was fighting on the east coast of the Adriatic as well. Meanwhile, the partisans of Antony and Octavian exchanged propaganda volleys at a growing rate. Octavia's status as Antony's wife grew shaky, while Cleopatra consolidated her position. The two great men forged new weapons to fight their respective foes, but those weapons could be turned against each other. The future of Rome hung in the balance.

Defeating Sextus Pompey

For Octavian and Agrippa, the year 36 BC was an annus mirabilis. When faced with the problem of defeating the fleet of Sextus Pompey, Agrippa did what Romans often did with a military dilemma: he dug. His engineers constructed a new port for a new fleet. Outside of Puteoli (modern Pozzuoli, north of Naples), they connected Lake Lucrinus to the sea by digging a canal, thereby creating a sheltered naval base where the shipbuilders could work unobserved by enemy spies. They called the base Portus Julius. Having built the new port in 37 BC, the following year they launched the fleet, but only after creating it almost from scratch. Italy had had virtually no fleet to turn on Sextus.

Romans were landlubbers at heart. To compete with Carthage, the great rival state and sea power, they had turned themselves into a naval power in the mid-200s BC and retained that power for a century while extending their empire across the Mediterranean. Then they let their naval forces languish. Gnaeus Pompey rebuilt the Roman navy in the 60s BC, but he relied in large part on non-Romans, as did Sextus, who inherited much of his father's naval power. These were Greeks who, with their strong naval tradition, constructed seaworthy vessels and deployed them in battle with great maneuverability and seamanship.

Agrippa's fleet, by contrast, was made up of Italians with little or no experience at sea. Agrippa himself had no naval background either: his military career had been entirely on land. His new fleet was heavier, clumsier, and less maneuverable than Sextus Pompey's. Yet Agrippa made up in sedulousness and ingenuity for what he lacked in grace. He trained his men in rowing. He invented a new weapon: a catapult-launched harpoon to prevent enemy ships from outrunning his attack, and thereby opening them up to boarding. Agrippa's new navy couldn't compete with Sextus's experienced captains when it came to maneuvering at sea and ramming the enemy. But what his men could do well was to fight essentially a land battle at sea. The standard Roman warship, the quinquereme, or "five," carried up to 120 legionaries. Those soldiers aimed to board, fight, and win control of enemy vessels. It wasn't pretty, but it worked.

Agrippa defeated Sextus in two great naval battles off the coast of Sicily in 36 BC. Between the two clashes, however, Sextus ambushed Octavian after he had landed forces on the island. Octavian was forced to flee, only to face defeat at sea, from which he barely escaped. One source says that, as a result, Octavian was "shattered in body and mind." He had to face the indignity of landing with only a single armor bearer and no retinue—imagine that! The sight of Octavian running for his life and abandoning his troops is one of the less edifying scenes in the annals of ancient warfare.

It was only a fleeting success for Sextus. Agrippa soon reversed his side's fortune and won a total victory at sea at Naulochus on September 3, 36 BC. For Sextus, it was a crushing loss, with perhaps the highest warship casualty rate of any major Mediterranean Sea naval battle for the previous three centuries. Sextus fled to Asia Minor with seventeen ships, all that was left of a fleet that had numbered in the hundreds. Many of his sailors were runaway slaves, and they met a worse fate: Octavian claimed that he captured thirty thousand runaway slaves in Sextus's fleet and returned them to their masters.

Although Sextus failed, his bold strategy might have succeeded against a lesser man than Octavian. Sextus had thought that by cutting off Rome's food supply and demonstrating Octavian's impotence, he could bring his rival to his knees. Another leader might have been willing to compromise or might have balked at the huge expense of building a fleet or at the risk of serving in it. Or he might have hesitated to entrust such power to a subordinate as Octavian did with Agrippa.

But in Octavian, Sextus faced a man of iron will and determination, with great political talent, few principles, and infinite cunning—and such a man was dead set against compromise. Although not the best of military commanders, Octavian was nevertheless courageous and indefatigable. It would be hard to say which was greater: his cunning, his unscrupulousness, or his ambition, all of them at the extreme end of human capability. In addition, he had a superb team of advisors and commanders. And so Sextus's spectacular effort to break Octavian's will failed.

One ancient writer called the war against Sextus the hardest struggle that Octavian ever faced. If so, he turned out to be fortunate, because it served as a school of war. Oftentimes militaries improve by learning from failure; that is, if they are guided by good learners. Octavian proved to be an excellent student.

The defeat of Sextus Pompey left Octavian the sole master of the western Mediterranean. Nobody knew it at the time, but Agrippa had created the Roman Imperial Navy. Misenum would become one of the fleet's two bases in Italy.

That lay down the road, however. In the short run, Agrippa had acquired the experience and self-confidence to fight and win at sea, and he bestowed those gifts on Octavian. It would be hard to overemphasize the importance of that development and also the irony. Octavian was the heir of Julius Caesar, and Caesar had displayed only a minimal interest in sea power. His senatorial opponents, especially Gnaeus Pompey, had enjoyed the naval advantage in the civil war—not that they used it effectively. For nearly a decade, Sextus Pompey ruled the seas, even identifying himself with the sea god, Neptune. Then the naval torch passed to the new Caesar, as Octavian called himself. He now ruled the waves.

The End of Civil War

After his victory over Sextus Pompey, Octavian gave welcome news to the Roman people: the era of civil war was over. There would be no more Roman fighting against Roman.

Maybe. Once Octavian won victory at sea, the odds of war with Antony increased. Because with Sextus gone, Octavian no longer needed Antony's cooperation. As for Antony, his work in the East would probably have kept him busy for a long time. Whether it would have satisfied him, and whether he would have been content to leave the West to Octavian, is an open question.

Rome's past history argued against peaceful coexistence. Marius and Sulla, Caesar and Pompey, now Antony and Octavian. The pattern was clear: Partnerships wouldn't work. Agreements were only temporary. One man would dominate Rome or die trying. Most of the senators who might have saved the republic were dead, fallen in battle during the civil wars, murdered in the proscriptions, or suicides who preferred martyrdom to surrender.

One thing is certain: Octavian wanted it all. From the beginning of his career, he said that he aimed at all of Julius Caesar's honors, and his actions over the years show that he meant it. Octavian could only look with concern as Antony captured the prize that had eluded every other Roman leader with the possible exception of Caesar: Egypt, the wealthiest independent country in the ancient Mediterranean.

Even with the war against Sextus Pompey over, Octavian hesitated to demobilize—not with Antony's legions ready to march on Parthia, and not when the shipyards of the East were building his rival a new fleet. Octavia lived near Octavian in Rome and was still married to Antony in 36 BC, regardless of his affair with Cleopatra. Octavia could have reported that, Say what you will about my husband, but he was crafting a lasting political settlement on Rome's eastern frontier. What would the young Caesar build in turn?

Octavian needed to add to Rome's empire, and he needed to keep his force intact and in fighting trim. He found the answer across the Adriatic Sea. Victory against Sextus was followed by a successful campaign of conquest on the coast and up the rivers of Illyria. The war, which took place from 35 to 33 BC, led to solid territorial gains and even greater propaganda victories.

Octavian conquered most of Illyria, enabling him to boast that he thereby protected Italy from raiders. He earned a much-needed boost to his reputation as a soldier by taking part in a siege and suffering the wounds to show for it. He scored a propaganda coup by recapturing several legionary standards that had been lost when an earlier Roman army had been defeated in Illyria about fifteen years before. There's some reason to think that his publicists compared Octavian to Alexander the Great. If so, that would have raised many an eyebrow. Still, Illyria gave Octavian's men additional military experience, self-confidence, and loot. They had more reason than ever to fight for their commander.

Using his thrust against a southern Illyrian people as a cover, Octavian probably helped himself to the key port cities of Dyrrachium (now Durrës, Albania), Apollonia, and Lissus. He thereby violated his 40 BC agreement with Antony, which assigned these areas to Antony. Never mind, the trade-off in security was worth it. By taking these cities, Octavian deprived his rival of the most convenient jumping-off points for any invasion of Italy.

This was an egregious breach, but neither triumvir abided by the letter of the treaty. Antony, for example, intervened in Italy and Hispania, while Octavian mixed into the domestic politics of the city of Aphrodisias in Asia Minor.

Information Operations

Although battered by the rule of a few strong men, Rome was still enough of a republic that public opinion continued to matter. Antony and Octavian each mounted a vigorous campaign to win the information war.

Given Octavian's dominance of the historical record, his actions are easier to reconstruct. Octavian controlled Italy, and, possession being nine-tenths of the law, the historical record is probably accurate when it shows Octavian overshadowing the publicity field there. Antony was almost 1,300 nautical miles away in Alexandria, if not farther afield.

Neither Antony nor Octavian needed any lessons about waging war through propaganda and pamphlets. From the moment Octavian first appeared on the political scene, about a month after the Ides of March, until well after the end of the war, charges flew between the two rival politicians and their supporters. That makes it difficult for historians today to separate fact and fiction, especially in regard to Antony, the eventual loser. The juiciest stories incite the least confidence.

Each man had a public relations staff working for him to promote his respective version of events and to sully the name of his adversary. These staffs included senators, orators, generals, historians, and poets. Octavian's people had included Cicero (from 44 to 43 BC) and the poet

Quintus Horatius Flaccus, now known simply as Horace. Antony's side—the losing side—is less well known today, but classicists may recognize Asinius Pollio, the general and author of a now-lost history of the era of the Roman civil wars, and perhaps Cassius of Parma (Gaius Cassius Parmensis), who was an admiral, an assassin of Caesar, and a poet good enough to win notice from Horace. Then there was Messalla (Marcus Valerius Messalla Corvinus), a poet, memoirist, orator, and patron of the arts as well as a politician and general. At first a supporter of Antony, he changed sides and then wrote pamphlets attacking Antony.

The war against Sextus Pompey had been a rehearsal for Octavian's war on Antony. Octavian portrayed Sextus as a pirate rather than a statesman. One wonders if it was Sextus and his supporters who first struck back with the charge that Octavian and Livia had put on a mime mocking the twelve Olympian gods at a lavish banquet—possibly even their wedding feast—while the city was starving under Sextus's blockade. Or perhaps the charge was the work of Antony and his friends. Each of the guests supposedly dressed up as a god or goddess, with Octavian playing Apollo and behaving adulterously. An anonymous ditty about this event made the rounds in Rome. Difficult Latin and obscure references make it hard to interpret today, but the poem must have stung, because it was still known 150 years later. Antony broadcast the accusation of Octavian's sacrilegious behavior in his letters, presumably a few years later, when his quarrel with Octavian heated up. Antony even identified all the guests by name.

The propaganda war was now nasty, now hilarious. Antony, it seems, criticized Octavian for the latter's weakness for playing dice. Octavian responded that an Egyptian soothsayer warned Antony that his daimon, or spirit, could not compete with Octavian's, which is why Antony kept losing to him in competitions of any sort, whether playing dice, casting lots, or fighting with cocks or quails.

Both sides weaponized information, but in Rome, Octavian did so to greater effect, controlling the narrative of the conflict. Perhaps he had to. In retrospect, Octavian might have looked like a giant, but, at the time, he was the underdog. To contemporaries, Antony and Cleopatra appeared to be powerful and frightening foes. We falsify history when we make Octavian seem the surefire and obvious winner. Octavian did not have a unifying master plan. Knowing Antony as well as he did, through his own observations and his sister's intelligence, he might have had a reasonable hope of predicting his enemies' behavior and thereby achieving success. But he couldn't be sure. He also knew that Cleopatra was shrewd, and he might have feared that she would steer Antony in the right direction.

Octavian turned his youth from a liability to an asset. Antony was a mature man, although hardly aged by Roman standards. That was all the more reason for Octavian to portray Antony as libidinous and irresponsible, as if he, young Octavian, were the adult in the room. He smeared Antony as a drunken womanizer who was in thrall to a foreign queen and for whom he had sold out Rome's interests. Antony, for his part, published a pamphlet, *On His Drunkenness,* in which he defended himself. Although we don't know the details, it is plausible that he explained that he was following in the footsteps of Dionysus, the god who had conquered Asia, and not Dionysus the drunkard.

Octavian turned every wrinkle in the marriage between his sister and Antony into an affair of state. Octavia was cast as the wronged but virtuous woman; Cleopatra, the foreign temptress. Octavian criticized Antony for his adultery with the Egyptian queen. Antony retaliated by publishing a litany of Octavian's alleged sexual misbehavior. These included his overly hasty marriage to Livia; his divorcing Scribonia merely because she'd objected to his affair with Livia; his using friends as procurers; and his seduction of a consul's wife before the man's eyes at a dinner party, where Octavian escorted her from the dining room into the bedroom for a quickie and then brought her back with her hair disheveled and her face glowing. Antony also named names of the women with whom Octavian supposedly cheated on Livia. Octavian's defense, made by his friends, was that his womanizing was merely political espionage, in order to gather information on his rivals through their wives, and so a prudent piece of statecraft.

Meanwhile, Antony expressed outrage at the charges made against him. Not only was Octavian a hypocrite, but also he was exaggerating and misrepresenting Antony's behavior. He referred specifically to his affair with Cleopatra. "What has made such a change in you?" wrote Antony in a letter to Octavian, at a time when the two of them were still on semidecent terms. "Because I lie with the queen?" he continued. "Is she my wife?" In other words, Antony defended his behavior as similar to Octavian's; it was adultery, but not bigamy.

Fire in the East

As Antony saw it, his mission was to complete Caesar's unfinished task in the East, where Rome's borders were sketchy and under threat. Doing so required an army and thus offered a chance for military glory, always the coin of the realm in Roman politics. It is difficult to disentangle Antony's plans or deeds from the surviving sources, as colored as they are by later Augustan propaganda. To this historian, the following is the likeliest reconstruction.

The strategic problem Antony faced was the contest with the Parthian Empire, as mentioned. Over the previous century, Rome had conquered a band of territory stretching from western Asia Minor in the North to Judea in the South. Some of it was annexed and became Roman provinces, but large parts remained client kingdoms—formally independent but subordinate to Rome. Egypt, too, was effectively a client state.

The one cloud on the horizon was Parthia. The Parthian Empire stretched from what is today eastern Turkey to eastern Iran, a distance of approximately 1,500 miles. It was the only empire left, west of India, that could rival Rome. The two states stared at each other warily across a long border from present-day northwestern Iran to Arabia. Sometimes they did more than stare.

In 53 BC the Roman general Marcus Licinius Crassus had invaded Parthian territory in an unprovoked attack. Superior in cavalry, especially horse archers and armored cavalry, the Parthians destroyed his army, capturing and killing Crassus himself. Julius Caesar planned a war of revenge, but his assassination in 44 BC stopped the expedition. Various motives impelled Caesar: Crassus had been a political ally; Parthia had maintained diplomatic contacts with Gnaeus Pompey in the civil war of 49 to 45 BC; the honor of Rome was at stake; there was glory to be won. The extent of Caesar's ambition against Parthia is unknown. We don't know if he envisioned something as grandiose as conquering all of the Parthian Empire, or only a part of it, or only inflicting a salutary defeat. In any case, after his death, Parthia struck next.

In 40 BC Parthia overran a large part of Rome's eastern provinces until an army organized by Antony and led by his general Ventidius defeated them decisively. By 38 BC, Rome was back in control of the region.

Antony's next move was a major act of statesmanship. He set up a series of client kings on the empire's eastern periphery. He required two qualifications: competence and loyalty. He installed Polemo in Pontus, Amyntas in Galatia, Archelaus in Cappadocia, and Herod in Judaea. This was the infamous King Herod of both Christian and Jewish traditions, but he was an efficient ruler and loyal to Rome. Each of these kings was given a generous amount of territory to rule; in the case of Amyntas, his kingdom included parts of Cilicia, a country located in what is now the eastern part of Turkey's Mediterranean coast. Cilicia had formerly been a Roman province, but it was more efficient for Rome to have a local ruler administer it.

To complete the project of securing the border, Antony turned to the northeastern marches. He chose as commander Publius Canidius Crassus, a self-made man who had risen to the top tier of Antony's generals. Canidius also snapped up a consulship along the way, thereby making him a member of the Roman nobility—in Rome, nobles were either ex-consuls or descendants of consuls—which was not bad for a man whose family had no roots in Rome.

Antony sent Canidius with an army to secure the frontier regions of Armenia and the southern Caucasus Mountains. Armenia was an independent kingdom covering a wide area that ranges today from eastern Turkey to Iran. Located between the two empires of Rome and Parthia, Armenians mastered the ability to play a double game. At the time, it was an ally of Parthia, but Canidius defeated Armenia, and its ruler, King Artavasdes II, switched his allegiance to Rome.

Antony now made his move. The sources claim that Antony wanted nothing less than to conquer the Parthian Empire, but he probably had something less grandiose in mind. The kingdom of Media Atropatene (today's northwestern Iran, also known as Iranian Azerbaijan) was a vassal state of the Parthians. Antony wanted to either conquer Atropatene or at least force it into an alliance with Rome. Either achievement would have threatened the Parthian Empire on its northwestern border, thereby reducing, if not eliminating, its further ability to invade the Roman East.

Victory would have brought Rome security on the frontier and Antony prestige, wealth, and seasoned troops. He would have faced his rival Octavian with a much stronger hand. He might have been able to compel the Parthians to return the battle standards that they had captured from Crassus. He demanded those before attacking Atropatene, but the Parthians refused.

Antony liked it big. While wintering with Cleopatra in Antioch, the capital of Syria, in 37–36 BC, he put the final touches on a massive invading army. Another piece of business in Antioch was for Antony to meet his twin toddler children by Cleopatra for the first time. It was perhaps only now that they received their epithets, Alexander Helios and Cleopatra Selene. Both names were full of significance. Alexander was, of course, the ancient world's greatest conqueror and the founder of Greco-Macedonian rule in Egypt. Cleopatra referred not only to the current monarch but also to several earlier and prominent Ptolemaic queens. Helios was the Greek god of the sun; Selene, the goddess of the moon. The sun, for many in the ancient world, represented the new golden age for which they yearned.

In the spring, Cleopatra traveled with Antony as far as the city of Zeugma on the Euphrates (near modern Gaziantep, Turkey), about a week's travel, where he drew together the army. Antony had ninety thousand to a hundred thousand men as well as siege engines carried on three hundred wagons—a train about five miles long—and an eighty-foot-long battering ram. The heart of Antony's army consisted probably of sixteen legions, or approximately eighty thousand men. In principle, legionaries were Roman citizens—that is, Italians. Octavian had cut off Antony from recruiting troops in Italy, so Antony had to include a certain number of recruits from the East. Some would be Italian settlers or their descendants living in colonies in Asia Minor, while others would be Greeks or one of the various other peoples of the East: for example, Arabs, Galatians, Jews, Macedonians, or Syrians. Romans believed that Italians made the best legionaries. That was probably just ethnocentric bias, since, in the following centuries, the tables would be turned: Imperial Rome would have no trouble recruiting excellent legionaries from every corner of the empire *except* Italy, whose inhabitants preferred peaceful pursuits. There is no reason to think easterners were lesser soldiers than Italians, but their loyalty could not be taken for granted.

Antony led the expedition himself. From Zeugma, they made the long march northeastward. King Artavasdes of Armenia joined Antony along the way with seven thousand infantryman and a crucial military arm that the Romans lacked: six thousand armored cavalrymen. Parthia had built its victory over Crassus at Carrhae in 53 BC on its strength in armored cavalrymen, so Armenia's contribution was key.

On the sound principle that speed kills, Antony and the bulk of his army pressed ahead toward the capital city of Atropatene, Phraaspa (exact location unknown). He was content to let the much slower siege train follow behind, protected by two legions under one of Antony's legates, or senior commanders. Unfortunately, the enemy followed another sound military principle: surprise. A Parthian army attacked and defeated Antony's siege train, killing the Roman commander and ten thousand men. They also took an allied king captive. That was enough for King Artavasdes to change his mind. He took his troops and went home, dealing a major blow to Antony.

It might still have been possible to take Phraaspa by building a mound around the city and cutting it off. But a Parthian relief army put paid to that by harassing Antony's troops while protecting themselves by refusing to fight a battle. Although Antony's men got in some good blows, he had to concede failure in the end.

With winter approaching, both sides agreed to a truce. The Parthians promised Antony a safe-conduct home, but they continually hounded him. It took four weeks for Antony's forces to straggle back to Armenia. Conditions were difficult: food shortages, enemy raids, and flagging troop morale and discipline. Yet Antony shone in failure; he did everything that was needed to save most of his men.

Still, the campaign cost Antony a quarter of his army, according to the Augustan tradition, which, considering the campaign's setbacks, might be accurate. It was a significant loss, but the bulk of the force was intact. Antony had bound his men to him by his extraordinary leadership during a difficult retreat. Everyone could take pride in the heroic effort to return to base.

Leaving to trusted subordinates the task of leading the army from Armenia to the Mediterranean, Antony hurried ahead to the coast, probably in today's Lebanon. He had sent a message to Cleopatra to bring badly needed supplies from Egypt, and she complied, arriving with a small fleet. After meeting the army and distributing Cleopatra's provisions, Antony retired with the queen to Alexandria for the winter of 36–35 BC.

Antony was probably in Alexandria when he received a message from his wife. In November 36 Octavia set sail from Italy on a mission to Athens. She brought for Antony's use two thousand legionaries as well as money, animals, and supplies. Plutarch says that she went on her own volition, with Octavian thinking that Antony might mistreat her and thus give him a propaganda advantage, but it's more likely that brother and sister coordinated their actions. Octavia was not easily manipulated, and Octavian did not need to risk losing her goodwill. It was, in any case, obvious that the mission might fail. The same year, 36 BC, Cleopatra gave birth to her third child by Antony, a boy, Ptolemy Philadelphus. He was named after the king whose reign in the early third century BC had marked the height of the Ptolemies' power.

Was Octavia trying to save her marriage? No doubt, but if the past five years were any guide to the future, she and Antony would spend little time together. More important, she was delivering a message. The power dynamic between her husband and her brother had shifted drastically. The message was: Octavian knew it, and so did she.

At Tarentum, Octavian had promised Antony twenty thousand legionaries, but he had been in no hurry to deliver them. When he finally did, via Octavia, he sent only one-tenth that amount. He broke his word and so risked a rupture with Antony, but by now, Octavian need not have cared—not after his victory at Naulochus and Antony's defeat in Atropatene.

Octavian had made a canny move. Sending no legionaries at all would have caused an open break with Antony, but his dispatching only *some* put Antony on the spot. Accepting the foot soldiers would be to admit weakness, but rejecting them would be to turn down badly needed reinforcements.

Octavian, therefore, offered Antony a gift from Octavia that was also an insult from his brother-in-law. Antony made a coarse response. He needed the troops, so he accepted the gift and the insult, but he did not come to Athens. He sent Octavia a letter, perhaps from Alexandria, instructing her to go back to Rome. And she did, in spring 35 BC.

Feeling that his sister had been humiliated, Octavian told her to divorce Antony. She refused. Or so Plutarch states. It is tempting to see this as a staged incident, agreed upon by brother and sister, that allowed Octavian to respond to Antony without actually breaking up the marriage. Neither Octavian's self-interest nor Antony's crude behavior justified divorce. Octavian knew that it was better to keep an enemy close than to set him free.

But Octavian had no intention of losing the opportunity to respond to a slight to his family. So, he reaffirmed his sister's dignity by having Octavia voted unprecedented honors. Adult Roman women had to have a male guardian for their property, but in 35 BC Octavia was freed from this obligation, which was a rare privilege. Legally, she could now dispose of her property as she wished. She was also granted the honor of a statue, a dignity that had been given to just one other woman in the Roman Republic, about a century earlier: Cornelia, mother of the Gracchi. But the most unusual thing of all was that Octavia was declared sacrosanct. That is to say, anyone who injured her could be tried for treason. Normally, this privilege was reserved for the ten people's tribunes, although it had also been granted to Julius Caesar and, just a year earlier, to Octavian himself.

Octavia's new status proved awkward for Antony. By acting as he did, Octavian went public with the problems in his sister's marriage. Antony's mistress might have been a queen, but his wife was now the equivalent of a Roman people's tribune. An insult to Octavia was now equal to an insult to a public official and an act of hostility to the Roman Republic. Perhaps in order to avoid jealousy, Octavian had the same honors voted as well to Livia, his wife. But Octavia was the real issue.

It would have been delicious propaganda to set up the statues of Livia and Octavia in the Forum of Julius Caesar. There was already a gilded statue of Cleopatra outside the Temple of Venus Genetrix, who was both the mother of the Roman people and the alleged ancestor of Julius Caesar and Octavian and Octavia. Assuming that the statues of Octavia and Livia were marble, and that they wore the traditional dress of a Roman matron, they would have made a sharp contrast to Cleopatra's eastern splendor.

High Noon in Alexandria

Antony's attempt to conquer Media Atropatene was a failure, but in the aftermath, the stars aligned in his favor. A breach between the victors, Media Atropatene and Parthia, led to an offer of alliance from the king of the former, Artavasdes the Mede (not to be confused with the Armenian king of the same name). Antony betrothed his young son Alexander Helios to Iotape, daughter of the Median king. With Atropatene now on his side, Antony could return with an army to settle scores with the king of Armenia.

It took another year before Antony was ready to move. His army needed to rest and recover and replenish its numbers through new recruits. Besides, Antony had to deal with the fallout from the defeat of 36 BC in Sicily, which, as will become clear, was considerable.

In 34 BC Antony was ready to march on Armenia with an army. If the Augustan sources are to be believed, he used treachery to capture King Artavasdes the Armenian, whom he defeated without a battle. When the Armenians chose a son of Artavasdes to replace him, Antony overcame the young man in a fight and sent him fleeing to Parthia. Antony then shipped the king, along with the rest of his family, off in silver chains to Alexandria, and proclaimed Armenia to be a new Roman province.

At the end of the campaigning season in autumn 34 BC, Antony returned to Alexandria. He entered the city with his captives on display in a victory procession. Both the Ptolemies and the Romans were masters of the processional art. Roman victory marches, the triumphs, are still famous, but the Ptolemaic equivalent, the Dionysiac Procession, is less well known. Yet such processions were a centuries-old and often spectacular tradition. The sources accuse Antony of hijacking a Roman triumph and conducting it in a foreign city. Surely this re-flects Octavian's propaganda that Antony was in thrall to the Egyptian queen. In reality, Antony probably incorporated elements of both east-ern and western traditions. He would show that, on the one hand, he was a Roman commander, while, on the other hand, his children were eastern princes who respected Alexandrian customs, as he did himself.

The procession supposedly climaxed at the feet of Cleopatra. An-tony is said to have presented the Armenian royal family—now in golden chains—to Cleopatra, who was seated on a gilded chair on a silver-plated platform. The proud and feisty captives supposedly re-fused to bend the knee or call her queen, for which they were punished. There is surely a healthy dose of Octavian's half-truth in these details.

Octavian had good reason to distort the facts. Antony's suc-cessful reentry into Alexandria represented a mortal threat. An-tony wasn't just setting up bastions on the frontier. Rather, he was building something magnificent with Cleopatra. The two of them could have turned Alexandria into a second capital of the empire—a Constantinople long before Constantinople. Even if Octavian had not declared war in 32 BC, he and Antony would most likely have come to blows eventually. If Antony had won and become master of Rome, he would not have forgotten Alexandria. He and Cleopatra could have sponsored a renaissance of Hellenism in that great city that could have advanced science and culture by centuries. It all de-pended, however, on their ability to defend their realm. Whoever said war never settles anything was not thinking of Actium.

And so, Octavian's propagandists set to work to vilify Antony. "Half-truth" is also the verdict for a related story that appears in the sources. Either at the end of the procession or shortly afterward, An-tony is supposed to have given away the store in public to Cleopatra and her children, and at the expense of Rome. Historians refer to this as the Donations of Alexandria. Details vary, but a composite picture goes as follows:

It took place before a crowd in the Gymnasium, a public building considered by some as the city's most beautiful. This large structure was a center of Greek civic life. Outside were colonnades over a stadium (606 feet) long. Inside, there were spaces for cultural and educational activities as well as athletic contests and also a dining room. It was perhaps at a public feast that the Donations took place.

Antony and Cleopatra were seated on gilded thrones on a silver-plated podium, with lower thrones for their children and Caesarion. There Antony announced that Cleopatra was to be called queen of kings and her sons each king of kings. These were common titles in the East. Cleopatra was declared queen of Egypt, Cyprus, and "Hollow Syria" (the fertile Beqaa Valley in eastern Lebanon), which she was to share with Caesarion. Of the queen's three children with Antony, Cleopatra Selene was given Cyrenaica (eastern Libya); Ptolemy Philadelphus was given Phoenicia (the coast of Lebanon), Syria, and Cilicia; and Alexander Helios was given Armenia, Media, and, as a future promise, Parthia. Alexander, at age six, was dressed in Median garb, while Ptolemy, only two, wore Macedonian costume. The boys embraced their parents and were given, respectively, Armenian and Macedonian bodyguards.

In the case of Cleopatra, the declaration merely restated what was already fact. She had long ruled Egypt and Cyprus, and Antony had granted her wealthy and strategic new territories abroad. In addition to the places mentioned above, these included the city of Ptolemais Akko (Acre, Israel), which had been founded by her ancestor; the oasis of Jericho; a mineral-rich region south of the Dead Sea; and two strategic harbor towns in Crete. She leased the valuable date-and-balsam-producing lands around Jericho to King Herod, while she also accrued income from the production of pitch south of the Dead Sea; pitch was used in architecture, agriculture, medicine, shipping, and mummification. Thanks to her control of these territories, Cleopatra presided over prosperity and was poised to project power abroad. Cyprus, Hollow Syria, and Cilicia were all rich in timber, and Phoenicia had several ports with a long naval tradition, so each of these places could play an important role in Antony's ship-building program. Cyrenaica, wealthy and fertile, also had important harbors.

Cleopatra did well, thanks to Antony, but she did not get everything she wanted. She was eager to wrest all of Judea from Herod. That would have given her a contiguous swath of territory from Libya to eastern Lebanon, while also fulfilling her dream of restoring the Ptolemaic Empire to its former greatness. But Antony refused and kept Herod on his throne. He might have shared the queen's bed and her luxurious lifestyle, but Antony put his own interests first. It was not to his advantage to give up an ally.

Plutarch says that the ceremony in Alexandria showed that Antony hated Rome—Octavian's propaganda at its finest. It showed nothing of the kind. The message was, rather, that Antony aspired to put his own children and (allegedly) Julius Caesar's on the thrones of allied kingdoms in the East, thereby strengthening Roman rule. True, it meant compromising with non-Roman rulers, but that was already Roman policy, and had been for centuries, even if it meant giving up formerly Roman provinces such as Cilicia and Cyprus. If the arrangements also served the greater glory of Antony, that was Octavian's problem, not Rome's.

Alexandria offered a superb base. It had a great harbor. As an administrative, economic, and religious center with a multiethnic population, it was teeming with useful intelligence. Even in decline, the Ptolemies still boasted considerable naval and technological know-how. Egypt offered an enormous amount of money. It had the richest agricultural land in the Mediterranean and a trading center, in Alexandria, that was second to none. The result was potentially enormous tax revenues.

It was not new for Roman generals to set up friendly princes in client states and then leverage those connections to improve one's power and standing in Rome; in fact, the pattern went back centuries. What was new was fathering those princes with a native queen and then installing one's children in power. It amounted to creating a personal empire.

It is unclear whether Antony and Cleopatra had a formal marriage or not. As pharaoh, Cleopatra was a goddess and had no need of benefit of clergy. In a way, the marital status of Cleopatra and Antony doesn't really matter, because theirs was less a marriage than a merger. Rome & Egypt Inc. is what the couple represented and what Octavian feared. Antony had achieved what the Senate had been trying to prevent for more than a generation: he had put the wealth of Egypt into one Roman's hands.

Antony and Octavian represented two different visions for the future of the Roman Empire. Antony offered the combination of a Roman noble and a Hellenistic prince, an imperator and a god, family that was half Roman and half Greco-Egyptian. His would be an empire that looked eastward and was anchored in Alexandria as well as Rome. Above all, Antony came with Cleopatra, which thrilled some and horrified others.

Octavian looked westward. He offered better Italian credentials than Antony but a worse noble pedigree. Without access to the wealth of Egypt and the East, he had much less money than his rival and was forced to squeeze taxes out of an unhappy Italy. Yet his political skills gave him a commander, Agrippa, who offered the possibility of winning what Antony had by force of arms. Octavian had learned from Caesar to open the most powerful positions to men whose talent outstripped their lineage.

Some senators preferred Antony as a way of preserving their narrow and aristocratic power. Not that they considered him a sincere republican, but they might have figured that, since he was far away, he would leave them breathing room in Rome. Octavian was not subtle about his intention of ruling the city with blood and iron, and about installing his family as all-but a royal dynasty. Both men left the world wondering if they would be able to practice the arts of peace as well as they had those of war. Which of them could better rebuild a war-weary world?

By the end of 34 BC, Antony's work on the northeastern frontier had borne fruit. Armenia was now under Roman control, destined to be a kingdom ruled by Antony's son Alexander Helios. Media Atropatene was a Roman ally. Young Alexander might one day inherit the throne of Media Atropatene for himself from his future father-in-law, the king. Meanwhile, for now, the road was open to an invasion of the Parthian realm. Armenia would serve as a reliable base, and Media could supply the cavalry that Antony lacked. The resulting campaign might have yielded a great prize: Mesopotamia, or at least the northern part of it. Had it succeeded, it would have been the capstone of a life's work for Antony. It's equally possible that he would have settled for something less: a combination of saber rattling and diplomacy that convinced the Parthian king to return the legionary standards lost by Crassus. In either case, from his base in Alexandria, a victorious Antony could have dealt with his rival in Rome.

But Antony's renewed Parthian campaign never happened. Instead, in 33 BC he withdrew his forces westward because Octavian had decided to make war on him. Octavian reached the decision to fight not so much because Antony was weak but because he was poised to become strong, even unassailable. To Octavian, it was now or never. And so, the war came.

Chapter 5

The Coming of War

Rome-Ephesus-Athens, 32 BC

AS THE YEAR 32 BC BEGAN, ANTONY AND OCTAVIAN were formally at peace, yet both prepared for war. It was probably on December 31, 33 BC, that the triumvirate had expired. It was not renewed.

Early in 32 BC the conflict between the rivals broke out in the Roman Senate. The two consuls for that year were both partisans of Antony. One of them was Gaius Sosius, who had served Antony as a commander in the East and as governor of two key provinces, Syria and Cilicia. On February 1 Sosius denounced Octavian in the Senate. Octavian was out of town, but, a few weeks later, he responded by attending another Senate meeting with an armed guard of supporters carrying daggers beneath their togas. He took a seat on the podium between the two consuls, which made clear his claim to power, even if the triumvirate was no more. In response, several hundred senators, and perhaps more than three hundred, now decided to flee Rome for Antony in Ephesus. Few of them loved Antony or even trusted him, but at least he belonged to the old Roman nobility and treated his senatorial peers with respect. Octavian was an upstart from the Italian bourgeoisie who made a specious claim of being a patrician but used violence on the Senate. Nor was the matter of age insignificant. The Romans generally looked down on youth. Antony was fifty-one at the time, which put him in the prime of life. Octavian was only thirty-one, an age at which a Roman could still be described as *adulescentulus:* "a very young man."

The refugee senators found an armed camp in Ephesus.

Ephesus, March 32 BC

Into the great harbor of Ephesus—ancient, venerable, and the largest port in Asia Minor—the ships poured in. You could hear the slowing beat of the oars, the cries of the boatswains, the thud of the rope lines as they were tossed ashore. Or you could hold your breath at the silence of a great ship gliding in on a breeze.

Already old at the time of the Trojan War, more than a thousand years earlier, the great port city had seen its share of seafarers and conquerors: a legendary Amazon queen; Hittite, Lydian, and Persian kings; the warrior-monarchs Alexander the Great, Ptolemy III of Egypt, Mithradates VI of Pontus, and the exiled Carthaginian general Hannibal. Yet Ephesus had never seen an armada like this.

There were five hundred warships and three hundred transport vessels. Most of the warships were quinqueremes—"fives," they were called, referring to the number of rowers in a cross section of the ship. These were big wooden galleys, each meant to carry 300 oarsmen and 120 marines as well as other crewmen. They had a technological edge. With reinforced timbers in their prow, the vessels were able to ram the enemy head-on. Yet there were even greater ships, too—in sizes ranging from "sixes" to "tens"—massive war machines meant to smash through the barriers of fortified harbors. Many of the ships were shiny and new, built with timber cut recently from the forests of Asia Minor's Mediterranean coast, or from Phoenicia and the lands on either side of Mount Lebanon, or Gilead (in today's Jordan) or Cyprus, or even from the sacred grove of the healing god on the island of Cos.

With all the personnel on these ships—up to 200,000 men—it would have taken a second city to provision them. Even more challenging to local resources, Ephesus was also the mustering ground for some 120,000 infantry and cavalrymen, for a total influx of around 300,000 men. They outnumbered the population of all but a handful of cities in the ancient world, including Ephesus itself, a city of perhaps a quarter million people. A miracle would be needed to feed them.

If any place could have heeded the call for the miraculous, it was Ephesus. Age-old home of the worship of the Greek goddess Artemis (Diana in Roman mythology), Ephesus housed the magnificent Temple of Artemis, which was one of the Seven Wonders of the World. The temple was an enormous marble structure with a portico surrounded by 127 columns. Although the temple also served as a bank, Ephesus might have been able to do without its resources to feed the soldiers and sailors, because it had another goddess to call on: Cleopatra.

She was flesh and blood, but, as far as her subjects were concerned, Cleopatra was the earthly incarnation of Isis, the supreme female deity of Egypt and a goddess popular around the Mediterranean. It was said that she had furnished a quarter of the warships and all their supplies as well as nearly two million pounds of silver. She was no passive partner: she had come to Ephesus to play an active role in the armada. It was not unusual for a Greek monarch to accompany a Roman general on a military campaign, but a queen was something new, especially if she planned to continue to the battlefront.

Cleopatra had proved her use to Antony already by putting her kingdom at his service as an engine of war. Although Ptolemaic Egypt had not invested in a big navy for two centuries, it retained its maritime know-how, from the great Mediterranean port of Alexandria, to the ships that plied the Red Sea and traveled all the way to India. Cleopatra had the money to finance a fleet and pay sailors. With her help, Antony outspent and outbuilt the enemy.

In addition to supporting her man and their three children, Cleopatra's greatest concern was that Antony not sacrifice Caesarion on the altar of reconciliation with Octavian. In spring 32 BC, with a military confrontation looming, her cause was strong. Still, politics is fluid, and Octavian was crafty, so the queen could not let down her guard. The safest policy was for her to keep close to Antony, wherever that might take her.

The Man Who Hated Cleopatra

The senatorial refugees who came to Ephesus included both Sosius and the other consul for 32 BC, Ahenobarbus. He hated and feared Cleopatra, despite her contributions to Antony's cause. As a Roman, Ahenobarbus looked down on Greeks. As a republican, he had no use for monarchs. As a proud man, he despised a powerful woman. He feared the queen's influence over Antony. Ahenobarbus's son was engaged to Antony's older daughter (by an earlier wife), but Ahenobarbus, as a politician, knew that Cleopatra was poison in Rome, where Octavian branded her a foreign witch who had seduced Antony. Many of Antony's men felt the same way, and they weren't shy about saying so. They joined their voices with Ahenobarbus in Ephesus.

The presence of both consuls made it easier for Antony to organize the refugee senators into a kind of counter-Senate, claiming, in effect, to be the real Rome. His partisans in Rome had kept his republican image alive in his absence. They celebrated triumphs—on one occasion including Antony in absentia—and sponsored public buildings. In Rome, it was possible to maintain the illusion of Marcus Antonius, a man loyal to the beeswax images of his ancestors that a Roman noble kept in a cabinet at home. No wonder some of his supporters were shocked when they fled eastward and came up against the gilded reality of Cleopatra and her consort.

The Roman Republic was dead, but no one had told Ahenobarbus. As a young man he had been captured with his father fighting against Caesar in a civil war. Caesar pardoned them and let them go. The father, alternately stubborn, insubordinate, ill tempered, and depressed, died in battle a year later. The son survived. Accused falsely of being one of Caesar's assassins—he had not taken part in the plot but approved of it afterward—he joined the assassins and commanded a fleet in their war against Caesar's heirs. Although they lost the war on land, Ahenobarbus kept on winning the battles at sea.

In 40 BC he finally made peace with Antony, who appointed him one of his top generals and administrators. But Ahenobarbus did not make peace with Cleopatra. She tried to win him over, but Ahenobarbus remained stubbornly opposed. He was the only one of Antony's supporters who refused to call her Queen Cleopatra, rudely referring to her instead as simply Cleopatra. He and his colleagues in Ephesus told Antony that she had to go. Having Cleopatra go back to Egypt would help Antony's case in Rome, because her absence would make clear that Octavian was fighting a civil war against Antony, not a foreign war against Cleopatra. And Octavian had vowed in public never to fight a civil war again.

Ahenobarbus and his like-minded colleagues might well have wanted Antony to invade Italy and defeat Octavian. They knew that it would be easier for Italians to accept such an invasion if Cleopatra were not part of it. They might also have feared that Cleopatra would oppose an invasion in order to preserve her fleet and protect the sea lanes to Egypt. They knew that, between her money, her ships, her men, and her influence on Antony, she would have considerable say. Hence, they had many reasons, in addition to their prejudices against a woman, an Egyptian, and a queen, to want to see Cleopatra gone.

Antony was still enough a part of the Roman establishment to hear the voices of his noble supporters, so he ordered Cleopatra to sail back to Egypt for the duration. She, however, would have none of it. She wanted to fight, and she feared leaving Antony. She also worried about Octavia. Cleopatra knew that if she went away, Octavia might swoop in and broker a peace agreement with Octavian, as she had done before. But Cleopatra didn't try to change Antony's mind on her own. She was too shrewd for that. Instead, she turned to his leading general, Canidius, a man as important to Antony on land as Ahenobarbus was at sea, and a man who called her queen.

Canidius had probably been in charge of Armenia, a key assignment. Following Antony's orders, early in 32 Canidius brought his army to Ephesus. Canidius was a practical person who recognized that Cleopatra brought money, Egyptian sailors, and hands-on experience governing a large state, all of which would be lost should she be sent away. He was the man Cleopatra chose to plead her case.

Canidius also argued that sending away Cleopatra would make the Egyptian contingent lose its heart for battle. This was no small thing, and it probably applied to many other eastern nations whose troops were joining the fight. The eastern Mediterranean had no shortage of people who hated Rome. Only about thirty years had passed since the death of King Mithradates VI of Pontus, the formidable enemy who fought three wars between 88 and 63 BC that shook Roman rule in the East. In Syria and Judea, some still remembered that their country had been free until Roman conquest in 63 BC. In Egypt, anti-Roman sentiment had blazed into a war against Caesar in Alexandria in 48 BC. Elsewhere in the East, people still resented the way Caesar's assassins had squeezed them dry to finance their war against Antony and Octavian.

To many, Cleopatra symbolized resistance. It was to her credit that she had tamed Antony and brought him to her side. He provided the muscle, but Cleopatra was the heart and soul of the fight.

Prophecy was a popular form of political messaging in the ancient world, especially in the East. A prophecy in Greek from around 33 BC claims that a "mistress" would "shear Rome's hair" and avenge Asia for the wrongs that Rome had inflicted upon it. The mistress would do justice by defeating the Romans and restoring a golden age of peace and reconciliation—an age, some said, of the sun. Although the mistress is not named, it is easy to see a reference to Cleopatra. No wonder her presence divided Antony's generals. For some, she was a force multiplier; for others, a dangerous revolutionary and a propaganda gift to the enemy.

Antony was willing to take the risk. He came down on Canidius's side, deciding that the queen could stay after all. For his pains, Canidius was accused of taking bribes from Cleopatra. Consider the evidence of a Greek papyrus document that survives by chance—it was reused in a mummy case in a Roman cemetery along the Nile. It records a royal order of 33 BC granting Canidius major tax breaks on his land in Egypt as well as on his import-export business (Egyptian wheat in exchange for wine from the Greek islands). The privileges included his tenants, animals, and ships. Perhaps the land represents an earlier royal gift. The order is signed by a different hand and says, in Greek, "make it happen." This may well be Cleopatra's own handwriting, but even if not, she was surely behind the order. The queen knew how to use Egypt's wealth to win Roman allies.

The thought might have crossed Cleopatra's mind to keep an eye on Ahenobarbus. Having lost his political struggle at Ephesus, he represented a security risk and might go to Octavian. After all, Ahenobarbus had changed sides before.

In the end, by pushing his agenda, Ahenobarbus only made Cleopatra's position with Antony stronger. In past wars, Antony always fought his own battles. His alliance with Cleopatra would cost him Roman supporters, some of whom now defected to Octavian. It was destiny, wrote Plutarch. It was Cleopatra.

Samos

In about April 32 BC Antony and Cleopatra and their staffs left Ephesus and sailed to the nearby island of Samos. It was the first step in the long westward move of the army and navy. It might take six weeks to get everyone across the Aegean, and much longer to reach and occupy the west coast of Greece. From there they could either defend the eastern half of the Roman Empire from attack or even invade Italy itself.

Antony had assembled a vast army of the East at Ephesus, calling to the colors all the kings, princes, cities, and nations from the Adriatic Sea to the Crimea, and from Syria to Armenia, as Plutarch puts it with dramatic flair. In a similar vein, Plutarch continues, Antony ordered all the "artists of Dionysus" to come to Samos. These were guilds of musicians, actors, and dancers. They were tight-knit, wealthy, and powerful groups in the Greek cities of the Aegean and beyond, representing the kind of influence that celebrities and professional sports teams do today. Antony rewarded them eventually with territory in the wealthy city of Priene (south of Ephesus, on Turkey's Aegean coast), but first came the spectacular on Samos. According to Plutarch, Antony and Cleopatra "made merry" on the island. Plutarch writes:

> [W]hile almost all the world around was filled with groans and lamentations, a single island for many days resounded with flutes and stringed instruments; theatres there were filled, and choral bands were competing with one another. Every city also sent an ox for the general sacrifice, and kings vied with one another in their mutual entertainments and gifts. And so, men everywhere began to ask: "How will the conquerors celebrate their victories if their preparations for the war are marked by festivals so costly?"

Plutarch here offers the Roman Empire's officially approved version of events. Antony and Cleopatra were frivolous, sybaritic spendthrifts who frittered away their military resources—so went the later propaganda. An impartial report might state instead that Antony and Cleopatra put on a brilliant rally to inspire their followers and to divert them during a lull in the campaign. It was part USO show, part send-off parade, part blessing the departing troops. As the new Dionysus, Antony could boast of his support from the followers of the god himself.

Divorce

By May or June, Antony and Cleopatra had transferred their base to Athens. Six years earlier, the city had housed him and Octavia, living together as a happy couple with a baby daughter, but those days were gone. Forgotten were the honors paid to Octavia when she was worshipped as Athena alongside Antony's Dionysus. Now the Athenian Assembly voted divine honors to Cleopatra. A delegation of Athenian citizens, led by Antony, who had been granted the citizenship about a decade earlier, came to the queen's house to announce the news. Antony stood before her and delivered a speech on the city's behalf.

Yet it was Octavia who attracted Antony's attention while he was in Athens. The Roman law of divorce was simple and blunt. Either spouse could inform the other that the marriage was over. "Take your things for yourself," went the legal formula of the partner announcing the divorce to the other. Antony communicated the message to Octavia via letter, which was common Roman practice.

From the Roman point of view, Antony's decision to divorce Octavia seemed tone-deaf. An unforced error. It underscored Octavian's argument that Antony had betrayed a virtuous Roman matron for a foreign seductress. From an eastern perspective, however, it made sense. By cutting his ties with the House of Caesar, the new Dionysus prepared to lead the East against the hated Romans. United with his true consort, Isis, he would embark on a holy war. Never mind the fact that Antony was, himself, a Roman. That fact could be buried under an avalanche of propaganda. Later on, when Antony got to Italy, he could reverse course and present himself as a loyal son of the republic.

Meanwhile, in Athens, statues of Antony and Cleopatra as gods were erected on the Acropolis, the city's holiest and most prominent site. One local joker took a shot at the two by scrawling under a statue of Antony, in Greek: "Octavia and Athena to Antony," followed in Latin by "take your things for yourself."

Upon receiving the notice that Antony had repudiated her, Octavia had to move. For five years, she had lived in Antony's house in an upscale part of Rome. There she received his friends and associates and put them in her debt—and that of her powerful brother—by helping them to obtain a public office or to manage some other business. Now Octavia and the six children that she was raising went to live with her brother. Those children included the two daughters she had borne Antony, a son and another two daughters from her previous marriage, and also one of Antony's sons by a previous marriage; the other son, Antyllus, was with his father.

At the news of divorce, Octavia is said to have cried tears of distress. Tears were more common and acceptable in Rome than they are today, and both men and women cried in public. The *miseratio*, or rhetorical plea for sympathy, often a weepy one, was as standard as it was suspect. More impressive is the sentiment that Octavia supposedly expressed: that she was wretched because it might seem as if she were one of the causes of the war that would soon break out. Note that Octavia didn't bewail the fact of the impending war itself but merely that *she* might be blamed for it. If this report is true, it accords with the emphasis that Romans put on their reputations.

Antony's divorcing Octavia played into Octavian's hands in Rome. In fact, it was such a bad move for Antony that one almost wonders whether Octavian didn't somehow trick Antony into it. Perhaps he started a rumor, with Octavia's connivance, that she was about to divorce Antony. That might have pushed Antony to act first, to avoid the humiliation of being rejected. How easy it would be then for Octavia to play the injured party. Then one remembers the huge propaganda advantage for Antony among his eastern followers by appearing to make a break with Rome and tying himself to Cleopatra, the avenger and savior. Antony might have wished that he could have had it both ways and have divorced Octavia in the East while staying married to her in Rome! He couldn't, of course, and Octavian could use Antony's action against him in the West.

If Octavia truly said that she felt miserable at being thought of as the cause of war, then it would take a heart of stone not to engage in a wicked thought. Maybe she would have felt even more miserable *not* to have been viewed that way. Maybe Octavia, no less than Helen, felt illicit joy at knowing that she made the world go around. A wicked thought, indeed.

As marriages go, Octavia's experience with Mark Antony had been a disaster: betrayal, humiliation, abandonment. But the marriage had also brought her motherhood, political power, celebrity, travel, and the odd deification. It had ended badly, but how many other divorcées could say that they had twice saved the Roman world from civil war? With perspective, perhaps many years later, Octavia could console herself with the knowledge that thanks to her sacrifices and hard work, the stage had been set for her brother to become the ruler of the world. Now, *that* was family loyalty that, even by Rome's strict standards, was worthy of the history books.

For nearly a decade after the divorce, Octavia is all but absent from the historical record. That is frustrating today but not surprising, because she had completed her mission. From her brother's point of view, Octavia's marriage had been a smashing success. It's no wonder that in the following decades, he treated her with the utmost consideration. Her mediation had kept Antony out of Italy when young Octavian needed a free hand against Sextus Pompey. She also got Antony to throw in a war fleet while allowing her brother to give almost nothing in return but promises, and those would be broken in due course. On top of that, by her good behavior and dignity in the face of Antony's humiliating treatment, Octavia had provided her brother a propaganda windfall. Octavia had not produced an heir for the Antonii, much less a boy to fulfill Virgil's prophecy. But she had done as much for the House of the Caesars as any military commander.

The Defectors

In June or July 32 BC Octavian welcomed to Rome the two highest-ranking members of Antony's entourage to defect. They were Lucius Munatius Plancus and his nephew Marcus Titius. Antony had trusted them both, to the extent that anyone could trust the slippery Plancus or his protégé. Together the two of them gave new meaning to the Latin word for deserter, *transfuga*, literally "one who flees across." Octavian, however, welcomed them as valuable intelligence and propaganda assets.

Besides, on the principle of "It takes a thief," Octavian was a good judge of turncoats. In a dozen years on the public stage, he had first supported Julius Caesar and then the Senate that approved of Caesar's assassination. He had made war on Antony and then joined forces with him against the Senate. He had allied with Cicero and then allowed him to be executed. He had made peace with Sextus Pompey and then fought a war to the death. So, Octavian could tolerate a few twists and turns on the parts of others. Or, in Plancus's case, more than a few.

In the space of the last dozen years, Plancus, too, had sometimes switched sides. A successful general, Plancus celebrated a triumph and was twice proclaimed imperator. After marching an army against Octavian at Perusia without actually fighting, he obtained Octavian's permission to escape from Italy and joined Antony in the East. He worked so closely with Antony in the following years that he was entrusted with Antony's signet ring and correspondence for a period, or at least so he claimed. Without doubt, Antony gave him the government of two important provinces, Asia (western Turkey) and Syria. Nor was Plancus out of favor with Cleopatra. Gossip told a delicious tale. Supposedly he was such a groveling flatterer that, to amuse her at a banquet once, Plancus imitated a merman by dancing naked, his body painted blue, his head encircled by reeds, while wearing a fish tail and crawling on his knees.

Plancus's nephew, Titius, who had been proscribed in 43 BC, raised his own fleet and went to sea; his father, who had also been proscribed, joined Sextus Pompey. Titius was captured by Sextus's men, but they spared him for the sake of his father, their fellow partisan. After the amnesty of 39 BC, Titius went back to Italy. He next went east, where he served Antony as quaestor in the invasion of Media. Antony gave Titius the job of dealing with Sextus when Sextus fled to Asia Minor after his defeat at sea off Sicily in 36 BC. Titius repaid Sextus's earlier generosity by having him executed, plausibly on Antony's order, or perhaps on Plancus's. Certainly Antony approved, because he made Titius governor of the wealthy province of Roman Asia.

Why then, did Plancus and Titius defect to Octavian? A hostile source says that Plancus got caught stealing and lost Antony's favor. But Roman officials tended to wink and nod at a little embezzlement, as long as they got their cut. A more plausible explanation says that Plancus and Titius broke with Antony over the divorce with Octavia. No one who cared about Italian opinion could have watched Antony make such a move without alarm. It might have seemed as if Antony were throwing away victory by acting in a way that would unite Italy behind Octavian. Like Ahenobarbus, Plancus and Titius had wanted Cleopatra back in Egypt after Ephesus rather than remaining with the expedition. Ahenobarbus continued to support Antony regardless, but Plancus chose to close his account. Perhaps the hostile source was right when he says that betrayal was a disease with Plancus.

The act of debriefing Plancus and Titius surely gave Octavian and his advisors precious information about Antony and his military plans. It also provided a juicy tidbit in the propaganda war: that Antony had left a will with the vestal virgins in Rome. Or perhaps Octavian already knew this, but he used the arrival of the two defectors as an excuse to wrest the will illegally from the vestals' safekeeping.

In a dramatic Senate meeting, Octavian announced the contents of the document. It recognized Caesarion, Octavian said, as the true son of Julius Caesar. It named Antony's children by Cleopatra among his heirs. Finally, it ordered that Antony should be buried in Alexandria beside Cleopatra. Even if he died in Rome, his body was to be shipped to Egypt. The upshot, as Octavian implied, was that Antony intended to move the seat of Rome's empire to the east.

That is, Octavian alleged that the will said all those things. Skepticism is called for. It is plausible that Antony left a will with the vestal virgins, but not that he put such damning words on paper, especially not in Rome, where they would be available to his enemies. In all likelihood, Octavian made most of it up, using Plancus's "revelation" as his excuse for finding the will. The one part that was certainly true was that Antony had already recognized Caesarion as Caesar's son.

Even with the flight in February of several hundred senators from Rome to Antony in Ephesus, there were still members left to criticize Octavian for his action. It didn't matter. The will could be claimed as tangible proof of Antony's enthrallment to a foreign queen. The remaining senators agreed to strip Antony of his imperium—the formal legal grant of power to command Roman armies abroad—as well as the consulship that he was supposed to hold in the following year, 31 BC. But they didn't declare him a public enemy because they didn't want to alienate his supporters; in fact, they offered to welcome those supporters to their side, as encouragement to them to defect.

The condemnation of Antony was quite a spectacle. Octavian loved the theater, and he might have remembered the vivid role of the letter in the Greek dramatist Euripides's play *Hippolytus*, from 428 BC, in which the female protagonist Phaedra falsely accuses Hippolytus, a royal prince and her stepson, of raping her. Antony's will made an equally effective prop in moving the drama along. Supporting actors, such as Gaius Calvisius Sabinus, who had tried to save Caesar's life in the fatal Senate meeting of the Ides of March, were called in to address the senators and to add details such as how the noble Antony had supposedly once stood up at a well-attended banquet in order to rub Cleopatra's feet.

It was all public relations. No one who had followed Octavian's career could have been surprised. He was a man who weaponized information.

The Declaration of War

After voting to declare war on Cleopatra, the senators took part in a formal ceremony steeped in tradition, although perhaps with an innovation or two. Once again, Octavian knew how to use theater.

The senators put on their military cloaks and went to the Temple of Bellona, the war goddess, located outside the walls of Rome. There Octavian carried out the official role of one of the priests known as *fetiales*, who supervised the laws and rituals of war and diplomacy. Before declaring war, these priests would make a public statement before Jupiter, Rome's chief god, that their cause was just. On this occasion, they did so, and then Octavian hurled a spear into a piece of land near the temple, symbolizing enemy territory. The symbolism was clear: Octavian's enemy was a foreigner, not a fellow Roman, and Octavian's cause was just. What is not clear is whether the spear toss was an archaic ceremony dredged up from the Roman past or a cultural appropriation from Greece. If archaic, it demonstrates Octavian's exploiting Romans' love for their heritage. If Greek, it copied the most famous spear toss in ancient history: Alexander the Great's beginning his invasion of the Persian Empire by throwing a spear after crossing the Hellespont strait and stepping onto the soil of Asia. Alexander considered Persian territory to be "spear-won" land. Either would have suited Octavian: reviving the Roman past or wrapping himself in the cloak of the world's greatest conqueror.

So, it was done at last. War with Antony, but only via the indirect route of striking at Cleopatra. The Senate, or what was left of it, acquiesced, at least in public. In all likelihood, they also voted Octavian the position of commander of the state's armies in the coming campaign. Evidently that was not enough. Octavian required that all

Italians and even the western provinces swear an oath of allegiance to him. In later years, he recalled this moment proudly:

"The whole of Italy voluntarily took oath of allegiance to me and demanded me as its leader in the war. . . . The provinces of Hispania, Gaul, Africa, Sicily, and Sardinia took the same oath of allegiance."

Focusing the war on Cleopatra rather than on Antony offered several advantages in Rome. Not declaring war on Antony allowed Octavian to keep his promise of not starting any new civil wars. In terms of publicity, the queen of Egypt represented an almost perfect enemy. As a female, a foreigner, a Greek, an Egyptian, and a monarch, she offered a rich target for Roman prejudices.

By the same token, Octavian gave the enemy a propaganda boost in the East. Antony was a Roman, and easterners didn't care much if one Roman attacked another. Cleopatra, however, was one of them. An attack on her was an attack on the East more generally as well as on the goddess Isis.

Antony and Cleopatra might have taken some credit for pushing Octavian into this corner. By asserting the legitimacy of Caesarion, they forced his hand, because it made Cleopatra and not Antony the real threat to him. They wielded information deftly and compelled their enemy to act in a way that strengthened their political base.

Octavian might have expressed outrage at Antony's treatment of Octavia. He might even have *felt* outrage, but sentiment did not push Octavian into war. Three things did: Rome, Egypt, and Caesar. The logic of Roman politics called for a showdown between two dynasts. Egypt was the treasure chest that Pompey and Caesar had each grabbed but were unable to keep over the Senate's opposition. Antony threatened to keep it, and with it the ability to outspend Octavian permanently. Caesar was the father claimed by two men, only one of whom could be his heir.

Caesarion threatened Octavian's claim to be Julius Caesar's son. Every day that the boy lived, he diminished the pretensions of the man known as Gaius Julius Caesar Imperator Divi Filius: Gaius Julius Caesar the Victorious General, Son of a God. If Caesarion was a flesh-and-blood Caesar, then Octavian was back to being merely Gaius Octavius, a minor member of a prosperous but provincial Italian family who just happened to be related to the great Julius, but only through his mother. Octavian didn't object to Antony's territorial arrangements in the East; in fact, after the Battle of Actium, he would keep almost all of Antony's client kings in place.

Octavian cannot be blamed for suspecting that war with Antony was inevitable. Antony's new fleet, his recognition of Caesarion, and his dynastic ambitions, all underwritten by Cleopatra's wealth, made the war inevitable. Yet the fact remains that Octavian struck first. He provoked the war at a time when Antony was fighting for Rome on the eastern front against Parthia. Some might call Octavian's move less than patriotic, but he hoped it would bring him the ultimate prize: the whole Roman Empire.

Part 2

A PLAN AND AN ATTACK

Autumn 32 to April 31 BC

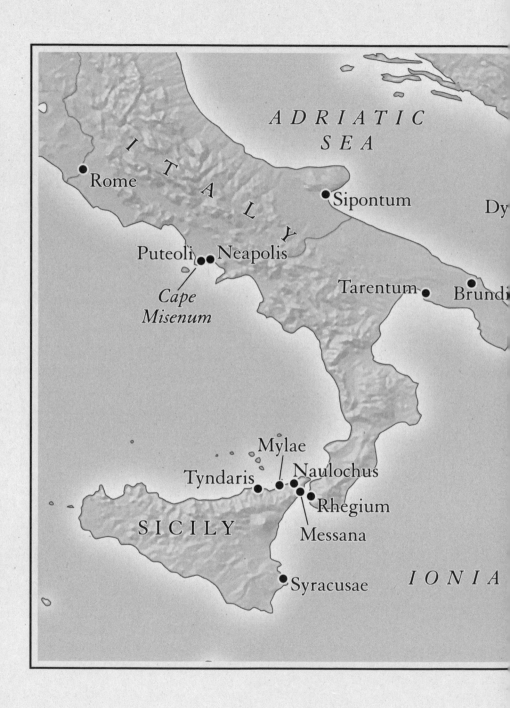

ADRIATIC
SEA

Rome

ITALY

Sipontum

Dy

Puteoli Neapolis

*Cape
Misenum*

Tarentum   Brundi

Mylae

Tyndaris   Naulochus

Rhegium

SICILY   Messana

Syracusae   IONIA

Western Greece and
Southern Italy/Sicily

0   MILES   200

0   KM   200

chium

pollonia
n

Philippi

PINDUS

EPIRUS

CORCYRA

Torune

Glykys
Limen

*AEGEAN
SEA*

PAXOS

NTIPAXOS

Actium

*M
T
S*

LEUCAS

ACARNANIA

ITHACA

Gulf of Corinth

CEPHALONIA

Patrae

Athens

ZACYNTHUS

PELOPONNESUS

SEA

Sparta

Methone

Taenarum

Chapter 6

The Invaders

Western Greece, Autumn 32 BC

ANTONY AND CLEOPATRA PURSUED TWO DIFFER-
ent strategies in 32 BC, one land based and one maritime. A land-
based strategy called for a thrust across the Ionian Sea and an invasion
of Italy, while a maritime strategy called for a base on the west coast of
Greece to defend the sea lanes to Egypt. All other things being equal,
a land-based strategy would appeal more to Antony, a land general
par excellence, whereas Cleopatra would favor a maritime strategy
because it protected the Egyptian homeland while emphasizing her
contribution in ships.

But all things weren't equal. The imperator and the queen had a
great navy, a proud Ptolemaic tradition at sea, and experienced admirals such as Ahenobarbus, but they faced a veteran and victorious
enemy fleet under Marcus Agrippa. Having conquered the greatest
admiral of his day, Sextus Pompey, and then having followed that accomplishment with a successful land-sea-riverine campaign in Illyria,
Agrippa had a fair claim to rule the waves. Only an alert, shrewd, and
determined force could mount a successful defense should he attack.
An invasion of Italy would transfer the initiative to Antony and Cleopatra while playing to Antony's strengths on land. Still, crossing the
Ionian Sea would be difficult and likely to be contested by the enemy.
Southern Italy had few ports, and the best of them, Brundisium and
Tarentum, were heavily fortified. Moreover, what if Agrippa and Oc-

tavian planned to bog down Antony and Cleopatra there while sending the bulk of their fleet to attack Egypt?

There was something to be said for a cautious strategy. Antony and Cleopatra could wait in Greece, threaten to invade Italy, and stir up opposition there to Octavian and his financial exactions. Ultimately, the enemy would have to come to them. A supreme effort of skill and alertness would keep them ready to contest the foe's crossing and any attempted landings. Even if Agrippa and Octavian were able to fight their way ashore and establish a base in western Greece, they would still need food and water. If Antony and Cleopatra could obstruct their access to those necessities, they would force them out to fight a battle on land. That would put Octavian and Agrippa exactly where Antony had wanted them in the first place, in a land battle, while also doing honor to the queen's naval contribution. Yet only a great military force honed to perfection could carry out such a strategy, and Antony and Cleopatra's navy was largely untested.

There was also a question of leadership. In Ephesus, Cleopatra had shown that she could make Anthony change his mind. A person might now ask, who was in charge?

Which would it be? A defensive stance in western Greece or an aggressive thrust into Italy?

The West Coast of Greece

Today's readers expect to be able to travel as directly as the bird flies, but ancient travel tended to be more roundabout. Modern maps are misleading about the realities of premodern transportation. Used to judging the ancient world by its famous cities—Rome and Athens, Ephesus and Alexandria—we might consider the west coast of Greece to be off the beaten path. In fact, it was prime real estate. Its islands and harbors marked the main navigational route between Italy and Greece and the eastern Mediterranean beyond.

The west coast of Greece was one of the most strategic waterways in the Mediterranean. Maritime traffic, especially naval traffic—that is, warships—knew it well, and for good reason. Galley warfare required control of the land. For this, there were several reasons. Warships were too light to carry many supplies. Navigation was difficult without the use of familiar landmarks. The open sea, even on the relatively gentle and tideless Mediterranean, could be rough and, on occasion, even generate fleet-destroying storms. So, naval commanders had to be able to control nearby beaches and ports and the markets to which they offered access. The sea lanes, with their mainland and island bases, held the key to victory. As a result, navies were also amphibious forces.

From time to time, ancient mariners sailed across open water between Sicily and the west coast of the Peloponnese. It was shorter and more direct than the coastal route. It minimized the risk of hitting rocks or going aground in hidden shallows. It was also a good way for merchantmen to avoid fast and fragile pirate ships, which had to stay clear of rough conditions. Still, navigators tended to prefer the coastal route, in particular along what is today the west coast of Greece and Albania.

Italy's east coast was dangerous and inadequate for ancient sailors. Even today it lacks harbors, offshore islands for shelter in a storm, prominent landmarks to guide navigation, and good anchorages. Worst of all, the prevailing winds make it a lee shore, with the risks of running aground and shipwreck. A better option beckoned. With its many harbors, islands, landmarks, good anchorages, and favorable winds, the eastern shores of the Adriatic and Ionian Seas offered everything the Italian coast lacked.

It's not by accident that so much of the ancient Mediterranean's maritime myth and history took place along the western coast of Greece. The most famous mariner of ancient legend, Odysseus, also known as Ulysses, lived there, on the island of Ithaca. The Peloponnesian War between Athens and Sparta was sparked by a naval battle in 433 BC off another island along that coast, Corcyra (modern Corfu, or Kérkyra). The western coast of Greece was also a major theater of the wars between Venice and the Ottoman Turks in the early modern era. The region retained its strategic importance during the Napoleonic Wars of the early eighteen hundreds, when it passed under first French and then British control. It became part of Greece in the mid-nineteenth century, then was occupied by Italy and Germany in World War II before returning to Greek control.

Whoever controlled that coast in ancient times held in his hands the fate not just of Greece but also of Italy. And by autumn 32 BC, it was firmly in Antony's grip. He had arranged his forces well. They dominated the eastern shore of the Ionian Sea, from the island of Corcyra in the north to the southwestern tip of the Peloponnesus, a distance of about 243 nautical miles. The main stations along this route were: Corcyra; Actium, at the entrance of the Gulf of Ambracia (Arta); the island of Leucas; the city of Patrae (modern Patras), just inside the entrance to the Corinthian Gulf; probably the island of Zacynthus, and Methone.

When Gnaeus Pompey held Greece in his war against Caesar in 48 BC, he made the port of Dyrrachium his base. It was a major harbor, close to Italy, and the start of the Via Egnatia, the Roman road that stretched eastward to Byzantium (the later Constantinople and Istanbul). Dyrrachium was located about 200 nautical miles north of Actium, a three-and-a-half-days' sail. Why did Antony and Cleopatra not occupy such valuable territory? For one thing, they might not have had a choice, if, as some evidence suggests, Octavian had helped himself to Dyrrachium and the nearby ports during the Illyrian War, breaking his agreement with Antony. Even if Dyrrachium was available to them, Antony and Cleopatra might have preferred a southern base, as it shortened their supply line from Egypt and forced Octavian to travel farther from Italy in order to reach them. Besides, a southern location made it easier to intercept an enemy fleet should it bypass Greece and try to invade Egypt.

Antony and Cleopatra spent the winter of 32–31 BC in Patrae, which had been the most important city of the Peloponnesus since the

Romans sacked Corinth about a century earlier. The main base of the fleet was at Actium, at a distance of about 126 nautical miles, or a day-and-a-half's sail from Patrae with a favorable wind.

By occupying these key harbors and bases, Antony had issued a challenge that Octavian had to answer, because his foe had, in effect, occupied the east coast of Italy without setting foot there. By putting a hostile fleet in control of the western coast of Greece, Antony threatened to sever Italian access to the east.

That Cleopatra and a strong Egyptian contingent were part of Antony's armada only made matters more serious for Octavian. For about a century, from the mid-200s to the mid-100s BC, the Ptolemies had controlled a naval base in the eastern Peloponnese. Now there arose the specter of a renewed Ptolemaic naval presence in Greece, but much closer to Rome.

Octavian might have remained on the defensive in Italy, but Romans liked their generals to attack. Besides, Octavian had declared war on the enemy, which put an onus on him. He might have tried to force Antony and Cleopatra back to Egypt by ignoring Greece and sending a fleet to Egypt, but that would have required a long journey, and he lacked allied assistance in the East.

All of that helped Antony and Cleopatra, but there were corresponding negatives. Supplying their force from Egypt and Syria required a herculean effort. The longer they stayed in western Greece—or in any one place—the more they risked seeing their force weaken and suffer desertion. Finally, the longer Antony and Cleopatra looked west, the sooner they would begin to face strategic challenges in the East, some potentially stirred up by Octavian's agents. There were, in short, reasons to invade Italy.

Invading Italy

Italy was not far off. Antony's northernmost base at Corcyra lay only 152 nautical miles and a two-day sail across the Ionian Sea from

Brundisium, the closest Italian port and Octavian's major naval harbor on the Adriatic coast. But this was not a journey to be undertaken lightly.

The peninsula bristled with defenses, both real and imaginary. The two main ports of southern Italy, Brundisium and Tarentum, were both heavily fortified, as Antony knew from personal experience. He was with Caesar in late 49 BC when Pompey held off their land attack on Brundisium until he was able to sail out to safety with his legions aboard his warships. Short of vessels, Caesar followed with only some of his legions in 48 BC and expected Antony to bring the rest, but Antony was blockaded in Brundisium. On the one hand, Antony won Caesar's praise for harassing the blockaders with men in rowboats and for lining the shore with cavalry and thereby denying the enemy access to water. On the other hand, Antony drew criticism from Caesar for excessive caution before he finally broke the blockade and crossed the Adriatic with additional legions.

Brundisium had closed its gates to Antony twice, in 40 BC and in 38 BC. The first time, Antony laid siege to the city and defeated troops sent by Octavian to drive him off. He also sent troops along the Italian coast to seize other strongpoints, including the Adriatic port city of Sipontum, about 175 miles north of Brundisium. Octavian dispatched veteran troops under Agrippa to retake the town, but they refused to fight their old comrade Antony. Affairs moved toward a political settlement. The next time Brundisium rejected Antony's fleet, in 38 BC, Tarentum received him, but possibly only because Octavian ordered the Tarentines to admit Antony for the meeting the two of them were about to hold there.

Then there was politics. After Octavian's successful smear campaign, it would be impolitic, to put it mildly, to invade Italy with a fleet including a large Egyptian contingent of ships, to say nothing of the queen of Egypt herself. That was surely one of the reasons why Ahenobarbus and others had argued back in Ephesus that she should go home to Egypt.

Nonetheless, Antony was considering an invasion. Maintaining a defensive posture and waiting for the enemy to attack was risky. His fleet was stretched out along a lengthy coastline, with many bays and inlets, thereby affording the enemy many places to attack. Antony's forces lacked the advantages of surprise and of popular support; the local inhabitants could hardly have been happy about the presence of a huge foreign army and navy in their country. Furthermore, by waiting, they would surrender the initiative to the enemy. This would surely depress morale among the men. As for Cleopatra, her presence in Italy might have been awkward, but people have accepted far worse things from a conquering army.

How might Antony have intended to win the war by invading Italy? Since he did not get to tell his story, and since Octavian has colored the historical record with his version of events, we need to engage in informed speculation.

Antony might have had a three-part plan for victory: financial, political, and military. On the financial side, he would squeeze Octavian by forcing him to levy hefty taxes in Italy to support his army and navy. To fund his forces, Octavian had required free people in Italy to pay one-quarter of their income, and freedmen (former slaves), one-eighth of their capital. The sources report how unpopular those taxes were. Freedmen rioted; murders and fires in public buildings in Rome were blamed on them. Octavian sent in troops against them, which is said to have convinced free people to shut up and pay. In addition, Antony sent money to Italy to support his old friends there or to buy new ones. He was doing this as late as autumn 32. There is evidence that during 33 and 32 BC, Antony was also minting coins of his own in Italy, to purchase additional support. This brings us to the second prong of Antony's strategy: politics.

Antony aimed at weakening Octavian's political base in Italy. Money was one way of doing so, propaganda was another, and creating a perception of victory was a third. That's where Antony's resources came in: the big numbers of his fleet and army and the well-known treasure of Egypt were meant to convey that Antony's was the winning side. The presence of his forces so close to Italy also fed the presumption that Antony was coming to Italy as soon as the weather improved and navigation became safe.

Octavian's response shows that he feared Antony's strategy. Octavian increased his vigilance in general and carried out one initiative in particular: he gave money to his soldiers. When it came time to leave Italy for the front, he carried out a unique departure. Sailing from Brundisium in spring 32 BC to fight Antony, Octavian brought with him all of the senators and many Roman knights. Some were supporters; others were virtually hostages. Rome had never seen anything like this. The Senate always sent out generals, while most senators stayed in Rome. It seems that Octavian did not trust business as usual. Even with his loyal supporter Gaius Maecenas remaining in Italy with an army, Octavian feared a rising in his rear by Antony's sympathizers.

Having softened up his opponent through financial and political warfare, Antony might have expected to achieve final victory by defeating Octavian in a military campaign. The sources state that he planned to invade Italy. According to a summary of the historian Livy (the original is lost), writing in the latter part of the reign of Augustus in the early first century of our era, "Antony intended to make war on the city of Rome and on Italy, and he gathered an equally huge number of naval forces as land forces." Marcus Velleius Paterculus, writing during the reign of Emperor Tiberius (AD 14 to 37), maintains that Antony decided to wage war on his fatherland, while Plutarch, writing around AD 100, says that Antony made a mistake in not forcing Octavian to fight before Octavian was ready. Although Plutarch doesn't say so, the only way to have forced Octavian would have been for Antony to invade Italy. Finally, Cassius Dio, writing in the early third century, contends that Antony set out to invade Italy unexpectedly. It could not be easy to move such a large fleet "unexpectedly." Yet Antony might have planned a feint toward, say, Dyrrachium, in order to mislead the enemy about his real target.

It's worth emphasizing the agreement of the ancient sources because several modern scholars reject the argument. True, it served Octavian's propaganda purposes to claim that Antony was going to invade the homeland. Cleopatra supposedly used to swear that one day she would dispense justice on the Capitoline Hill, the religious center of Rome. If this invasion plan was merely Octavian's invention, then it was a brilliant one, sure to make some Italians shiver.

Perhaps Antony wanted merely to create the impression that he intended to invade Italy, just in order to stir up fear, but without ever seriously meaning it. He had reason to hesitate before invading, but he also had reason to hesitate at the thought of facing Agrippa in a naval battle. If Agrippa agreed to meet Antony's fleet head-on in open water, with both crews fit and in fighting trim, then Antony's big ships with reinforced prows had a chance of prevailing. But the wily and experienced Agrippa was unlikely to be so obliging. With his veteran crews and knowledge of the sea, he could find a way to force Antony to fight on unfavorable terms. Antony, the commander in chief of his forces, was not proficient in naval warfare. His men, too, were largely inexperienced. Cleopatra's ships probably included a large contingent of officers and seamen from Egypt's Red Sea–India trading fleet, and they knew the sea, but their know-how was in commerce, not warfare. The advantage of having experienced men in ancient warfare cannot be overstated. A crew of novices was likely to make mistakes or, worse, panic in the stress of their first battle.

A How-to of Invasion

If Antony opted for invasion, how could he force his way into an Italian port? In an ideal world, his political and military pressure campaigns would have won him enough friends in Italy to open the gates of Brundisium or Tarentum. Failing that, however, a military victory would be difficult but not impossible.

The nature of Antony's ships tells the tale. A combination of archaeology (meticulous measurement of the size of the ram sockets on Augustus's Actium Victory Monument) and history (analogies to earlier Ptolemaic fleets) gives us a rough idea of Antony's naval building strategy. As noted earlier, the typical ship of a Roman fleet was referred to as a five. On a plausible reconstruction, they were two-level warships with three men on each oar on the top level and two men per oar on the bottom level. They typically carried 300 oarsmen and 120 marines. There were also some smaller ships, including "threes," or triremes, galleys that each carried 180 oarsmen arranged on three levels, with one man per oar. There were also lemboi: smaller and faster ships with rowers arranged either on one or two levels, for a total of roughly 50 rowers, depending on the particular type of craft. Finally, there were a few larger vessels, ranging from "sixes" to "tens."

Fives were versatile ships, ably adapted for the various stages of a naval battle. They had a big, heavy, reinforced ram in the bow, which allowed for frontal ramming of the enemy when the two fleets sped toward each other at the start of an engagement. Fives were also capable of using grappling and boarding tactics, often preceded by a barrage of catapults. The quinquereme or five was the warhorse of Mediterranean naval battles in the last centuries BC. As for the catapult, it was a heavy missile weapon, powered by tense springs made of twisted rope from hair or animal sinews, and capable of releasing great power. Roman catapults in use during this era could fire either stones or bolts.

The largest ships, the sixes to tens, were not much use in battle. Big and slow, they made easy targets. Their main purpose, instead, was to engage in a naval assault on a fortified port. They could be used to break through harbor barriers, such as chains or lines of boats, to crush smaller warships in the way, and even to ram the foundations of city walls. Their covered decks served as protection for marines, while their towers allowed the emplacement of catapults to shoot at the enemy. It is with these ships that Antony planned to attack.

The evidence shows that Antony's fleet contained at least four to five tens, four nines, five eights, six sevens, and perhaps eight sixes, for a total of twenty-seven or twenty-eight large ships—only a little more than 5 percent of Antony's total force of five hundred warships. Although he might have had still more big ships, he probably wouldn't have had too many more. Not only were big ships expensive to build and maintain, but also they were vulnerable to enemy attack and needed to be protected by a large guard of smaller ships. Most of Antony's fleet, therefore, probably consisted of fives.

Octavian's propaganda made much of these big ships, which far outnumbered the few similar vessels in Octavian's fleet. But it's not true that Antony's fleet consisted mainly of lumbering monsters.

To an ancient observer, the size and character of Antony's fleet sent a clear message, and that message was: invasion. The target was Italy. One might have suspected that he was bluffing, and one might have doubted Antony's willingness to test his ships against the stout walls of Italian ports, but his threat was clear.

An ancient observer would have read another message in Antony's fleet as well. And that was that it hardly seemed Roman. Roman admirals tended to avoid naval sieges and preferred to face enemy ships in battle. It was a throwback to the glory days of the third century BC, when the fleets of Alexander's successors, the Ptolemies and their rivals, vied for naval mastery of the eastern Mediterranean. All of these fleets were run by Greek speakers, and each fleet eventually lost its power to the Romans. But under Antony, they seemed to have a sudden and unexpected revival.

Naturally that would lead an ancient observer to attribute the strategic difference to the influence of Cleopatra. The queen symbolized a naval tradition ready to rise from a long sleep in the shipyards of Alexandria. They would provide the large workforce of craftsmen and engineers needed to build a fleet, particularly one including big ships capable of conducting a siege.

Cleopatra embodied the ancient aspirations of the Ptolemaic dynasty. Most important of all, she alone had the treasury to pay for such a fleet. Because whatever else they were, big ships were expensive. Navies in general were the costliest part of ancient warfare, and none more so than navies designed to lay siege. In fact, their very existence was meant to intimidate on the financial front as well as militarily.

If things went according to plan, Antony would sail across the straits to Italy. Whether Antony chose to attack Brundisium or Tarentum, he would have been wise to send a squadron to the other in order to mislead the enemy. Likewise, as mentioned, he could have detached part of his fleet to sail toward Dyrrachium as a feint.

Antony might have decided to bypass both ports and to lay siege to one of them while the bulk of his army marched on Rome. That, however, would deny him a supply base, as well as leave the enemy free to enjoy two good harbors and to move his ships by sea at will. It would also have exacted a price in the loss of prestige to be gained by capturing a port. Attacking made the most sense.

Antony knew every inch of Brundisium and its defenses. He probably was less familiar with Tarentum, but his visit there with a fleet only five years earlier had given him and his commanders a chance to inspect the city and its fortifications. Such knowledge would help him greatly in any attack.

Ideally, traitors would betray the city to Antony. If not, he would execute a complex, joint land-sea assault. He would land most of his legionaries on shore at a safe distance from the city but near enough for them to march to it. Fives were light enough to be drawn up on a beach. Antony would also unload his siege equipment and pack animals. They would proceed to carry out a siege by land, while being ready to fight a battle first if need be. Meanwhile, a naval siege unit would attack the harbor. The mere approach of the fleet would incite terror. Writing about a looming naval attack on a fortified city in an earlier period, one historian describes the soldiers and old men and women lining the city walls, "terror-stricken at the magnitude of the fleet and the gleam of the shining armor, . . . [and being] not a little anxious about the final outcome."

The unit would consist of a combination of ships, from large sixes, eights, and tens, to smaller vessels able to protect the largest ships and fight enemy warships. The largest ships would attack obstacles blocking the harbor entrance and then launch catapults at the city walls. The other ships would fight via a variety of tactics, from ramming, to shooting stone missiles or bolts, to grappling and boarding enemy ships. They might also land marines on shore to try to scale the walls with ladders.

The battle would be horrific: a cacophony of shouts, trumpets, and battle cries set to the pounding rhythm of oars; the whoosh of catapults and the crash of ships; and, everywhere, the screams of the dying. With luck, Antony could achieve victory in days or weeks, but a longer siege, one taking months, was not out of the question. In order to avoid that, Antony needed to achieve enough local success here and there along the city's walls to encourage his most influential supporters in Italy to come forward and defect. If he emerged victorious, Antony could march on Rome. No doubt many Italians would decide that they really didn't mind having Cleopatra around after all.

Yet it must be admitted that a joint land-sea attack was highly risky. Would Antony have taken the chance? One would like to answer yes, for like all great men, Antony did not think small. Nor was he humble. Another factor is that, when it came to sieges, Antony had unfinished business. He was with Caesar at the Battle of Alesia in Gaul in 52 BC—an epic engagement that set the standard for successful sieges. But Antony's own sieges had failed: first at Mutina in 43 BC and then at Phraaspa in 36 BC. And Brundisium had shut him out twice, leaving him a score to settle. Invading Italy offered redemption.

So why did Antony and Cleopatra not invade Italy? A joint land-sea assault would require a long preparation. By the time Antony got his forces into position, it was already autumn 32 BC—probably too late in the season to mount a major naval operation. Sailing would be safer in the spring, especially beginning in May. So, Antony might have put off the invasion. One source contends that Antony probed the possibility of invasion in late autumn, but the presence of enemy scout ships off the island of Corcyra frightened him away, since he suspected that Octavian and his entire fleet were nearby. This sounds suspiciously like a later attempt to portray Antony as a coward.

Gifted with hindsight, Plutarch blasted Antony's delay as a mistake. Maybe so. In the past, Antony had been an aggressive commander, but even the most bellicose warrior can grow cautious when everything is at stake. Experience, moreover, is often a harsh teacher. When he invaded Media Atropatene in 36 BC, Antony had sped ahead, leaving his siege train to follow and, as it turned out, to be attacked and destroyed by the enemy. Now, four years later, he might have concluded that it was better to wait than to forge ahead. At the age of fifty-one, Antony was unlikely to be impetuous. A cautious general can always find a reason to switch to a defensive stand: bad weather, the failure of sufficient traitors in Brundisium or Tarentum to have materialized, the success of Octavian's propaganda campaign against foreign invaders of Italy's sacred soil, the risk of overextending already stretched supply lines, the presence of enemy scout ships off Corcyra, the lack of enthusiasm on the part of Cleopatra and her Egyptian contingent. Any or all of these possibilities could have justified shelving the invasion of Italy. Perhaps Antony even thought it was still possible that Octavian would back down and offer to negotiate rather than risk an invasion of Greece.

Cleopatra's influence on the decision cannot be calibrated, but it is likely to have been considerable. Her ships, her propaganda value in the East as Isis, her personal influence with Antony—however much or little that might have been—all mattered. Most important, the queen held the purse strings. If she did not want to risk an invasion of Italy, she and her treasury might have made the difference.

The alternative to attacking Italy was to stand on defense in western Greece. That, it seems, is the choice that Antony and his high command had made in winter 31 BC. They would wait for Agrippa. But he would not arrive when or where they expected. He was about to teach the truth of an oft-quoted military maxim: "The enemy gets a vote."

Chapter 7

The Naval Crown

Italy, March 31 BC

HE WORE THE NAVAL CROWN. BEFORE HE CROSSED the sea to confront Antony, Marcus Agrippa was already Rome's most decorated naval officer. After defeating Sextus Pompey, Agrippa had taken part in a campaign to wipe out the pirates of the eastern Adriatic coast by driving into their hinterland and taking over their swift ships. He had rebuilt the Roman navy from scratch, trained its men, and devised tactics that would allow a less experienced fleet to defeat a navy of master mariners. In short, he was already a great admiral.

Upon returning to Rome from victory against Pompey in 36 BC, Octavian gave Agrippa a highly unusual military honor. It was the naval crown, a golden wreath featuring a prominent decoration shaped like the prow of a warship. The Senate gave Agrippa the right to wear the crown in triumphal parades. Coins and statues show him sporting the crown. Only one Roman had received the honor of a naval crown before, but Agrippa's was the first made of gold.

The poet Virgil describes Agrippa wearing the "naval crown, that binds his manly brows." Shown in profile on coins, the three-finned ram (which might also be described as trident shaped) and curving stem post of a galley, in the crown's front, stand out prominently above Agrippa's forehead. Wearing such a creation could hardly have been comfortable, but with the vigor implied by the image's full head of curly hair, classical profile, and thickly muscled neck, Agrippa appears to be having no trouble bearing the burden. The conflict ahead would indeed require fortitude along with skill and cunning.

It is a tribute to Octavian's propaganda in later years that today we can hardly appreciate what a thunderbolt Agrippa's seizure of Methone represented. Taking the enemy's key supply base there in March 31 BC was a military coup of the highest order—as daring and risky as George Washington's crossing the Delaware or Japan's surprise air attack on Pearl Harbor. Octavian, as Augustus, wanted to portray Antony's defeat as inevitable, because, he said, Antony was the emasculated love slave of Cleopatra and hence incapable of posing a serious threat. The truth was that Antony represented a mortal danger. So, forced to act, Octavian approved Agrippa's risky plan to strike first, and it worked.

Methone was the keystone of Antony and Cleopatra's logistics; the most important link in the chain of bases, stretching from Egypt to western Greece. Tucked in the southwestern corner of the Peloponnese, the town sat on a rocky peninsula beside an excellent harbor. Three nearby islands served as a natural breakwater, protecting the harbor from the rough sea. Methone lay on the shipping lanes from Egypt and Syria, via Crete and the Peloponnese, to Patrae and Actium. Antony's forces in Greece could not live off the land; they needed to have food shipped to them.

Methone served two military purposes. It provided a safe harbor, and ancient ships had to make frequent stops at coastal anchorages. Its strategic location allowed Methone to protect supply ships coming around the Peloponnese. So it was important to hold the town in order to ensure that Antony's men were fed. In later centuries, when Venice controlled Methone, the Venetians considered it to be one of "the eyes of the republic" (along with the nearby seaside fortress of Corone).

Octavian and Agrippa had devised a plan to prevent Antony from attacking. They knew that the enemy's strong position at Actium lay on a weak foundation. Antony's forces depended on a logistical and supply chain stretching a thousand miles southward and eastward, mainly by sea: from Antony's northernmost position on the island of Corcyra in northwestern Greece all the way to the ports of Syria and Egypt. A series of bases along the route secured the chain. Though the bases were all defended, individually, they were vulnerable, for with so many places to protect, Antony was limited in the number of men and ships he could put in each. A shrewd adversary would take advantage of this weakness, and Agrippa was shrewd indeed. If he could cut the supply chain, he could starve the enemy.

Antony and Cleopatra had more and bigger ships than the enemy and far more money, so Octavian and Agrippa engaged in the classic competitor strategy. Having become specialists in naval warfare, they knew how to craft a strategic riposte. They began their attack via an indirect approach, aiming to put the odds in their favor before the final reckoning.

By attacking Antony's rear, Agrippa was, although unbeknownst to him, following the advice of the great, ancient Chinese military strategist, Sun Tzu: he was attacking the enemy's strategy rather than immediately attacking the enemy. Agrippa had an excellent intuitive sense of the strategic landscape.

And by attacking Antony's supply chain, Agrippa was anticipating the advice that Publius Flavius Vegetius Renatus, author of an influential military treatise, would give Roman generals many centuries later: "A great strategy is to press the enemy more with famine than with the sword." Roman commanders had employed such a strategy since the days of the Punic Wars against Carthage in the third century BC. Agrippa and Octavian had used it just a few years previously to set the stage for ultimate victory in the war against Sextus Pompey, when, according to the Greek historian Appian, they cut off his food supplies on Sicily "by first capturing the towns that furnished them." This strategy proved so effective that Sextus had to fight or starve, and so he decided to stake everything on one battle, at Naulochus, where Agrippa crushed Sextus's fleet.

Against Antony and Cleopatra, Octavian and Agrippa planned

something similar but on a grander scale. But if they saw the enemy's vulnerability, why didn't Antony and Cleopatra?

History is full of examples of generals done in by their own blind spots: from a willingness of the Persian fleet to sail into the Greeks' trap in the Salamis straits; to the legions that marched into Arminius's ambush in the Teutoburg Forest; to the American warships and airplanes that were easy pickings for the Japanese attackers at Pearl Harbor. There were reasons why Antony and Cleopatra failed properly to appreciate their rivals' success against Sextus Pompey and the Illyrians. They had an enormous and fully supplied fleet, as well as the services of the best admiral on the side of Caesar's assassins, Ahenobarbus, a man with particular experience of fighting in the Ionian Sea.

"Infinite variety": Shakespeare applied these words to Cleopatra, but they fit Agrippa, too. He was the rare general who turned into a successful admiral. In addition, he was the rare conqueror who didn't mind becoming a sort of water commissioner (aedile) for Rome, or, later, an urban planner, architect, ambassador, and both indispensable associate and son-in-law to Rome's first emperor. Agrippa was versatile, brilliant, and pragmatic. Now, confronted by an enemy in Antony and Cleopatra whom he couldn't defeat head-on, he mastered the indirect approach and deployed it with a bold and creative solution when he chose to attack Methone.

Located in the southwest corner of the Peloponnese, Methone was about 385 nautical miles from Brundisium by coastal sailing routes. As far south as Methone was, Antony might have considered it safe. More likely, he expected an attack in the north—say, at Corcyra, which was closer to the crossing from Italy—but if so, he underestimated the enemy.

Octavian surely gave his approval to Agrippa's audacious plan. Octavian respected his admiral's acumen, but Octavian was the boss. A clear and undisputed chain of command is the recipe for a successful partnership.

To take Methone, Agrippa had to transport his troops undetected; overrun a fortified city; and, along the way, gather the necessary intelligence. We would like to reconstruct Agrippa's attack on Methone in detail, but the sources are too scanty. Still, they offer clues, and important information comes from other, similar, better-documented operations.

Agrippa knew how Antony's mind worked. Both he, and even more so, Octavian, had worked with Antony directly. High-profile defectors such as Plancus and Titius brought inside information about Antony's plans and the disposition of his forces. Perhaps most precious of all was the insight that Octavia could have provided to Octavian.

As a result, a shrewd and bold commander was in a position to operate inside Antony's frame of reference, and to disorient, disrupt, and ultimately defeat him. Agrippa is likely to have begun by employing deception.

We don't know what route Agrippa took to Methone, but it was surely one that the enemy did not observe. One might imagine him beginning in Brundisium. He is likely to have increased operational security in his port of embarkation by strictly limiting access to the naval harbor there. From Brundisium, Agrippa could have followed the coast a short distance to the southeastern tip of Italy, the Sallentinum Promontory (modern Cape Santa Maria di Leuca). From there, it is a distance of about 320 nautical miles to Methone. Agrippa's ships could have headed southeastward, taking care to give a wide berth to the Ionian Islands with their enemy forces.

An even better way to avoid detection was to take the open-water route from Sicily to the Peloponnese. As long as one brought along sufficient supplies for several days at sea, such trips were possible. Since the southeastern tip of Sicily and Methone lie on roughly the same latitude, it was easy for mariners to navigate by the stars. That route was roughly the same distance as the trip from southern Italy to Methone. It would have required a long detour from Italy at the outset, followed by an open-sea voyage, which was not without risk in bad weather—especially for warships, which were less sturdy than merchant ships. So, that route is a less likely choice.

If they steered clear of the Ionian Islands, how did Agrippa's ships keep from getting lost at sea, without either compass or sextant, let alone GPS? Ancient navigators could look for mountains and other landmarks—and Greece's high mountains were visible even far out at sea. They could note the direction of the winds or the presence of land breezes (and hence of the nearness of land), observe the direction of the current, notice the formation of clouds (often formed over land), pay attention to the flight path of birds (either seabirds who nest on land and feed at sea, or migratory birds following regular paths). They study directions left by prior navigators in the various published sailing manuals (*Peripli*), use lead lines to take soundings when nearing the coast, and, most important, steer by the sun and the stars. Experience was vital. Agrippa surely recruited professional mariners who had sailed the route before (whichever route he took), knew its details well, and were likely to stay calm in the face of trouble.

How many men would be needed to capture Methone? In 200 BC a Roman fleet took the Macedonian stronghold of Chalcis on the island of Euboea, not far from Athens. They had twenty Roman threes (triremes), and four allied fours, three undecked Athenian ships, so probably about two thousand marines. Those men proved to be enough to storm the city's poorly guarded walls and to kill the enemy commander, but not enough to garrison the place with sufficient troops left over to hold Athens, so the Romans withdrew after their quick and violent success.

Since Agrippa wanted to keep Methone after capturing it, he probably brought a stronger force. Scholars have long surmised that Agrippa brought only fast, light, highly maneuverable vessels. Yet, traveling across open water with lighter ships than threes (triremes) would have been too risky. This is particularly the case because Agrippa probably attacked early in the sailing season, perhaps in March, when conditions could still be rather rough. But there are other ways to travel light aside from sailing in small ships.

A Roman war fleet of forty quinqueremes or fives is known to have sailed in wintertime 171 BC from Naples to the island of Cephalonia, off the western Peloponnese. Perhaps Agrippa too, sailing 130 years later, had forty of the fives, if not fewer. A Roman five normally carried about 120 marines. With forty of them, Agrippa could have brought about 4,800 marines, a strong force. They could have carried their own food and water, in order not to slow the force with merchant ships. He might also have brought a small number of light, fast ships to serve as reconnaissance vessels along the enemy coast. He might even have had those ships, their sails, and their rigging painted sea blue, with the crews' uniforms dyed a similar color, to avoid detection.

In 171 BC that Roman war fleet of forty quinqueremes sailed from Naples to Cephalonia in five days during wintertime. At an average speed of four knots before a favorable wind—fast, but not unprecedented—Agrippa's fleet could have reached Methone in as little as about three and a half days. The prevailing wind during March in the Sicilian Sea is northwesterly, which would have sped Agrippa's fleet southeastward.

Agrippa's strategy was not entirely new: Romans had, after all, attacked their enemy's supply lines before. But it was bold and ambitious. It surely demonstrates the capability of both Agrippa and Octavian to think creatively. They would also have had to plan meticulously, because an amphibious operation requires nothing less. Fortunately, Agrippa was a master planner. He would assemble, we imagine, a small but strong force, staffed with experienced legionaries with a sense of adventure, a commitment to Octavian's cause, and a taste for a good fight.

In addition to planning, a successful military operation requires nimbleness and adaptability. After all, few plans survive contact with reality. Experience, training, and leadership gave Agrippa's team most of what it needed in order to make adjustments on the fly, but one more ingredient was required: good intelligence.

Agrippa needed to know as much about Methone in advance as was possible. Several sources were promising: defectors from Antony's camp, and Romans familiar with the province of Achaea (Greece), from former governors down to slaves, could have supplied information on the situation at Methone. Some of Agrippa's crews might have been to the town, as it was on a major shipping route in the center of the Roman Empire. A man of Octavian's status surely also had what the Romans called "clients" along the west coast of Greece: free people who were tied to him by a web of mutual obligations. Octavia, who knew Greece, might also have provided useful sources. Agrippa could debrief them as well as other persons who disliked Antony or Cleopatra or who simply wanted to hedge their bets. There were spies, too. A report says that Octavian caught a spy sent by Antony, and presumably Octavian sent spies to Antony in turn. Perhaps the most vital source of information was the pilots, who could guide Agrippa's ships along the coastal waters around Methone.

With luck, one or more of these sources could have reported on the whereabouts of Ahenobarbus and Antony's other experienced admirals, which would better help Agrippa avoid them, should they be in the vicinity of his route. Still, he would have known that, however careful his navigators, he still might not be able to hide his fleet from Antony. A prudent commander would have taken additional steps to deceive the enemy about his intended target, perhaps by planting spies to spread disinformation.

A surprising situation awaited in Methone.

Chapter 8

The African King

Methone, Greece, March 31 BC

THE CAPTURE OF METHONE HAS OFTEN BEEN SEEN as one of the jewels in Marcus Agrippa's nautical crown. Little attention has been paid to the man who lost it. He was an experienced general with one great success to his name but with some failures as well. Given the consequences of the loss of Methone, he deserves a closer look.

He was Bogud, a Moor, and an African king.

Moors lived in Mauretania, in what is nowadays Morocco and western Algeria, a land with variegated marble that the Romans prized. Historically, Moors have been a multiracial group, including both darker- and lighter-skinned individuals, a mixture of peoples of sub-Saharan-African and Mediterranean descent. About Bogud, we cannot be more precise.

In 49 BC he and his brother or cousin Bocchus were recognized as kings by both Julius Caesar and the Roman Senate; they were Bogud II and Bocchus II. Bogud ruled western Mauretania, and Bocchus ruled eastern Mauretania.

If the report is true, Caesar was not shy in what he asked for in return. He is supposed to have had an affair with Eunoe, who was Bogud's wife, or perhaps one of his wives, since Mauretanian kings were known for polygamy. Given Caesar's reputation for bedding politician's wives and foreign queens alike, the story is plausible. Caesar is supposed to have bestowed many splendid gifts on both husband and wife in exchange.

But the main thing that Caesar asked for and received from Bogud was military and political support. Bogud's greatest battle came when he fought for Caesar at Munda in Farther Hispania. At this encounter on March 17, 45 BC, the two sons of Pompey forced Caesar into a long, tough fight that lasted the whole day. A key moment came with a cavalry attack on the Pompeian camp, which unleashed a chain reaction of fear among the enemy that soon caused them to break and run. It was Bogud who led that crucial cavalry attack.

Bogud commanded a unit of Moorish cavalry. Moors were famously light, fast, and lethal horsemen. Bogud's cavalry attack helped Caesar win the battle, but the outcome was not achieved easily. Afterward, the Roman dictator supposedly said that while he had often fought for victory, this time he'd fought for his life.

After the Ides of March, Bogud decided to back Antony, while his relative Bocchus sided with Octavian. Bogud crossed over to Hispania in support of Antony, although whether he did so on Antony's instructions or his own initiative is unknown. Bogud was involved in heavy fighting in Hispania, but he had to turn back to Africa when a rebellion broke out at home, supported by Octavian and Bocchus. Bogud was forced to concede, and Octavian confirmed Bocchus as the new ruler of Bogud's kingdom. In 38 BC Bogud left his homeland and made his way in exile to Antony in the East. And in 31 BC he was in charge of Methone.

As long as its wall was well maintained and defended by a strong force, Methone was highly defensible. In 431 BC, for example, an Athenian and allied fleet of more than 150 ships proved unable to take the town, in spite of a weak wall and the absence of a garrison, thanks to the arrival of a small but tough Spartan relief force. A few centuries later, when the town was well walled, Illyrian raiders didn't even try to assault the place. Instead, they pretended to be traders in order to lure out the population of the town: captivity and probably slavery followed. In the year 1500 it would take a siege of twenty-eight days for Methone to fall to an Ottoman Turkish fleet supervised by the sultan himself.

Given Methone's strong position, how did Antony lose it to Agrippa? One source claims that Antony stationed a very strong garrison in Methone, but if so, it was outmatched. However, that source, *History Against the Pagans*, by the Roman historian Orosius, was written around AD 400 and was likely based on an earlier source favorable to Augustus: either the emperor's own *Memoirs* or a later text based on it, which might have exaggerated the opposition that Agrippa faced in order to make his achievement look better. Perhaps the garrison was "strong" in numbers of men, but there is reason to think that Methone was underpowered in terms of quality.

Antony should have placed a Roman in charge and supplied him with a force of legionaries. Instead, he chose an ally, and one who no longer had a country behind him to supply manpower. Bogud was an experienced soldier, but one suspects that his main job qualification was his loyalty to Antony; after all, Bogud had nowhere else to go.

Modern armies are notorious for putting their least experienced troops in the rear. In the American Civil War, Union generals Ulysses S. Grant and William T. Sherman placed raw troops at the back to get them used to soldiering, but that left them vulnerable to veteran Confederate raiders. A hundred years after that, the US war in Vietnam gave rise to the acronym REMF, or "rear-echelon motherf—ers." Today they are mocked as "fobbits" because they stay on the FOB: forward operating base, where everything is safe, and supposedly never "leave the wire."

Ancient armies are unlikely to have been different. Then, as now, the most ambitious soldiers want to fight where there is glory to be won, and that is on the front lines. So, Bogud is unlikely to have had many, if any, legionaries. Instead, most of his soldiers were probably light-armed troops. But Agrippa had legionaries. Outfitted with heavier weapons and armor, probably better trained and better disciplined, legionaries could outfight light-armed troops both on land and in boarding parties at sea.

Even if the manpower defending Methone was stronger than just suggested, the place might have had other weaknesses. Some of Bogud's light-armed troops might have doubled as rowers, but Bogud is unlikely to have had many ships at his disposal: Antony simply had too many places to defend. Nor do we know the state of Methone's walls at the time. We hear nothing of the various defenses used to protect a fortified place in this era, such as any barriers erected in the harbor, nail-studded doors to serve as traps for invaders, spikes on the shore, and stockades on landing places. We don't know how careful the lookouts were.

To be sure, Antony and Bogud should have attended meticulously to all of these factors. Antony knew as well as any commander just how vulnerable waterborne supply lines were. He was cocommander with Octavian at Philippi in 42 BC when a relief force, en route to resupply their army, was attacked and destroyed by the enemy navy. Another example that should have been on Antony's mind was the enemy's harassment of his supply lines during the Parthian campaign. But even careful commanders make mistakes or take risks when they have to man far-flung bases with limited resources.

The several hundred senators who fled Rome for Antony's camp, as well as other sources, would have brought information of their own, including detailed reports of Agrippa's success as an admiral against Sextus. It should have been clear that Agrippa would make a formidable opponent, but clearly Antony didn't prepare sufficiently. As far south from Brundisium as Bogud was, he might have felt safe, but if so, he underestimated the enemy.

Agrippa might have taken several simple steps to increase the surprise factor. "Time is everything," the great admiral Horatio Nelson said later, and it is likely to have played a key role at Methone. If, as is often thought, Agrippa timed his attack for the very beginning of the sailing season, in March, he would have been all the more unexpected. Agrippa also might have timed the attack for a quarter moon, the lunar phase that offers just enough light to navigate but without making ships visible to the enemy until they are close.

Agrippa is likely to have moved his ships at night, as much as that was possible. To begin with, when arriving at the Peloponnese, he might have made landfall at night. That was risky because rocks and shoals would be hard to discern, and darkness would make it hard to be sure exactly where one had landed. Still, night sailing along the coast is attested, and Agrippa's fleet might have taken the risk, especially with sufficient moonlight.

It was not easy to take a fortified place by storm. Successful ancient examples involved taking advantages of gaps, breaches, or other weaknesses in defensive fortifications (for example, walls with parts in ruins, or a breach in the walls caused by a mistake on the part of the defenders, or gates incautiously left open); making a surprise attack, usually at night or just before dawn, as stealthily as possible; or the massive use of catapults and ballistae or battering rams and mining operations. In his treatise on fortifications and defense, Philo of Byzantium, the author of a book on siege warfare ca. 200 BC, advised attacking a city when most men were outside the gates—for example, during a festival or during the harvest or vintage—and preferably when the enemy was drunk. He also recommended approaching the wall secretly, with ladders ready, either by night or during a storm. Philo advised the commander to offer rewards to the first men over the wall. He wrote that it was best to make the first assault by placing ladders against the weakest spots on the walls, in order to storm the city while those inside were still afraid. Philo also recommended the use of special climbing equipment, such as leather and rope ladders with hooks on the ends in order to catch on the battlements when thrown up and over; tempered and sharpened iron pegs to place into cracks and joints in the wall; and iron hooks thrown onto the battlements on ropes with loops in them.

Launching a successful amphibious assault on a fortified place is even more difficult than attacking by land. Agrippa knew this from personal experience. In 36 BC he captured Tyndaris, a strategic stronghold in Sicily, although it took two separate attempts. Tyndaris sits on a promontory, and ancient sources say it was admirably situated for naval warfare, and well stocked with provisions at the time. On the first occasion, Agrippa got inside the town, presumably through the help of supporters within, but the defending garrison fought bravely and drove him out. Then, not long afterward, Agrippa came back and finally took Tyndaris, but no details of the operation survive. To take another example, in 35 BC, during the Illyrian War, Agrippa and Octavian seized the city of Siscia (now Sisak, Croatia), which sat at the confluence of two rivers. After gathering a large navy, they attacked the town both from the land and from the river. The defenders put up a stout resistance but eventually surrendered.

Methone was walled. Nowadays a large Venetian-Ottoman fortress is there, covering a flat promontory that juts a thousand feet into the sea. This was not the first fortification in this strategic location. Literary sources refer to fortifications there as early as the fifth century BC. There are reports of Hellenistic revetments and of second-century AD Roman walls as parts of the Venetian fortress, but there has been no systematic excavation. A fishhook-shaped breakwater curved around the east side of the fort in antiquity, and was built perhaps after the year AD 175. We surmise this, since it is not mentioned by the Greek geographer and historian Pausanias, who visited the site shortly before then. We simply don't know the extent of the fortification or harbor works in 31 BC. Still, we can be sure that then as now, there was a natural harbor on the east side of the cape on which Methone sits, and a beach stretching northeastward from the harbor.

Agrippa's capture of Methone would reverberate in Roman memory, but no detailed contemporary account survives. Although not much is known of his activities in the campaign before the Battle of Actium, the seizure of Methone is mentioned in four separate sources:

by Strabo, a Greek geographer who was a contemporary of Octavian; Cassius Dio, active around the year 200; the Phoenician philosopher Porphyry of Tyre, active around 300; and Orosius, active in the early 400s. That suggests that these events figured prominently in Augustan accounts, perhaps in Augustus's *Memoirs*.

We might imagine that Agrippa captured Methone in one of several possible ways. After crossing the sea from the west, Agrippa might have stopped on the coast of the Peloponnese to take on water and give his men a brief rest. He then sailed directly into Methone. He might have relied on the shock of his unexpected arrival providing enough of a force multiplier to overcome the advantage that daylight offered to the enemy. Several centuries earlier, an Athenian general had recommended that the best way to capture the city of Syracuse was to sail right in and attack as soon as possible. Shock and panic, he said, would paralyze the enemy. Since the general's plan was not accepted, we do not know if it would have worked, but Agrippa might have followed a similar reasoning at Methone. A bold and direct daylight assault is the simplest way to construe the ancient sources' reference to his capturing the place "by an attack from the sea" (*ex epiplou*). Strabo, who uses this phrase, is the earliest surviving source for the capture.

A more complex operation is also possible. We might imagine Agrippa sailing not directly to Methone but rather to Sapientza, one of the Oenussae islands that lies only about two miles offshore from Methone. Perhaps he sailed to Sapientza at night. Indeed, in the prelude to the Battle of Mylae in 36 BC, Agrippa sailed his fleet from the island of Hiera (modern Vulcano, one of the Aeolian or Lipari Islands) at night, thereby using darkness to surprise the enemy off the northern coast of Sicily. To take another example, Rome's successful attack on the Greek city of Chalcis in 200 BC began with a nighttime sail. Sapientza was a good place to hide ships, as illustrated by the island's heyday as a pirate's nest in the early modern era. The island was inhabited already in the Hellenistic era. From Sapientza, Agrippa could sail to Methone and reach it by first light, as long as he had the assistance of local pilots.

We might imagine a calm March night with a quarter moon. Perhaps it was either March 14 or March 29, which in 31 BC marked the first and last quarter moons of the month. No one at Methone expected an enemy attack so far from the ports of southern Italy, so their guard was down. Agrippa might have timed his attack for first light, when the enemy troops were likely to be groggy and unprepared. The Romans timed their attack on Chalcis for just that hour. Runaways had told Agrippa where the city was most sparsely populated, and he had one unit of marines attack there. They scaled the wall with their ladders, captured a tower, killed the sleeping enemy guards whom they first encountered, and fought their way through the rest. Meanwhile, another unit attacked Bogud's ships. By the time the enemy sounded the alarm, it was too late. Besides, their light-armed troops were no match for Agrippa's legionaries. In short order, they reached a gate, tore it down, and admitted the rest of their troops inside the walls. Confusion and slaughter followed, and it didn't end before Agrippa's men had killed Bogud.

At the other end of the scale of possibilities, we might imagine a much-better-prepared Bogud and a beach too well armed for Agrippa to employ a direct attack. In that case, he might have landed at an offset site and then marched his men overland to Methone. It is also possible that Agrippa divided his forces to keep Bogud guessing. He might have launched one attack by sea and another from an offset site on land. In 259 BC a Roman general captured Sardinian towns by just such a stratagem. After landing troops secretly at night, he attacked the cities when his ships drew off the defenders. But such an operation was difficult indeed for an ancient navy.

The sources state that Agrippa killed Bogud, but they don't indicate whether that happened in the course of battle or as an execution afterward. In either case, the Moor died a long way from home.

The consequences of the seizure of Methone rippled outward.

Like some ancient Sir Francis Drake, the English sea captain whose 1587 raid destroyed Spanish supply ships and slowed the sailing of its armada against England, Agrippa had seriously discomfited the enemy.

Methone was only the beginning of Antony's troubles in the rear. Agrippa was now able to use the town and its fine harbor as a base for raiding the enemy's supply ships. In addition to the ships that he had brought, he now also had at his disposal whatever ships he had captured from Bogud. In an era in which men were often forced to change sides, he probably also had Bogud's manpower to help his as well. He might also have sent word of his victory to Italy and received reinforcements in order to carry out further attacks.

In the following months, Agrippa captured Antony's base at Patrae—after Antony had left it—and raided Corinth. Agrippa seems to have worked in a methodical manner to prevent Antony from off-setting the loss of his southern sea lines of communication to Egypt by establishing an alternate route. That is, we might suppose that Antony off-loaded supplies at the Corinthian isthmus and reloaded them on the other side, allowing him to resupply his forces via the Gulf of Corinth. This would explain Agrippa's raids north and the capture of Patrae and his raid(s) on Corinth itself. Agrippa surely did this either in response to Antony's efforts to reconfigure his supply route or in anticipation that he would do so, thus preemptively denying Antony this option.

Antony, in return, had to withdraw warships from his other bases in order to counter Agrippa's moves. In fact, Agrippa's quick and multiple thrusts flooded Antony with uncertainty and doubt. One source writes that after taking Methone, Agrippa "was now watching for the merchant vessels that came to land and was making descents from time to time on various parts of Greece, all of which disturbed Antony greatly."

Agrippa's attacks can be considered a form of swarming: a seemingly amorphous but actually highly structured and coordinated series of attacks that appear to come from all directions. Agrippa moved with great speed and unpredictability, whereas Antony's commanders reacted more slowly and with less success. The result was to disrupt the enemy's ability to respond effectively.

In order to feed his men, Antony had to levy a grain tax on Greece, whose poor soil could not compensate for the loss of the rich produce of the fertile Nile Valley. It is probably to this period that we should date an anecdote of the Actium campaign in Plutarch's *Life of Antony*:

> At any rate, my great-grandfather Nicarchus used to tell how all his fellow citizens were compelled to carry on their shoulders a stipulated measure of wheat down to the sea at Anticyra, and how their pace was quickened by the whip; they had carried one load in this way, he said, the second was already measured out, and they were just about to set forth, when word was brought that Antony had been defeated, and this was the salvation of the city; for immediately the stewards and soldiers of Antony took to flight, and the citizens divided the grain among themselves.

The period after the loss of Methone was probably also the time when Antony's trusted associate, Quintus Dellius, offended Cleopatra by complaining that they had to drink sour wine while, in Rome, one of Octavian's favorites was drinking a fine Italian vintage.

There was more. It was a day's journey from Methone to Sparta, the key city of the southern Peloponnese. One of the city's leading men, Gaius Julius Eurycles, held a grudge against Antony for having executed his father as a pirate. It was probably now that he defected to Octavian. The Spartans illustrated their change of heart by changing the name honored on their coins from ATR, for the Antonian general Lucius Sempronius Atratinus, to AGR, for Agrippa. Eventually Atratinus defected to Octavian as well.

Velleius Paterculus, writing about fifty years after the Battle of

Actium, says that Octavian's victory "was a certainty long before the battle." That is an exaggeration. The prolific British author Michael Grant is more on the mark when he concludes that "the capture of Methone in itself meant that the war was half lost already." It wasn't just the capture of Methone, though, but also Agrippa's initiative in building on that success to achieve further victories and Antony's failure to stem the bleeding.

Antony did not retake Methone. If it was as well fortified as the sources state, then all Agrippa had to do to hold on to it was to be more prepared than Bogud had been. By keeping his guard up, Agrippa could have kept the city secure. Then, too, Antony had to divide his resources in order to defend his other bases, however unsuccessfully. Most pressing of all, it wasn't long until his greatest challenge took shape. Sometime later in the spring of 31 BC, when sailing conditions were generally safer, Octavian crossed with the bulk of the fleet and reached the east shore of the Adriatic. The main confrontation now loomed.

Chapter 9

Sitting on a Ladle

Western Greece, April 31 BC

FOR ABOUT SIX MONTHS BETWEEN OCTOBER 32 AND April 31 BC, Patrae was the center of the universe or at least of its eastern half. While Antony and Cleopatra were there, Patrae became the nucleus of finance, information warfare, and intrigue, as well as a hub of feasting and religious ritual.

It was a far cry from Alexandria. Patrae was a sailors' town at the entrance to the Corinthian Gulf from the Ionian Sea, a city of merchants and bankers and Roman dignitaries passing through en route to and from Italy, until Antony and Cleopatra and their undoubtedly enormous entourage arrived.

The army and the navy were mostly elsewhere. Actium, located farther north up the coast at the entrance of the Ambracian Gulf, was the main station of the fleet, but Antony's ships were scattered up and down the western coast of Greece, continuing south around the Peloponnese and eastward to Crete, Libya, and Egypt. The legions camped in various locations around Greece. But a campsite was no place for the queen and her consort, so they wintered in Patrae.

Located in the foothills of the mountains of Achaea, Patrae offered dramatic views northward across the gulf to the mountains of Acarnania. The city has a typical Mediterranean climate, with hot, dry summers and mild, wet winters. Looking across the sea on a winter's day, Antony might have thought about the fighting that lay ahead. Or he might have turned to happier thoughts on a rainy evening, lying beside Cleopatra on banqueting couches in a hall glittering with candlelight and warmed by the heat of charcoal braziers.

Even in winter quarters, military campaigns are busy places. Business always pressed, and at Patrae, Antony took care of a crucial matter: paying his troops. He had millions of coins struck while he was in the city. These were almost all silver denarii (a small denomination), except for a small number of gold coins. They all bore the image of a galley on one side, with its oars extended as if off to battle. The reverse showed two legionary standards flanking a legionary eagle. The standards were long poles with flags or symbols of the legion it represented; the eagle topped a pole. Both the standards and the eagle represented a legion; they were symbols for which men fought and died. Around the galley, the legend proclaimed Antony as both triumvir and augur (a religious official), while the other side named the particular legion by its number; for example, LEG III, the third legion. Caesar too, had been an augur, so Antony might have been trying to borrow a little of the great man's glory with their shared title. He could not, however, borrow Caesar's vast fortune. Even with Egypt's wealth, Antony could not pay his many soldiers and sailors without inflating the currency, which he did by lowering the coins' silver content and adding copper. That could not have pleased the men.

The coin images were propaganda meant to advertise the power of Antony's army and navy, while hoping, perhaps, to distract attention from the debasement of the silver. But they weren't the only propagandistic coins issued at Patrae. Antony struck other coins there claiming the consulship of 31 BC, the office that Octavian had forced the Senate to take away from him. One side of these coins bore Antony's image; the other, Cleopatra's. The queen figured on other coinage issued by the city of Patrae. The town celebrated its royal visitor by minting coins with her image and the legend "Queen Cleopatra"; the reverse depicts the crown of Isis.

Both Antony, as augur, and Cleopatra, as Isis, decorated their coinage with religious symbols, a reminder that they had the gods on their side. One imagines that the new Isis and the new Dionysus made the case more vividly while in Patrae and presided in person over rituals in honor of Isis.

Whatever else they did, the two looked westward to Italy, where they sent agents to disperse bribes, gather intelligence, and stir up trouble for Octavian. No doubt they also interrogated couriers who had braved the winter sea to bring news of Rome.

Omens were weapons in information warfare. We hear only of those that favor Octavian, but there must have plenty of pro-Antony omens as well. Reports describe various alleged prodigies, including bloody or sweating statues of Antony; wind and storm damage to images of Antony's patron gods, Hercules and Dionysus; and an earthquake in an Italian city in which Antony had established a veteran's colony. Swallows are supposed to have made a nest on Cleopatra's flagship, the *Antonias*, but then other swallows came and drove out the adult birds and killed the nestlings. Swallows symbolized the goddess Isis, but they also symbolized death. In addition to these portents of doom for Antony, there were signs of death for Romans more generally, including an owl flying into temples, storm damage to various statues and trophies, and, allegedly, an eighty-five-foot-long, two-headed serpent in central Italy. Octavian's partisans even trotted out the news that after two days of fighting between children's teams in Rome, the "Caesarians" beat the "Antonians." Cut from the same cloth is the charge that Antony left Italy because he kept losing to Octavian in games ranging from dice to cockfighting, which supposedly proved to an Egyptian seer that Antony's spirit could not stand up to Octavian.

Trash talk was part of the information environment as well. Octavian offered to let Antony land unmolested in Italy's harbors and anchorages after Octavian had withdrawn his forces about a day's ride by horseback (about fifty miles). Antony, for his part, challenged Octavian to single combat; failing that, Antony said, he defied Octavian to land in Greece and then to march his army to Pharsalus, in central

Greece, where they could fight it out on the very battlefield where Caesar had crushed Pompey's army in 48 BC. Antony played a big part in that battle, leading Caesar's left wing, while Octavian, aged fourteen, was living safely in Rome. A second battle at the site was an utterly impractical proposal, since the trip from western Greece to Pharsalus took, by the fastest route, well over a week, and a lot longer by the slow route. But neither man's offer was meant seriously.

If Antony was planning to invade Italy in 31 BC, he had not gotten very far when the enemy struck at Methone in March. Still, a defensive strategy was not despicable. It might have worked had his forces been prepared for the unexpected. But they were not, as the events of March made plain.

Antony and his team had had time to respond to Agrippa's victory at Methone when a thunderclap sounded in the North: Octavian and his fleet had crossed the Adriatic Sea.

Octavian Arrives

In spring 31 BC Octavian prepared to go to war. He gathered his forces in Brundisium, the preferred port for travel between Italy and the East. Octavian had an army and a fleet there, but his stay was as much political as it was military. He ordered all the most important knights and senators to join him in the port city. They were to cross the sea with him on campaign, with each bringing a stated number of servants as well as their own supplies. If the bit about servants sounds like the outfitting of a bunch of prima donnas, it should. From a military standpoint, the gathering of grandees spelled nothing but trouble. But Octavian wasn't thinking like a military man.

This drafting of the senators to go to war was unprecedented and only slightly less odd than if, say, Winston Churchill had ordered the members of the House of Commons to join him on the D-day expedition in 1944. But Churchill, unlike Octavian, was not faced with the possibility of a coup d'état against him in his absence. So, Octavian essentially took the Senate with him as hostages, as well as the most capable Roman knights.

Not wanting to leave Italy on a sour note, Octavian turned the conscription of the Roman elite into a celebration of Italian unity. He hammered home the message that he had repeated frequently since the "discovery" of Antony's will: that the consensus of Italy was behind him. That, he let out, was the meaning of the extraordinary gathering at Brundisium. No one knew better than Octavian how incomplete Italy's supposed unity was.

It was probably not long after the good news about Agrippa arrived from Greece that Octavian set sail with the main part of his fleet. It was, roughly, April 31 BC.

Octavian had 230 warships and an unknown number of transports. If all went well, he would link up across the Adriatic with Agrippa and his fleet, consisting of the vessels that Agrippa had left port with (or at least the surviving ones) and any that he had captured from Antony. When Octavian was joined by Agrippa's forces, the combined fleet had more than 400 ships.

Antony, meanwhile, had stationed most of his fleet in the Gulf of Ambracia at Actium. He had departed Ephesus almost a year earlier with five hundred warships. After posting detachments in his far-flung bases, he was left with a smaller but still substantial armada, but he had also to cope with losses from desertion and disease. As a result, he was able to muster far fewer than five hundred ships at Actium in spring 31 BC.

Octavian had fewer soldiers than Antony—about eighty thousand to a hundred thousand men—but they made up in quality what they lacked in quantity. Octavian had fewer allied troops, who served largely in light-armed roles, but he had about the same number of heavy-armed legionaries. He probably had sixteen legions of about four thousand to five thousand men each, that is, roughly at full strength. Antony had nineteen legions, but they were probably below strength, so each side came to war with about seventy thousand to seventy-five thousand legionaries. Antony had twenty thousand to twenty-five thousand light-armed allied infantry. Each side had twelve thousand cavalrymen. Both sides had a large number of veterans: Antony's served in the campaigns against Brutus and Cassius and the Parthians; Octavian's, in the wars of Perusia, Illyria, and the struggle against Sextus Pompey. Octavian, however, probably had more veterans than Antony, since his losses in his previous campaigns had been relatively low.

Antony had suffered heavy losses fighting in Media: 25 percent, according to hostile but plausible sources. Since he had as many troops in 31 BC as in 36 BC, it follows that he had refilled his ranks, largely by recruiting new soldiers but probably also by stripping Macedonia of its three legions. Aside from those legions, few of Antony's new recruits would have been Italians, although some would have been Italian colonists in the East or their sons.

Antony's allied forces represented a diverse group particularly strong in cavalry. Yet each allied leader came with a private agenda. None could be counted on for loyalty. Nor would forging them into a unified force be easy. For all they added to Antony's power, they also represented a challenge.

A half dozen allied kings and tribal rulers, from Asia Minor and Thrace (roughly, Bulgaria) were present at Actium with their troops. Many if not most of them brought cavalry. Each of them had been chosen by Antony to rule a client kingdom. The most important of them in the events to come was Amyntas, king of Galatia in central Asia Minor. He had supported Brutus and Cassius at Philippi at first but then switched sides before the final battle. Antony rewarded him with his kingdom and expanded its borders for good measure. Amyntas brought to Actium two thousand Galatian cavalrymen, a group known for their excellence fighting on horseback.

Four other kings were not present themselves but had sent armies. Two of them would cut important figures in events to come.

Malchus was king of the Nabataeans, in northwestern Arabia, a wealthy region that controlled trade with the valuable spice-producing areas of southern Arabia. Befitting a ruler in a border zone, Malchus had complicated loyalties. He had supported Julius Caesar, then the Parthians. Antony gave part of Malchus's territory to Cleopatra and forced him to lease it back for an annual rent of two hundred talents of silver—more than fifteen thousand pounds. But he fell behind in his payments, and Antony had his neighbor King Herod of Judea attack Malchus and defeat him. Herod was probably happy to oblige, as he held a grudge against the Nabataean ruler for refusing to support him a few years earlier when Herod was a refugee from Parthian attack. No doubt hoping to get on Antony's good side, Malchus sent troops to support him at Actium.

As for Herod, he and Cleopatra were enemies. She had coveted his kingdom, but Antony kept it from her. The Judean king, in turn, could not have been happy at what Antony did give her: the rights to the groves of balsam, a valued medicinal, found around Jericho. Herod, too, had to pay an annual rent of two hundred talents of silver. Neither Herod nor Cleopatra could have been sorry that he stayed home from Actium, while sending troops in support of the cause.

As Octavian landed on the eastern shore of the Adriatic, he received another gift from Agrippa. His loyal friend had defeated Antony's ships off the island of Corcyra and then diverted part of the rest of Antony's fleet as he continued to sail and attack in the waters around Greece. It was a perfect opportunity for Octavian to cross the Adriatic in safety. He landed first on the mainland, at the foot of the mountains opposite Corcyra. There his ships disembarked their cavalry. Agrippa had already captured Corcyra, thereby freeing Octavian of worries of an enemy attack from the island. Then Octavian and his ships sailed south for approximately two days along the mainland until Octavian based his fleet at a place called Glykys Limen, "Fresh Harbor" (Modern Fanari), near the mouth of the Acheron River. The army occupied a place nearby called Torune, in northwestern Greece. Probably the modern town of Parga, Torune lies about thirty-five miles north of Actium, about a two-days' march by land. Antony and Cleopatra's main fleet was docked in the Gulf of Actium, about 125 nautical miles from Patrae, or a day-and-a-half's sail for a fast ship under oars.

Antony and Cleopatra's fleet responded passively. They didn't challenge Octavian or prevent him from establishing a camp. The ancient historian Cassius Dio claims that they were too confident to accept Octavian's invitation to parley and too fearful to take up his challenge to fight a battle. Perhaps they were outnumbered and waiting for Antony and the rest of the force to arrive, or perhaps they were awaiting orders.

After the disaster at Methone, Antony should have been ready to hit back hard. He had to be prepared to counterattack and to repel the enemy, wherever else he struck, especially in the North, where a crossing from Brundisium was predictable. Instead, he appeared to be asleep.

By doing nothing to hinder Octavian's landing or his establishing camp, Antony hardly impresses. It was as if he had tacitly conceded command of the sea to the enemy. Perhaps he justified his passivity by recalling his own experience crossing the Adriatic in 48 BC. Pompey's ships made it difficult for Antony to make the journey, but, in spite of their massive superiority in numbers, they couldn't stop him. Antony might have concluded that it wasn't worth trying to stop Octavian. It's true that he was eager to fight a land battle, and Antony might have reasoned that the sooner Octavian and his army were within his reach, the better. Yet, if that was Antony's strategy, he was not displaying the aggressive spirit expected of a Roman commander (and of most commanders).

Antony and Cleopatra and their staffs now had to hurry northward, but the Egyptian queen kept calm and made a joke. Her cutting wit was on display.

"What's so terrible," she said, "if Caesar [that is, Octavian] is sitting on a ladle?" The joke has multiple meanings. A person looks ridiculous sitting on a ladle. A man looks less than warlike, since a ladle is a poor substitute for a spear or a sword. But most important, *ladle* was, it seems, obscene, if obscure slang for "penis," which means that Cleopatra was accusing Octavian of being a *cinaedus*, the passive partner in a male, same-sex, sex act. In other words, she was saying, it was no big deal, since Octavian was used to sitting on "ladles." To Greeks and Romans, that behavior was utterly unacceptable for a grown man. Antony had already accused Octavian of having been Julius Caesar's passive partner in bed, and one wonders if Cleopatra, who knew Caesar intimately, was the source of that story. (The double meaning of *ladle* apparently goes back to fifth-century BC Athenian comedy, so Cleopatra's joke showed off her scholarship.)

The Lay of the Land

As mentioned, Actium sits beneath the mountains of Epirus. Epirus was war country. It was the homeland of Olympias, the woman who gave birth to the conqueror of the world, Alexander. A generation later, Epirus would be ruled by the warrior-king Pyrrhus. He killed an enemy chief in single combat and crossed the Adriatic in search of an Italian empire, only to be driven out of Italy and, upon his return to Greece, to be killed by a roof tile dropped on his head by an angry woman standing on her terrace during an urban brawl. Epirus was the home, too, of the entrance to the underworld—via the Acheron River—or so the priests claimed.

But it was not in the highlands of Epirus where the gods of war would battle on this occasion. This combat would take place near the coast. The shore is low and sandy, ringed by an undulating layer of hills. The entrance is so narrow—less than a half mile wide—as to hide the gulf's presence from the unsuspecting traveler. At about twenty-five miles long and nine miles wide, the Ambracian Gulf is a perfect bay. Here Antony and Cleopatra kept the pride of their war fleet. Octavian and Agrippa had their armada nearby.

At Actium, as often in the history of battle, topography tells half the story. The name Actium refers broadly to the opening of the Ambracian Gulf to the Ionian Sea, a narrow strait. More precisely, though, Actium was the southern of the two promontories that guard the entrance to the gulf, like two arms reaching out and almost touching. The area around Actium had numerous good harbors offering safe anchorages for foreign fleets. Actium was most famous, however, for the Temple of Apollo and the annual festival associated with it.

The Two Camps

Antony and Cleopatra made their camp on the cape of the southern, or Actium, promontory. Their camp was substantial enough that, nearly fifty years later, it was still possible to visit its remains. (Nowadays, a more amusing memorial marks the site: the Cleopatra Marina.) On either side of the entrance, guard towers, capable of firing volley after volley of missiles—stones or bolts (short, heavy arrows)— kept most enemy ships from entering the gulf, and, if necessary, patrol ships sent in the channel could cut off the rest.

Roman military camps were austere, masculine places, famous for their order and regularity. This one was different. Not that it lacked discipline, but it was certainly colorful, with its range of allied soldiers and their different uniforms and equipment. And then there was Cleopatra, with her retinue and her royal ways. She would hardly have subsisted on the grain-heavy diet of a Roman legionary. We can imagine the imperator and the queen dining on the local delicacies: sardines, succulent shrimp, and other tasty fish from the Ambracian Gulf and the duck of the Louros River marshes.

That rich fare would have made quite a contrast to the conditions in camp, especially as they worsened over time. Despite its strategic advantages, the Actium promontory was not an inviting place. It was a flat, sandy, and largely empty piece of land. It lacked trees and fresh water, and its small and enclosed area might render waste removal a challenge for a large army. Its marshes bred mosquitos. All of this would spell trouble if the army was still there in the hot months of the summer. Trouble too, if they couldn't ensure a steady supply of food and water.

Octavian sited his camp at a place known today as Michalitsi. Surely he would have liked to control the entrance to the Ambracian Gulf, but that lay firmly in Antony's hands. Michalitsi sits about four miles north of the mouth of the gulf. Michalitsi is composed of a range of ridges reaching more than five hundred feet at the highest peak. Octavian's headquarters tent—his *praesidium*—was probably located at the site of the victory monument, at an elevation of about three hundred feet. The rest of his camp probably stretched along the slopes of Michalitsi over the land of modern Nicopolis (Smyrtoula). In addition to being easily defensible, the heights offered several other advantages. The site provides a panoramic view, no small benefit in an age before binoculars. Standing on the hill, one can see the Ambracian Gulf directly below, the Ionian Sea nearby, the rugged ridges of the islands of Leucas in the distance to the south, and Paxos and Antipaxos to the northwest, with the mountains of Acarnania to the south and those of Epirus rising in the haze to the north. In addition to the view, the cool and breezy hill also offered protection from the mosquitos that frequented the lowlands and brought malaria.

On the minus side, Michalitsi didn't provide access to a protected harbor on the sea. Octavian kept some of his ships at Glykys Limen, "Fresh Harbor," a sheltered harbor about twenty nautical miles away to the north. The closest harbor to Michalitsi was less than ideal. It was Gomaros, just about a mile to the west but exposed to the elements if a strong wind from the west was blowing. It is possible that Agrippa built a mole or stone breakwater there to offer some protection to ships; a modern mole there may perhaps obscure ancient remains. To connect harbor and camp, Octavian had a set of long walls built, the sort of engineering feat at which the Roman army excelled. The walls meant that supplies could be delivered safely to Octavian's camp.

Fresh water provided a greater challenge. As surface inspection shows, today there are springs in Michalitsi and on the slopes and plain below. Assuming the same was true in 31 BC, they would have proven useful but insufficient for the needs of Octavian's large army. Knowing this, Antony tried to cut off Octavian's access to water sources outside his camp. About two miles away from Michalitsi, there was fresh water in the Louros River, which empties into the marshes at the northern end of the Ambracian Gulf. It was vulnerable to enemy action.

Antony did nothing to stop Octavian from taking the high ground at Michalitsi, but with his legions not yet at Actium, Antony was in no position to prevent Octavian's move. Antony might also have concluded that his opponent had fallen into a trap. Without a good harbor and with the real danger of having its water supplies cut off, Michalitsi might have looked like the site of Octavian's last stand. All Antony had to do was to block his enemy's access to fresh water.

March and April 32 BC had been bad months for Antony. He failed to contest Octavian's crossing, to impede his army's march southward, and to prevent his seizure of the high ground at Michalitsi north of Actium. It was a failure of leadership, but it could be repaired.

Antony Strikes Back

Roman military doctrine emphasized the offensive. Octavian was the first to take an aggressive stance, and he started with his ships. He approached the mouth of the Ambracian Gulf at daybreak, but Antony was prepared for him. Since his legions had not yet arrived in full strength, Antony improvised. He lined the entrance of the gulf with his warships, their prows facing the enemy and their oars raised as if ready to take a stroke. On deck, rowers were dressed to look like legionaries, so the overall impression was of a fleet ready to fight. Octavian halted his offensive. Whether he was taken in by the ruse or whether he was stopped by Antony's catapults on either shore, we don't know.

Octavian had to settle for picking off Antony's transport ships. On land, meanwhile, Octavian drew up his infantry in battle order, but Antony refused to cross the strait from Actium and engage him. Until all his legions were in place, Antony knew better than to risk a general engagement. He contented himself for the time being by sending a few troops to skirmish against the enemy.

Then, about three weeks later, the tables were turned. Antony's legions had all arrived, so he crossed the Actium straits—the narrow entrance to the Ambracian Gulf—to the northern shore. There he proceeded to build a second camp in addition to his main camp on the southern peninsula. This camp lay around two miles south of Octavian's camp at Michalitsi. Then Antony lined up his army and offered battle, but now it was Octavian's turn to refuse. It was all a matter of strategic advantage.

It would be understandable if Antony was hoping for a second Philippi, where he had defeated the army of Caesar's assassins in 42 BC. Octavian was present there too. Brutus, the enemy commander, should have been willing to wait to starve out Antony and Octavian. Instead, he attacked rashly and was defeated.

If Antony could have provoked Octavian and Agrippa to come down from their camp on the high ground at Michalitsi, he might have expected a good outcome. But Octavian knew not to repeat Brutus's mistake. Better to make Antony wait while his army deteriorated from hunger and disease.

But Octavian could not have afforded to be patient without victory at sea. Fortunately, Agrippa gave him victory once again. The admiral achieved a momentous success by defeating Antony's forces at the island of Leucas, south of Actium—winning the prize "before the eyes of Antony and his fleet." Clearly, Antony and his ships were outmatched at sea. Agrippa gave Octavian access to the fine harbor at Leucas, only about ten nautical miles away from Michalitsi. Not only did this guarantee Octavian's access to supplies but also it allowed him to tighten the blockade of Antony's fleet. Octavian was far less reliant on the harbor at Gomaros, where his ships were at risk from storms.

Meanwhile, any of Antony's supply ships coming from the south and trying to sneak into Actium now had to avoid Agrippa's fleet and take a longer route around the island of Cephalonia, which was unprotected from the sea and the winds.

Shortly afterward, Agrippa defeated a squadron of Antony's fleet near Patrae under Quintus Nasidius, a former naval officer for Sextus Pompey. Nasidius had fled with Sextus to Asia Minor after the defeat at Naulochus in 35 BC. Once he realized that things were hopeless there, Nasidius defected to Antony, along with a number of other prominent men, including Sextus's father-in-law. Now Nasidius fell once again to Agrippa, the victor at Naulochus. Agrippa took control of the city of Patrae, which until recently had been Antony and Cleopatra's headquarters. It was a blow to their prestige and reduced even further their ability to get supplies, by taking away another stopping point for transport ships en route to Actium.

Antony's preferred plan, to provoke the enemy into fighting a pitched battle, had failed. His alternate approach, to lay siege to the enemy and starve him out, had run into a major obstacle, for Octavian could replenish his food supplies by sea. Yet there was still a way of forcing Octavian to fight.

Antony could try to block Octavian's access to fresh water. Antony had his troops throw up earthworks around the spring below Michalitsi, and he sent his cavalry to try to cut off the enemy from the Louros River. The marshes, usually the haunts of ducks, herons, pelicans, and many other bird species, were suddenly the site of the bloody clashes of horsemen. The sources record only the eventual failure of these maneuvers, but they might have met with some initial success. Coin evidence shows that Antony's men saluted him as imperator at some point in the campaign. It's a fine silver coin, with Antony's head on the obverse, and a nicely wrought winged victory standing on the reverse, holding a wreath with a fillet (or headband, such as might be worn by a champion athlete) in one hand and a palm branch in the other. If Antony achieved success over Octavian near Michalitsi, it was a fleeting moment. To cut off his foe completely, it was necessary to hold a line five miles long—no mean feat. We must imagine a series of engagements over time along the line. Eventually a successful cavalry charge by Octavian's men led to the defection of King Deiotarus Philadelphus of Paphlagonia (in what is now northwestern Turkey) and his cavalry. Another king, Rhoemetalces of Thrace, also defected to Octavian around this time.

Like Paphlagonia, Thrace was known for its horsemen. Cavalry was the key to controlling access to the Louros River, so the desertion of the two kings and their men to Octavian struck a blow to Antony's hopes. We should not imagine that they changed sides by accident, nor that they decided on their own that the wind was blowing in Octavian's favor. No doubt they defected only after negotiations with Octavian. Surely there was an exchange of messages; perhaps also Octavian had secret agents in Antony's camp. It is also likely that Octavian had sent out feelers to Antony's allies long before they got to Actium.

Octavian was a past master at suborning treason. Indeed, a key moment in his rise to power occurred late in 44 BC, when he was not yet twenty years old. Hearing of discontent in Antony's camp, Octavian's agents there talked two legions into defecting to the young heir of Caesar. Naturally, they promised the men a major pay raise. It worked, and it gave Octavian a private army—an invaluable tool in the turbulent period after Caesar's assassination. Now an experienced man in his early thirties, Octavian would have found it easy to poach units from Antony once again.

Another low moment for Antony, if the following anecdote is true and not merely propaganda, came when he was almost captured. Two long walls connected his camp to one of his harbors, perhaps on the northern promontory. He was used to walking down the walls without a large guard. A slave noticed this and reported it to Octavian. He, in turn, arranged an ambush. The men lying in wait nearly captured Antony, but they struck too soon, and he escaped by running away, which was below the dignity of an imperator. Octavian's men had to be satisfied with capturing only the man who was advancing in front of Antony.

In order to draw off Antony's troops, Octavian sent forces into Greece and Macedonia, which proved a temporary distraction. Later, near Michalitsi, Antony tried again to cut off the enemy from his water supply. This time he led the attack in person, but it failed because of yet another defection: King Amyntas of Galatia joined Octavian. Amyntas was a practiced traitor; he had deserted Brutus and Cassius at Philippi.

Amyntas's treachery at Actium proved consequential, because he took with him two thousand horsemen. They were Celts, and highly reputed as cavalry. In Rome, the poet Horace wrote of two thousand Gallic (Celtic) cavalrymen chanting "Caesar" as they rode to his camp, disgusted, he wrote, by Antony's subservience to a woman and her eunuchs.

Men defect because they like to follow a winner. In spring and summer 32 BC, that looked to be Octavian. He could offer political support, money, and the promise of victory. Each new success by him or Agrippa tipped the balance in his favor for kings and princes who wanted to survive on their thrones. And then there was Cleopatra. The rulers of the East were probably not lining up in support of the expansion of her kingdom and her power under Antony. Their jealousy, discontent, and fear surely provided rich grounds for Octavian's agents.

By summer 32 BC, Octavian and Agrippa had displayed a model of leadership and teamwork. In contrast, Antony had disappointed. He had failed to prevent the enemy from cutting his supply lines, from establishing a strong base opposite his main harbor, and from winning strategic successes over squadrons of his fleet. Although Antony appears to have had a victory of his own on land, it offered only a temporary advantage. And Antony's alliance was showing cracks.

As he crossed the strait again and returned to his camp at Actium, Antony had to wonder how he could win the war.

Part 3

THE BATTLE

August to September 2, 31 BC

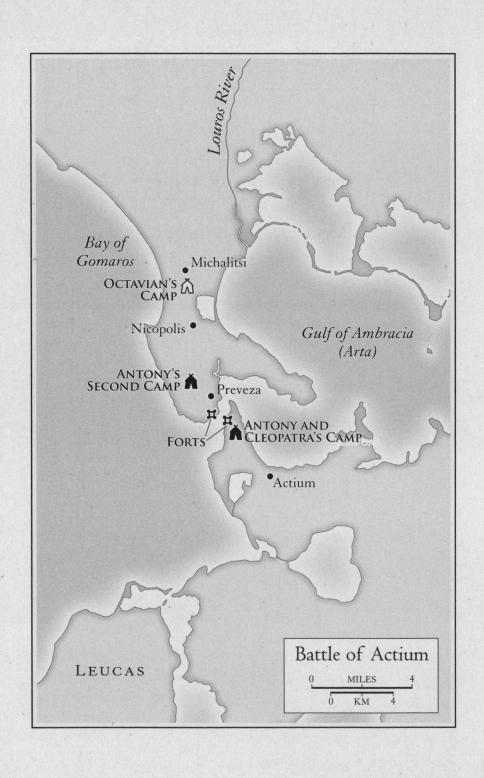

Louros River

Bay of
Gomaros

Michalitsi

OCTAVIAN'S
CAMP

Nicopolis

Gulf of Ambracia
(Arta)

ANTONY'S
SECOND CAMP

Preveza

FORTS

ANTONY AND
CLEOPATRA'S CAMP

Actium

LEUCAS

Battle of Actium

0   MILES   4

0   KM   4

Chapter 10

Apollo's Revenge

Actium, August 31 BC

SOLDIERS WERE DYING. HERE AND THERE AROUND the camp, they were struck down, some with malaria, others with dysentery. Many were hungry and thirsty, which weakened their resistance further. The heat of summer no doubt accentuated the bad situation. It might have been a scene from the opening of the *Iliad*. In that great epic, the poet Homer describes how the god Apollo struck the Greek encampment with disease in revenge for the mistreatment of the god's prophet. Homer writes:

> *The fleet in view, he twanged his deadly bow,*
> *And hissing fly the feathered fates below.*
> *On mules and dogs the infection first began;*
> *And last, the vengeful arrows fixed in man.*
> *For nine long nights, through all the dusky air*
> *The pyres thick-flaming shot a dismal glare.*

It wasn't the Greek army at Troy that was dying, though: it was the Roman army at Actium—in particular Antony's army.

Throughout history, more soldiers have been killed by disease than in battle. Antony's force at Actium was a case in point. We have no precise data, but we do have an indication of the depth of the crisis.

At Ephesus in March 32 BC, Antony had gathered five hundred warships. When it came time to fight at Actium, he was able to man less than half that number. Some ships were stationed elsewhere on his long supply lines, and some were lost to enemy action, but the sources specify that his ships lacked manpower. They also state that Antony's agents fanned the Greek countryside to entice or press-gang able-bodied men into serving as rowers. Antony supposedly remarked that as long as there was a man in Greece, he would not be short of rowers. Around the same time, his agents had to whip free men in central Greece to hurry up and haul sacks of grain down to the sea in the Corinthian Gulf to be shipped to Antony's camp at Actium.

Perhaps Antony did think of the *Iliad*. He was an educated man, and, like any Roman of his class, he had studied Greek literature. If so, he would have remembered that it was Apollo who inflicted the disease on the Greek army at Troy. He could hardly have forgotten that Apollo was also the favorite god of Octavian; Antony, of course, preferred Dionysus and Hercules. A man of action like Antony probably didn't dwell on that, but it might have occurred to others in his camp, and it surely did not boost their spirits.

Octavian's strategy was working. By refusing to fight on land while unleashing Agrippa to win victories at sea—capturing enemy bases, defeating enemy squadrons—Octavian's forces were suffocating the enemy. Control of the sea meant that Octavian could largely deny the import of food to the enemy's camp. At the same time, his men enjoyed a healthier location on higher ground. Their food supply was ensured, unlike Antony's, and they beat back Antony's efforts to cut them off from water. All the while, disillusioned allies defected to Octavian.

Antony might have hoped to stem the wrath of the gods, but he knew the realities of war too well to expect that prayer alone would save his men. Instead, he reached the same conclusion that Achilles did in the *Iliad*: it was time to go. As Achilles asked his fellow commanders in a council of war:

Why leave we not the fatal Trojan shore,
And measure back the seas we crossed before?
The plague destroying whom the sword would spare,
'Tis time to save the few remains of war.

Change "Trojan shore" to "Greek shore," and we have Antony's situation at Actium. It was time to leave and save what he could.

It had been a period of six months that shook the world. At the end of February, Antony's forces were getting ready to awaken from their winter slumber and prepare for either an invasion of Italy or a climactic land battle in Greece. Then came the assault on Methone, the forays around western Greece, and Agrippa's victories over Antony's naval squadrons, the successful crossing of the Adriatic by Octavian and his rendezvous with Agrippa, and the failure of attack after attack to dislodge the two from their elevated campsite north of Actium. All the while, Antony's army and navy degraded. Key allies defected to the enemy. By August, it was clear: Octavian and Agrippa—especially Agrippa—had outgeneraled the great Mark Antony. Antony had gone from besieger to besieged.

Agrippa seemed to have the magic touch at sea, and, no doubt with his help, Octavian held his position on land in the face of Antony's attacks. As a final insult, at some point during these months (we don't know when), Agrippa sailed boldly into the Corinthian Gulf and briefly captured its crown jewel: the city of Corinth. Antony's forces soon regained it, but even a temporary loss was a blow to his prestige.

How could the hero of Philippi have fallen so low? On the one hand, Octavian and Agrippa had mastered the art of war during the past decade. Between Agrippa's service in Gaul and on the Rhine, his contribution to Octavian's victory in the Perusine War, Agrippa's titanic engineering and operational success in defeating Sextus Pompey, and their joint pushing inward of the Roman frontier in Illyria, the two men could have sent off a virtual archive of laurel-wreathed victory dispatches to the Senate. On the other hand, Antony had left himself vulnerable by relying on a supply chain with too many links to defend efficiently.

Antony had wanted to win a quick victory in a land campaign. Instead, he got a war of attrition fueled by the enemy's ability to seize control of the sea.

Magnanimity and Severity

Domitius Ahenobarbus had had enough. At Ephesus a year earlier, he had expressed his open disapproval of Cleopatra. Now some new grievance against her arose in his mind; the sources don't provide details, but it was enough to make him defect. It could hardly have been an easy decision, because Octavian had condemned him to death for the assassination of Julius Caesar, even though Ahenobarbus was guiltless. Then too, Ahenobarbus had been consul in 32 BC and had fled Rome to Antony rather than tolerate Octavian. Reasoning that Octavian wanted to encourage further defections, Ahenobarbus might have concluded that his former enemy would treat him courteously.

Although Ahenobarbus had a fever, he was not deterred. He boarded a very small oared galley—probably one with fewer than twenty oars—and was rowed, arguably by disembarking right across the Actium straits, and walked up the hill to the enemy's camp.

It's possible that Ahenobarbus escaped undetected, but, if so, his absence was soon noticed. Antony was displeased, to put it mildly, as Ahenobarbus was his most experienced admiral. Nonetheless, Antony decided to engage in a beau geste. He sent Ahenobarbus's baggage after him, accompanied by his loyalists and servants. Cleopatra supposedly did not approve, but Antony was following the example of Caesar, who had done the same when his second in command deserted him. Antony's high-mindedness might have been meant to show him as a better claimant to Caesar's mantle than Octavian. It also might have carried a sting of contempt, as if to say that Ahenobarbus meant so little to Antony that his departure was no cause for anger.

Yet Ahenobarbus's defection indeed harmed Antony, even though Ahenobarbus was sick and died not long after joining Octavian. For one thing, Ahenobarbus either brought actionable intelligence to the enemy or left Antony worried that he had done so. For another, by showing how much he disapproved of the state of things in Antony's camp, Ahenobarbus encouraged others to follow him to the enemy—and they did.

In order to stop the desertions, Antony turned to torture. He put to death two prominent men whose loyalty he suspected: Iamblichus, the Syrian king, and Quintus Postumius, a Roman senator. It didn't work. One source claims that there were daily desertions from Antony to Caesar but none in the other direction; no doubt an exaggeration, but perhaps not by much. The chronology of who went when is unclear, but other defectors included Marcus Licinius Crassus, a former follower of Sextus Pompey who had joined Antony, and Marcus Junius Silanus, who had quarreled with the supporters of Cleopatra. There would be at least one other defector as well.

Only three ex-consuls (consulars, as they are called)—men of the highest political status—remained with Antony: Canidius, Gaius Sosius, and Lucius Gellius Publicola. Publicola, like many figures of the era, would make a good subject for a novel. In addition to the usual political treachery—first Publicola supported Brutus, then he switched to Antony—there was family drama. Born into an old patrician clan, Publicola was adopted by a prominent man who was not, however, a Roman noble. Later on, according to rumor, Publicola committed adultery with his adoptive father's second wife. Publicola's brother, Marcus Valerius Messalla Corvinus, had also supported Antony, but by 35 BC, he had switched to Octavian. In 31 BC Corvinus was coconsul with Octavian, and Corvinus surely served with his colleague at Actium. So, the two brothers faced off on opposite sides of the Actium straits.

Failed Breakouts

Short of soldiers, Antony sent Dellius and Amyntas into Macedonia and Thrace to recruit mercenaries. Antony decided to follow them, supposedly because he questioned their loyalty. Although that suspicion turned out to be justified, he might simply have wanted a break from Actium. Or perhaps he thought he could induce Octavian into following him—and into a trap. If so, it didn't work: no influx of mercenaries, no trapping Octavian.

That left the sea as a place for Antony to make a move. So he did, but without leading the naval counterattack in person. Perhaps he preferred to save himself for a final battle, but, more likely, Antony knew that he was no admiral. He preferred to entrust the navy to someone who knew the sea. He placed his fate in the hands of Gaius Sosius. Ahenobarbus was even more experienced in naval affairs, but he was no longer available. Sosius, like Antony, was better known as a land commander, and a successful one, but he did have a maritime connection, and he was loyal.

Sosius had built his career around Antony. He served first as Antony's quaestor in 39 BC. Antony then chose Sosius for important assignments: governing Syria and Cilicia, and providing the military muscle to place Herod on the throne of Judea against Parthian opposition. In reward, Sosius was allowed to celebrate a triumph in Rome in 34 BC. Sosius also served his chief by next restoring the Temple of Apollo in Rome, which reminded the Roman people that his patron Antony still cared about them. In 32 BC Sosius took up the consulship, in which role he attacked Octavian. When Octavian struck back, Sosius fled Rome and went to Antony at Ephesus.

That Sosius knew something about navies is suggested by his connection with the island of Zacynthus, which was strategically located off the northwestern coast of the Peloponnese. His name appears on coins struck on the island between 39 and 32 BC. The coins display an image of Antony and an eagle—a symbol of the Ptolemies, and, therefore, of Cleopatra. Blessed with ports, Zacynthus was surely a naval base, and Sosius's coins suggest that he was in command.

So, Antony chose Sosius to try to break the blockade. It was midsummer; perhaps early August. Professional that he was, Sosius timed his attack well. He waited for a thick mist and sailed out of the straits in the predawn hours. His target was a small squadron of the enemy fleet that was anchored opposite him, under the command of Lucius Tarius Rufus. A man of humble origins, Tarius was a comer, and he had probably already risen to the Senate. This was not his day, however. Sosius caught him unawares, routed his force, and was pursuing him when, suddenly, Agrippa appeared with a superior force. Tarius escaped, but Sosius was lucky to do so. He suffered heavy losses, including King Tarcondimotus of Amanus, who was killed.

It was a major victory for Agrippa and Octavian, and a corresponding defeat for Sosius and Antony. Both breakouts, by land and by sea, had failed. It was probably at this point that Antony decided to withdraw his legions to the southern promontory, a move that was carried out at night. Antony was surely reluctant to take the pressure off Octavian in his camp at Michalitsi, but there was no choice.

Antony's Strategic Failure

The state of things at Actium in summer 31 BC was extraordinary. Antony had begun the campaign with an excellent harbor and the advantage of having been ensconced on the western coast of Greece for months. Octavian was a new arrival, with only a mediocre port. Yet, after a few months, Octavian held the upper hand, and Antony was struggling to survive.

The real blame for the state of the expedition lies with Antony. He wasn't prepared to fight a maritime war. It seems that, for him, the navy was a transport service and, perhaps, a siege weapon, should he actually invade Italy. Why was Antony unprepared? In the 48 BC campaign that culminated in victory at Pharsalus, his side had won without a maritime strategy, and the other side had not used its naval resources effectively. The same had been true in the Philippi campaign of 42 BC. So, maybe Antony just assumed that he could get Octavian to engage in a land battle, whether in Italy or Greece.

Nor did Antony set the right tone for his men. As the supreme commander, he should have projected daring and enterprise to inspire his admirals. He should have reinforced the vulnerable points along the coast after the defeat at Methone. He should have tried harder to save Patrae, Corcyra, and Leucas, and to prevent Corinth from suffering the humiliation of an enemy raid.

Once Octavian achieved command of the sea, he took the offensive and put Antony on the defensive. In the era of the Actium War, it was in general more advantageous to be on the offensive than the defensive. Rarely could one win a defensive war without coming up with some way to take the war back to the enemy. The defender could deploy a scorched-earth strategy to deny the attacker food or somehow lure the attacker into fighting a battle on unfavorable terms. He could open a second front, engage in an ambush, draw the enemy into a trap, deploy a technological innovation, turn a tactical defeat into a moral and therefore strategic victory, or acquire new allies and new resources. Antony tried to deny Octavian water, tried to get him to fight a pitched battle on land, and tried to acquire new allies, but failed in all his efforts.

Having failed, Antony should have made the painful but necessary decision to withdraw from Actium. Had he done so in May, for example, he could have moved the army into central Greece and waited for the enemy, as Caesar did after losing at Dyrrachium in 48 BC. Alternatively, he could have pulled back both army and navy to a defensible perimeter in the Aegean, in a line running from Athens, to Crete, to Cyrene (modern Libya). He would have lost both face and territory (in western Greece) and would probably have suffered defections, but he would have lived to fight again another day. By August, it was too late.

Among the qualities of a successful general are good judgment, audacity, agility, and a leadership that is both courageous and decisive. In the spring and summer of 32 BC, Antony proved deficient in these qualities. Why? Perhaps it was the challenge of fighting his first real naval campaign. Even with experienced sailors such as Ahenobarbus and Sosius, learning how to coordinate land and sea operations could not have been easy. Perhaps he was past his prime. Perhaps he was simply overmatched by Agrippa's daring, experience, and sheer skill. At the start of the war, there was a question as to whether the naval experience of Agrippa and his veteran forces would outweigh the material and financial resources of the other side. That was a question no longer.

And then there was the matter of leadership. In the decade before Actium, Octavian had only improved in deciding strategy. He fended off Antony's political challenge in Italy and peeled off Antony's allies at Actium. Agrippa had proven to be a masterful tactician.

Antony's previous career bears the mark of a good general but not a great one. He displayed pluck and intelligence when he ferried Caesar's legions across the Adriatic from Italy in 48 BC. He showed his mettle when still encamped at Brundisium. There he foiled the enemy's attempted blockade by cutting off his water supply. Then, after crossing the Adriatic from Italy with his warships, nimbly avoiding the enemy fleet and landing on the eastern shore, he sidestepped an enemy ambush and joined Caesar. Soon afterward, Caesar's army came under siege at Dyrrachium, and Antony played a brave role by shoring up the lines at a moment when the enemy was threatening to break through. A few months later, Antony went on to command the left wing of the legions at the Battle of Pharsalus in central Greece. He served well but did not make the decisive contribution to victory, nor was he in command: Caesar was. However, Antony does get the credit for victory over the forces of Caesar's assassins at the two battles of Philippi in 42 BC, and it was a great success indeed.

But the outcome at Philippi can be attributed to the good fortune of Cassius's suicide and Brutus's impatience as much as to Antony's military skill. Conspicuous in Antony's military record are two failures: the siege of Mutina in northern Italy in 43 BC and the siege of Phraaspa in Media Atropatene (northwestern Iran) in 36 BC. He failed to take either city. In both cases, he is better remembered for his steadiness in retreat than for his achievement on the offensive. All in all, Antony displayed bravery, ingenuity, and a cool head in adversity, but rarely was he the architect of victory.

Antony's strategic failure at Actium is not unique. Military history is full of campaigns marked by ill-conceived strategies and poor logistical planning, and that holds true even for campaigns led by veteran generals. It is depressingly common to find bold and ambitious plans that take insufficient account of the reality of geography or local conditions. Consider the case, during the American Revolution, of the two failed British commanders at Saratoga, New York, in 1777, John Burgoyne and Henry Clinton. Each had rendered distinguished service in battle during the Seven Years' War against France as well as in earlier stages of the Revolutionary War. And yet they failed at the central battle at Saratoga.

To turn from military to psychological arguments, there is the explanation of the hostile sources: Antony had been unmanned by Cleopatra. The queen supposedly kept him under her thumb and repeatedly vetoed all plans that didn't keep them on the coast of western Greece, where they could best prevent a thrust southeastward toward Egypt and where her navy could win a share of glory that would be denied in a land battle. Worse still are the claims that Antony had sunk into drunkenness and self-delusion.

A reader doesn't have to swallow this tabloid version of history in order to conclude that Cleopatra's presence had a deleterious effect on good order and discipline in Antony's army and especially in his high command. Even Canidius Crassus, a staunch supporter in Ephesus the year before, now reached the conclusion that Cleopatra had to go. Canidius's dismissal of the queen was not an attack on her personally but rather a decision to send her, the bulk of the fleet, and the Egyptian treasure off to safety while that might still be possible. Yet there certainly were those in Antony's high command who disliked Cleopatra, even after the defection of Ahenobarbus.

Council of War

By late August, it had become clear that Antony had no choice but to leave Actium. The only question was, how? He called a council of war. It would have taken place in the commander's tent (*praetorium*), which was located in the center of the camp, surrounded by rows and rows of soldiers' tents. The tent was made of leather, typically goatskin or calfskin, and was situated on a plot measuring forty thousand square feet, or two hundred feet per side. Caesar claimed that in Pompey's camp at Pharsalus in 48 BC, there were officers' tents decked out luxuriously, with freshly cut strips of turf for floors and silver tableware. It would not be surprising if Antony's tent was similarly plush.

Antony presided over the council. We can reconstruct its members. They included Canidius Crassus, the commander of the legions, and Sosius and Publicola, the highest-ranking naval commanders, as well as two other important officers, Marcus Insteius and Marcus Octavius. A former people's tribune, Insteius was a loyalist who had served Antony at the siege of Mutina. Octavius was possibly the distant relative of Octavian's who had commanded fleets against Caesar's forces in the Adriatic and off the North African coast during the civil war in 49 to 46 BC.

Then there was Quintus Dellius. He had served Antony in important positions as a diplomat and officer in the East, especially during the Parthian War. He dispatched Dellius to Alexandria in 41 BC to summon Cleopatra to her fateful meeting with Antony at Tarsus. The following year, Antony sent Dellius on an important mission to support King Herod against the king's rival. He next trusted Dellius to go to Alexandria at the start of Antony's Median campaign in 36 BC and ask Cleopatra to come to Antony's headquarters in Syria. Trusting Dellius wasn't easy, though, because the man had deserted two other commanders *before* joining Antony. Another public figure of the era gave Dellius the label "Trick Rider of the Civil Wars" because he changed "horses" so often. For what little it's worth, gossip said that Dellius wrote smutty letters to Cleopatra, which some think meant they were lovers.

It's possible that Antony also included certain senior centurions in the council, as Caesar sometimes did. Centurions, the equivalent of captains, were the only professional officers in the Roman army. Presumably, other allied commanders were there, but the only ally whose presence is confirmed is Cleopatra. It was not the first time in ancient history that a female ruler took part in a council of war—for instance, Queen Artemisia I of Caria was at the war council of King Xerxes I of Persia before the Battle of Salamis in 480 BC—but, still, it was hardly a common practice.

Other commanders were notable by their absence from the war council: some having deserted, some fallen in battle, and one executed by Antony. Surely there had been earlier councils of war in which all had been present. The knowledge that they were gone, and why, could not have improved the mood of what was already a grim occasion.

Canidius argued for a withdrawal into Macedonia or Thrace, where they could decide the war by a land battle. He even promised the help of a certain King Dicomes of the Getae. Nothing is known of Dicomes; the Getae were a wealthy and warlike people who lived between the Hister (Danube) River and the Euxine Sea, in what is today Bulgaria and Romania. One source says they turned out to be too divided among themselves to help Antony. Still, one could hope. There was no shame in avoiding a naval battle with so experienced an admiral as Agrippa, as Canidius is supposed to have said. He urged Antony to use the force of his large number of legionaries instead of dividing and wasting his strength among ships.

But it was too late. Dicomes was a very long shot, while Octavian was unlikely to do Antony the favor of agreeing to fight a pitched battle on land, something that Octavian had been deliberately avoiding. Besides, even if Octavian suddenly did agree to fight, Antony's army was too far gone. His forces were hungry, disease ridden, shorthanded, and demoralized. If Octavian refused to fight, the men would still need to find their way back to Egypt, which would be nearly impossible without a navy. And to be clear, a retreat by land meant giving up the fleet.

Neither army nor navy was in a good position to fight and win a battle. The navy, however, had better prospects. The enemy would, of course, contest their departure, but at least *some* of the fleet should be able to break through and escape. It was even possible that Antony's fleet could defeat Octavian's; stranger things have happened. The army, by contrast, faced annihilation. Those of Antony's ships that escaped would be far more mobile than the army, and they could reach a food supply more quickly. Antony still had a naval base at Cape Taenarum in the southern Peloponnese, about a three-day voyage from Actium for a fleet of warships that stopped ashore at night.

We would expect that Antony planned to man the ships with his best and healthiest men. Perhaps he even ensured that they received adequate rations.

The sun in Antony's camp at Actium gleamed on the legionaries' shining helmets. The sea had turned the bronze beaks of the warships to a dull bronze-and-brownish-green color. From a strategic point of view, the real light was shining on the camp's vast store of gold and silver: Cleopatra's treasure, which she had brought with her from Egypt. It was undoubtedly substantial and probably included other moneys as well—gifts from the allies and taxes that Antony had collected in the East and declined to send back to Rome.

Everybody wanted that money. The queen and Antony would need it if they were going to hire more troops, as they would have to in order to continue the fight. Octavian had practically broken the back of his support by squeezing Italy dry to pay for his army and navy. He was no less eager than his enemies to get his hands on their fortune.

Rarely would a navy carry so consequential a reward as Antony and Cleopatra's fleet did in their attempted escape from Actium. They could have chosen to transport the treasure by land, but the sea seemed less chancy. Although sea travel was never without risk, it was still summer, and the Mediterranean was relatively calm. Given the army's perilous state, the navy was the logical choice.

The sources claim that it was Cleopatra who persuaded the commanders of the plan that they eventually adopted. She proposed that they leave garrisons in the best strategic positions, perhaps to force Octavian to expend resources on blockading them, and that the rest of the fleet depart to Egypt with her and Antony. If it really was Cleopatra who proposed the prevailing opinion, that is a remarkable testimony to her analytical skills, her persuasive ability, and her influence. It was also, of course, a sign of the importance of her treasure. Rare as it was for a woman to attend a war council in the ancient Mediterranean, it was even more singular for her to win the argument.

Cleopatra might have made an additional case to Antony in private. It was too late to save the army, she might have said. Therefore, by abandoning the legions, they weren't leaving Octavian a windfall but rather a poisoned chalice. To obtain the troops' surrender, he would have to offer them terms including land and money, neither of which he had. Once again he would have to raise taxes in Italy, which might drive his opponents into a renewed struggle against him.

As far as what lay ahead at sea, Antony and Cleopatra might have hoped to be lucky enough to sail the fleet to safety before the enemy could bear down on them. They had to be prepared for battle, however.

The sources, predictably, discredit the motives of Antony and

Cleopatra. Antony, says Plutarch, was a mere appendage to Cleopatra, and he wanted the fleet to win the victory only in order to please her. Cleopatra was supposedly just a frightened female who gave in to bad omens. This was untrue, nor was she selfishly thinking only of her escape, as a hostile historical tradition alleges. Antony and Cleopatra simply recognized reality. A land battle was no longer an option. There was only one way out of Actium, and that was on the water.

The Plan

We'll never be certain of Antony's battle plan at Actium. The sources are too few and too hostile. The best we can do is to piece together a plausible reconstruction, which the work of generations of scholars makes possible. About a century ago, a debate raged as to whether Antony thought he had a chance of destroying the enemy's fleet or if he felt that the best he could do was to punch his way through and bring as many of his ships as he could to safety in Egypt, where perhaps they could fight again another day. Since then, a consensus has emerged in favor of the latter, with room for an opportunistic twist should the gods prove favorable. In other words, Antony's plan at Actium was to break out; but if the enemy made a mistake or if the weather should provide an opening, enabling him to defeat his enemy as he escaped, well, Antony would certainly take advantage of good fortune.

Antony could not have expected to flee Actium without Octavian's fleet trying to stop him. Nor could he have planned to take the enemy by surprise—not with the presence of spies and the visibility from a distance of some of his preparations. But he might have hoped to keep the enemy guessing about his tactics.

That hope was dashed by one last high-profile defection: Dellius. The veteran traitor had engaged in his final and most profitable act of treachery, by bringing Octavian the details of Antony's plan of action. Octavian now surely called a war council of his own.

The attendees no doubt included Agrippa and the two other commanders of the fleet: Lucius Arruntius and Marcus Lurius. Arruntius had the usual civil war story: He came from a town near Rome where his family was wealthy but not senators. He escaped a death sentence from the triumvirs in 43 BC by fleeing to Sextus Pompey in Sicily. After the amnesty of 39 BC, Arruntius returned to Italy and ended up fighting for Octavian. As for Lurius, while serving as governor of Sardinia in 40 BC, he had lost the island to one of Sextus's commanders, who defeated him at sea. No doubt Lurius hoped to improve his reputation at Actium.

Titus Statilius Taurus, commander of the army, was surely also at the council of war. He was a notable commander whose military record made him second only to Agrippa in prestige. Like Arruntius, he came from a nonsenatorial family, probably from southern Italy. He had distinguished himself by his service to Octavian. An admiral in the war against Sextus Pompey, he afterward pacified Roman Africa (modern Tunisia), for which he celebrated a triumph, followed by service in the Illyrian War.

The most important of the defectors from Antony might have taken part in the council as well, among them Amyntas of Galatia and Dellius.

There was no doubt that Octavian's fleet would try to stop the enemy from escaping. The only question was one of tactics. At the war council, or perhaps only later, after they had seen how Antony had prepared his ships, Octavian and Agrippa had a debate.

According to the sources, Octavian proposed that they let Antony and Cleopatra sail out unopposed but then overtake them with their fast ships and attack their rear. Antony and Cleopatra would flee, and the rest of their fleet would be easily persuaded to change sides. Octavian thought that he could win without fighting.

Agrippa, however, put it otherwise. The enemy's ships would be prepared for flight, with sails to hoist, while their own would be stripped for battle. Presumably, Antony would wait for a favorable wind to speed his path. Hence, their own ships would be unable to catch Antony and Cleopatra's fleet. The only choice was to block the enemy's exit. Octavian agreed. Once again, he showed his quality as a leader by his willingness to admit that he was wrong and his subordinate was right.

Antony's best bet at Actium was to take advantage of his ships' greatest asset. Because his larger units had reinforced timbers in the prow, they could pack a punch in prow-to-prow ramming. They could start the battle with a charge into the enemy's line that might rip open a hole in it. Then they could follow up with marine boarding parties. They might even start a panic that could turn the enemy fleet to flight.

They could do so, however, only if the enemy was unprepared. But Dellius had brought Agrippa crucial intelligence. Once Agrippa understood Antony's battle plan, he knew exactly how to counter it.

Information had dominated the conflict before the fleets sailed, when the struggle for the Roman Empire was fought through pamphlets, speeches, public ceremonies, and religious rituals. Now, on the eve of the great clash of arms, information played a key role once again.

And so, the stage was set for battle.

Chapter 11

The Clash

Actium, September 2, 31 BC: Morning

LIKE CHILDREN, BATTLES HAVE MINDS OF THEIR own. Commanders can make every preparation beforehand. They can set their forces in perfect order. They can calculate the odds of success or plot an escape route in anticipation of failure. They can harangue the departing heroes passionately as they head off to face the foe. They can worry over the last detail, and yet they cannot be certain of the outcome. Things go wrong. Soldiers and sailors blunder, winds blow in without warning, a lucky arrow, slingshot, or catapult shot fells a leader. The two sides might each think they can predict the outcome, and yet the fortunes of war resist prophecy. So it was with Actium. Octavian and Agrippa, Antony and Cleopatra might each have thought they knew what to expect in the great battle, but none of them could be sure.

Octavian and Agrippa had advantages, including experience of war at sea, veteran crews that were healthy and well fed, a series of recent victories, a steady boost of defectors, and information dominance. Antony and Cleopatra had only a navy on the ropes, but even such a force could still prove dangerous. The odds of victory might have been slim, but for them and their forces, it was a matter of pride and survival. Smaller and leaner, their navy still contained some big ships capable of crippling the enemy via prow-on-prow ramming, and it still had an advantage in missile-throwing catapult towers. Agrippa and Octavian had to be sure to anticipate their every move and to avoid making any mistakes.

Let us follow the two sides' actions as they made ready at last for the fateful clash.

Sources of Evidence

In order to make sense of the battle, first we need to consider the sources of evidence. There are two detailed literary accounts: those of Plutarch in his *Life of Antony*, and Cassius Dio, in his *Roman History*. Neither account is contemporary, but both authors read no-longer-extant contemporary accounts—in particular the biased *Memoirs* that Octavian (as Augustus) later wrote. Neither Plutarch nor Cassius Dio offers a satisfactory narrative, but they provide a great deal of useful information. The historian Livy wrote a detailed account, and probably a good one, if biased in favor of Octavian, but only a very abbreviated summary survives. The poet Horace describes the battle in two poems, as do Virgil in a brief section of his epic *Aeneid* and the poet Sextus Propertius in several poems. These texts are of limited value, as they are impressionistic pieces of flattery for Octavian. Returning to historical accounts, brief—and biased—ones are found in several later works, in particular writing by Velleius Paterculus (who lived from approximately 20 BC to after AD 30), Florus (lived during the late first and early second century AD), and Orosius (lived in the late fourth and early fifth century AD).

Archaeology provides additional evidence. A few objects have been found underwater. A bronze boat fitting with a figurehead depicting the head and shoulders of a female figure armed with helmet and breastplate—possibly the goddess Athena—was discovered in the outer bay of Preveza, the modern city on the northern peninsula at the entrance of the Ambracian Gulf, in the area where the battle was fought. Because it is relatively small, only about nineteen inches long, it probably comes from a small ship. Stylistically, it appears to date to the first century BC, and from a Greek and perhaps a Ptolemaic workshop. So, it might come from one of Antony or Cleopatra's ships. Another set of artifacts that might date from the battle is a series of small, egg-shaped stones photographed on the sea floor in the same area in 1997, but not recovered. These might be catapult balls used in the battle. Meanwhile, underwater archaeology has discovered about thirty ancient warship rams—not at Actium but elsewhere in the Mediterranean—dating in the main from the third century BC. These three-bladed rams sat on the waterline and allowed galleys to strike an enemy vessel without suffering damage to their own ship. Finally, coins and frescos also provide important if indirect information.

By far the most important piece of material evidence, however, is the victory monument that Octavian erected on the site of his camp after the battle. Over the past quarter century, it has been systematically excavated by Konstantinos Zachos of the Greek Archaeological Service. The finds of Zachos and his team, especially by the archaeologist William M. Murray, provide key new evidence, particularly about the warships. Octavian also erected a second monument, the so-called *dekanaia,* or "ten-ship monument," on the southern promontory at Actium itself. The ruins of that monument no longer exist, but a literary source states that it included one example from each of the classes of ships in Antony's armada, from a one to a ten.

Alas, these items don't provide a solid foundation for reconstructing the battle, as they are either one-sided or incomplete. It's not surprising that scholars have disagreed vehemently about what really happened during the sea fight. Still, as a result of more than a century of research and debate, a consensus has emerged about the general picture, if not the details.

Preparation

Antony and Cleopatra had to prepare the fleet for battle without letting the men know that their plan was for a breakout, because in a breakout, some men would be left behind. A successful breakout battle against a numerically superior foe was likely to be costly. Antony and Cleopatra knew that they would lose ships and men—possibly a large part of their force. Worse still, unless they defeated the enemy navy, they would have to leave behind an enormous army to find its own way out by land. Hobbled as they were by hunger, disease, and desertion, that army would be unlikely to escape Octavian's and Agrippa's vengeance if they survived Actium largely intact.

They had to prevent their forces from panicking or mutinying before the battle began. It was a delicate operation. The first thing they had to do was burn some of their ships. A painful choice, but they simply lacked the manpower to take all of their vessels. Better to lose the ships than to leave them behind for the enemy. Antony chose to save his largest and best ships, ranging in size from threes to tens. These are variously described as 170 ships or less than 200 ships, so, roughly, three squadrons of sixty ships each. He also chose to save Cleopatra's squadron, which consisted of approximately sixty Egyptian warships, for a total of around 230 ships. The rest, the smaller warships and most of the merchant ships, would be burned.

There was a good case to be made for burning the largest ships too. Tens were too big for a prow-to-prow charge unless they were manned by a full complement of healthy, rested rowers, which Antony did not have. Nor were they good candidates to make a fast escape under sail. Yet the psychological impact of burning his tens would have been devastating and would have made clear to the men that Antony had scant hope of victory. Perhaps Antony found it impossible to admit to himself as well that his cause was lost, as burning the largest ships would have conceded. Hence, he took his tens into battle, however limited their military value.

Antony was famous as a commander for his bond with his men, so he might even have told them the truth. For what it is worth, the sources state that in the dark of night, Antony and Cleopatra had their considerable war chest loaded onto their ships. This included Cleopatra's royal treasury and personal wealth, payments from the allies, as well as taxes and tribute that had been collected from the eastern provinces and which Antony had no doubt not forwarded to Rome. It surely consisted of jewelry and precious stones as well as coin. It might well also have included the accumulated pay of the twenty thousand legionaries who fought aboard the ships. In the Roman Empire, a legion's commander retained a large part of a soldier's pay to make sure he didn't spend it all in the same place—or that he didn't desert.

They are supposed to have carried out the operation as secretly as they could. They couldn't burn their ships secretly, however.

Another action undertaken was to load the masts and sails aboard the ships—highly unorthodox for going into battle. Normally, warships relied on oar power during battle rather than unwieldy sails with their heavy masts and tackle. Yet when his helmsmen wanted to leave the masts and sails behind, Antony forced them to bring the equipment aboard. He explained that conditions off Actium were windy, and their ships were heavy, so, after winning the battle, they would need wind power to chase enemy ships. "Not one fugitive of the enemy should be allowed to make his escape," he supposedly said, although he was probably more concerned about being able to sail off quickly and escape.

Around the same time or shortly afterward, Antony had the rest of his fleet loaded for departure. Given the differing sizes of the ships and the likely shortage of manpower, it is hard to know how many rowers and crewmen were on board, but an estimate of forty thousand is reasonable. In addition, Antony boarded twenty thousand heavy-armed soldiers and two thousand archers. Boarding and missile launching were essential parts of naval warfare in the era, along with ramming and shearing off enemy ships' oars, which explains the choice of personnel.

One soldier was unhappy with Antony's decision to board the ships. In an anecdote picked up later by Shakespeare, Plutarch reports that a centurion approached Antony as he was walking by. Each commanded a century: a unit of eighty men. Responsible for administration and discipline, they kept the legion going on a daily basis. Julius Caesar respected his centurions and included senior centurions in his war councils, and Antony probably behaved similarly. Hence, what the centurion said on this occasion mattered. He was a veteran with scars to show for it, which added weight.

"Imperator," he is supposed to have addressed Antony, why are you putting your hopes in "miserable logs of wood?" He begged Antony to give them land on which to fight and either conquer or die. Antony supposedly did not reply but merely gave the man an encouraging gesture and a heartening look. Perhaps something like this really happened. It's not implausible, as Roman soldiers and especially centurions did sometimes speak frankly to their commanders. Plutarch (or his source) was not above inventing speeches from whole cloth, however.

Certainly the plea is a likely echo of what Antony's soldiers really felt at the time. Most would have lacked the experience of a naval battle, and men who have never been to sea tend to magnify its terrors. As an ancient writer on naval warfare said, it was particularly important to have combat veterans when choosing marines—the men who would fight on deck. With so many novices at sea, Antony's men might have agreed with the centurion, and would have preferred to fight on land.

No details survive of the preparations in Octavian's camp. Their intelligence was good enough to know the enemy's plans. The smoke of Antony's burning ships was visible to all. Octavian's scouts on the northern promontory opposite Actium could obtain a more detailed picture of Antony's fleet and its ships' positions. With a long string of victories at sea behind them, and with all the defections from the enemy, Octavian's men had reason for confidence. They were too realistic, however, to underestimate the danger posed by the ramming power of Antony's ships or the fight that his marines could give them in boarding parties. So, they had to prepare carefully and with a well-thought-out battle plan. They knew that Antony's primary goal was to break out and escape. His secondary goal was to do serious damage to their fleet, but only if the battle broke his way. Thanks to Dellius's intelligence, they knew that Antony would stay close to shore at first in order to prevent them from outflanking him—a real danger, since Octavian's fleet outnumbered his by almost two to one. Antony hoped to tempt the enemy to draw close, so that he could launch a successful enough charge to allow his fleet to sail off to safety.

Numbers, experience, recent victories, and the relatively good health and nutrition of their men all favored Octavian and Agrippa.

Dawn of Battle

All was ready on August 29, but Antony's ships did not depart that day nor on the three days following. A strong wind, probably a westerly, prevented the navy from sailing out of the Ambracian Gulf. The men must have gone back to shore to wait, thereby ratcheting up the already high state of tension. Finally, on the fifth day, there came "a windless, waveless calm." It was finally time to launch the ships. It was September 2, 31 BC.

Dawn broke at Actium at 6:07 a.m. We can be sure that the men and their commanders were awake well before then. They needed to be ready to go as soon as the light allowed for navigation.

Ancient commanders always addressed their men before battle. Without an efficient means of amplifying their voice on the water, and with tens of thousands of men in hundreds of warships, they could be heard only by a small selection of those present. Seated below deck, for example, few if any rowers would have heard a thing.

Plutarch records that Antony made the rounds of his ships on a small galley. He exhorted the soldiers to fight from a still and steady position—as if they were on land because their boats were heavy. He told the helmsmen to meet the ramming attacks of the enemy as calmly as if they were lying quietly at anchor and to keep to the narrows around the entrance to the gulf. All good advice, but the last directive was tricky. On the one hand, it made sense to stay close to land in order to prevent the much larger enemy fleet from spreading out and surrounding them. On the other hand, the water was rather shallow inshore, so the helmsmen had to take care not to run their boats aground. They probably stood at least a half mile out to sea.

Plutarch does not report what Octavian said, but Cassius Dio offers two prebattle speeches, one by Antony and one by Octavian. Speeches in Greek and Roman history were meant to be light fiction, recording more what the speaker *should* have said than what he actually did say. Cassius Dio's speeches deserve no trust as fact, but they are plausible, based as they seem to be in the warring propaganda of the era, including Octavian's memoirs.

Cassius Dio has Antony tout his experience and impressive record as a commander compared to Octavian's youth and slim military achievements—while, of course, neglecting to mention either Antony's failures or Agrippa's successes. Antony compares his side's vast financial resources with the enemy's relative poverty. He points out his advantage in equipment: ships so thickly timbered as to be resistant from ramming either bows-on or on the side (actually, they weren't resistant on the side); higher decks on which to position catapult towers; superiority in numbers of archers and slingers. He downplays Agrippa's victory over Sextus Pompey, alleging that Sextus had inferior ships that were manned by slaves (neither of which was really conclusive, and the comment about slaves is rank prejudice). While conceding an advantage to the enemy in infantry, he promises that, after winning at sea, Antony would lead his men to success on land. He notes that despite the official declaration of war, Octavian was really fighting Antony and his followers. Cassius Dio has Antony slyly omit any mention of Cleopatra's name. Antony complains of Octavian's past treatment of both himself and Octavian's other rivals, and paints a dire picture of what would await the men in defeat. Finally, he sounds the old Roman theme of liberty—*libertas*—a reminder that, strange as it seems, Antony's cause appealed to the last die-hard supporters of the republic.

Plutarch continues the story with Octavian. In the predawn hours, while it was still dark, Octavian left his tent. He was on the way down the hill to make the rounds of his ships when he met a driver and his mule. He asked the man his name; the mule driver replied that he was named Eutuches ("Prosper") and his mule, Nikon ("Victory"). Omens were beloved in the ancient world, and this was such a good omen that we have to wonder if it was staged. Perhaps Octavian's men were more nervous about the battle than their record of victory might suggest. Years afterward, Octavian had bronze statues of the man and his mule erected somewhere at his victory monument on the slopes of Michalitsi.

Cassius Dio offers another version of what Octavian might have said to his troops before battle. After enumerating some of Rome's past military successes, Octavian draws a contrast with the present enemy: a woman and an Egyptian, and, therefore, doubly unworthy of Rome's attention. He bemoans the submission to Cleopatra of many noble Romans and, above all, of Antony, his former brother-in-law and partner in government. By declaring war on Cleopatra alone, Octavian had hoped to bring Antony to his senses, but he had failed. In any case, there was nothing to fear from a foe as decadent as Antony or from his coalition of easterners whom Rome had often conquered in the past. As for Antony's ships, they were big, thickly built, and tall, but they were too heavy to maneuver in battle and so would offer easy targets. (Octavian fails to say that if the initial charge of these heavy ships succeeded, they could crush the bows of his own ships.) Besides which, Octavian's men had already defeated Antony's ships at sea more than once. (True, but they had never faced his full fleet.) Finally, says Octavian, the enemy had loaded his treasure aboard ship, a sign of lack of faith in victory.

The main audience for such speeches was usually the commanders. Some probably listened attentively; others only pretended to pay attention. Some prayed to their gods, and others thought of the joy of action or of the payday that would come with victory. The commanders spoke, but the time for words was rapidly coming to an end.

The two fleets sailed out to battle, each to the sound of trumpets.

Preparing the Battlefield

Later propaganda offers a false picture of the two fleets, arguing that Antony's armada consisted of gigantic battleships against the plucky frigates of Octavian's fleet. As the second-century AD historian Florus put it, Antony's vessels were so clumsy and unwieldy that they made the sea groan, while Octavian's ships were maneuverable and easy to handle. Octavian's fleet is said to have featured a large number of light and nimble vessels. This fit Octavian's propaganda narrative of grandiose, unrestrained Oriental despotism versus disciplined republican virtue. All of this is untrue.

In fact, most of the ships in the two fleets were probably similar in size and capability. In both fleets, fours and fives predominated. Perhaps 30 of Antony's 230 ships were larger. Based on the evidence of the Actium Victory Monument, a reasonable estimate is that he had four or more tens, four nines, five eights, six sevens, and perhaps eight sixes. Although Antony had burned most of his smaller ships, no doubt he maintained a few small, fast galleys to serve as scouts or messengers during the battle. He should also have retained a number of small boats to pick up men who had fallen overboard.

Octavian's fleet was little changed from the navy that Agrippa had built to fight Sextus Pompey. The sources describe that fleet as "heavy." The fleet also included a certain number of liburnians. Those fast ships were based on pirate vessels used by the peoples of Liburnia on the Adriatic coast, conquered by Octavian and Agrippa in the Illyrian War of 35 to 33 BC. Octavian himself spent the Battle of Actium on a liburnian, which gave his propagandists added incentive to exaggerate those ships' role in the fight. In fact, the main and decisive part of his fleet consisted of heavy ships.

In a typical naval battle of this era, the two rival fleets would line up opposite each other. In each fleet, the ships would be arranged side by side, in line-abreast formation. Then they would approach and join battle.

The most significant differences between the two fleets at Actium lay in number, manpower, and construction. Antony's ships had an advantage in prow-to-prow ramming, which was the preferred way for navies in this period to begin a battle. This also deterred the enemy from engaging in a similar maneuver. Instead of ramming the enemy's prows, Octavian's and Agrippa's captains would attempt to get through or around Antony's ships and ram them in the side or attack them from behind. They might also engage in the more elegant and difficult maneuver of shearing off the enemy's oars on one side, which would cripple the ship. In addition to ramming, both sides would come up close to the enemy's ship and attempt to board it and fight on deck. As they neared each other, the two fleets would be shooting bolts and stones from catapults and slings, as well as—at a closer range—arrows and javelins.

Antony's ships were at a disadvantage at both ramming and boarding because they were short of rowing manpower, especially fit and healthy manpower. Antony needed to take measures to protect his ships from an enemy whose fleet was larger, faster, and more mobile, powered as it was by a full complement of healthy oarsmen. So, he sought help from the lay of the land. He had his fleet hug the shore after leaving the entrance to the Ambracian Gulf, as planned. He arranged his ships on a north-south line stretching about three and a half miles long, according to one estimate. By anchoring either end on a point on shore or at a point where they were protected by shallow water to the left or right, he prevented his fleet from being outflanked. And by keeping his ships close to one another,

Antony left little room for the enemy vessels to slip through and attack the sides.

Antony commanded the right wing, with the help of Publicola. Insteius and Marcus Octavius commanded the center, and Sosius the left. Given the weakness of his fleet, Antony might have done well to mass his forces to deliver a strong blow on one wing and then hope to sow panic in the rest of the enemy fleet. Alternatively, he might have tried to force the enemy to concentrate its attack in one place, thereby opening a gap where the rest of Antony's ships could escape. In either case, Antony would have placed his biggest ships at one point: say, with him on his right (northern) wing. This is a plausible if unproven hypothesis.

Antony had 170 ships, or three squadrons, in his front line. In the rear, closely behind the front line, was Cleopatra and her squadron of sixty Egyptian ships. Their job was to respond to any breakthrough maneuvers by the enemy. No doubt Cleopatra had an expert (male) admiral or admirals to rely on. It was, to put it mildly, unusual to find a woman in command of a flotilla in battle.

Opposite Antony, about a sea mile away, lay Octavian and Agrippa. Marcus Lurius commanded the right wing, Agrippa the left wing, with Lucius Arruntius in the center. As Agrippa faced opposite Antony, he held the most important position. Octavian was positioned in a liburnian on the right, where he could watch the action while leaving overall command to Agrippa.

The reality was the opposite of the arrangement that Virgil immortalizes in the *Aeneid*. He wrote the poem a decade or so after the battle. In it, he describes the scene thus:

> *Young Caesar [Octavian], on the stern, in armor bright,*
> *Here leads the Romans and their gods to fight:*
> *His beamy temples shoot their flames afar,*
> *And o'er his head is hung the Julian star.*
> *Agrippa seconds him, with prosp'rous gales,*

And, with propitious gods, his foes assails:
A naval crown; that binds his manly brows,
The happy fortune of the fight foreshows.

It was, of course, Octavian who seconded Agrippa and not vice versa.

Antony could not maintain his inshore position forever, not if he wanted to fight the enemy, and not if he wanted to break out of Actium. For one thing, Agrippa kept his fleet about a mile away from Antony's prows. Commanding the larger and faster fleet, Agrippa was better off fighting the battle in open water, where there was room to maneuver. Thanks to Dellius, they knew that the enemy wanted to unleash a prow-to-prow charge, so they kept their distance to force him into a longer, harder, and more tiring row. By the time Antony's rams reached them, they would have lost their force. And then there was the wind.

Wind is not a subject that is top of mind for most people nowadays, but it was different in ancient times, especially for people who lived on the coasts and, above all, for mariners. The economy depended on transport by sea, where the wind was as important a source of power as oil is to the trucking business today. Winds, moreover, were part of the agricultural year as well, so winds were common knowledge, down to their names and their vagaries. After having spent months in the vicinity of Actium, the men in the two fleets knew the local winds well.

Antony had prepared to outrun the enemy by loading his sails aboard ship, as mentioned. His rowers could not hope to outpace the enemy's, especially with the bigger ships in Antony's fleet and with the handicaps of poor nutrition and ill health. They needed to be able to sail, and in order to sail at a rapid pace, they needed a favorable wind.

To Antony and Cleopatra, the most important detail was the wind that blew in from the west-northwest every afternoon in a more or less predictable pattern. Ancient ships were square rigged and so had little ability to tack—that is, to zigzag through the wind. Medieval and modern ships, with their triangular sails, are much more maneuverable. To reach maximum speed, the ships of 31 BC needed to have the wind at their back or on their rear quarter.

Geography provided an additional complication. The island of Leucas lies about five miles south-southwest of Actium. To go south of it, a ship has to go around the island's west coast. Antony and Cleopatra's ships, therefore, could not escape if they stayed close to shore. They needed to row out to sea before catching the wind and turning south. That sounds simpler than it was.

To row out to sea, Antony and Cleopatra's ships would have had to struggle against a strengthening wind and an enemy that was waiting for them. What lay ahead was a task to challenge the cunning mind of Odysseus.

The Men

Octavian embarked about forty thousand men—the soldiers of eight legions and five praetorian cohorts on his ships. Antony boarded twenty thousand legionaries and two thousand archers on his ships. Octavian had nearly twice as many fighting men, but he also had nearly twice as many ships—400 versus 230—so the average number of deck soldiers on each side's ships probably was roughly similar: about a hundred men per vessel. The legionaries would have worn bronze or iron helmets and chain mail armor. Each one carried a large shield, a javelin, and a short sword, or *gladius*.

One anonymous legionary who fought for Antony has left us his coin hoard of forty-one denarii, the standard Roman silver coins, which was found at Actium. Among them are coins issued by Julius Caesar, by Antony, or by Antony and Cleopatra, and they include thirty-one of the legionary coins minted the previous winter in Patrae. We might guess that the soldier buried them before the battle, thinking they were safer there than on board his ship, and hoping to come back and retrieve them after victory. It was an idle hope.

Antony's legionaries included veterans of his campaigns, from Mutina and Philippi to Media and Armenia, as well as new recruits to replace those lost in the Median defeat. They included Italians, Roman settlers and their descendants in the East, and non-Romans trained as legionaries. The archers were allied troops. So, although Latin was the predominant language aboard ship, other tongues would have been heard too. No ordinary soldiers can be named.

We can do better with Octavian's legionaries. In most ways, Actium has been stingy with its secrets, but historians have had a few lucky breaks. Actium is one of the rare ancient battles where the names of some ordinary participants, and not just officers, survive. Five gravestones from northeastern Italy state that the deceased was an Actium veteran. That is distinctive in and of itself, for as far as we know, Actium is the only battle in Roman history to give its name to its veterans. Each of the five men calls himself an "Actium Fighter" (*Actiacus*). They all received land in a northern Italian colony set up by Octavian after the battle.

It's all but certain that three of them fought aboard ship, and perhaps all five did. One specifically states in his epitaph that he served in a "naval battle." To be sure, he might have exaggerated, but he also states that he served in the eleventh legion, and if there was ever a unit to rely on in a tight spot such as a crucial naval battle, it was the eleventh. Two of the other Actium Fighters also state their enrollment in the eleventh, so they probably also served at sea as well. The other two don't specify a legion.

The eleventh had a proud history. Originally raised by Julius Caesar to serve in Gaul, it also fought in the bloody civil war battles in Greece and the Balkans. Disbanded in 45 BC, it was reconstituted by Octavian in 42 BC. The new eleventh legion proved itself in some of Octavian's great victories. No wonder men were proud to list the eleventh on their gravestones.

They were probably country boys, no doubt of humble origin; otherwise they would not have been mere legionaries, nor would they have needed land in a colony. Still, they all have names that were of some prominence in Roman history, perhaps pointing to distant relatives.

Marcus Billienus, for example, the soldier of the eleventh who specifies that he fought in a naval battle, recalls a Gaius Billienus, who, oddly enough, is the first name in Roman history that we can assign with certainty to a statue of someone in armor (around 100 BC). Quintus Coelius, another soldier of the eleventh, has a family name that recalls distinguished Roman statesmen, generals, and a historian. His legionary colleague Salvius Sempronius brings to mind one of the great families of the republic, the Sempronii. One of them, Lucius Sempronius Atratinus, actually served Antony as an officer and then, at an unknown date, deserted to Octavian. As for the two Actium Fighters who don't list their legion on their gravestone, one, Quintus Atilius, shares another prominent name in Roman history, most memorably the admiral Atilius Regulus, who defeated Carthage at sea in a great battle of the third century BC. The other, Marcus Aufustius, has a less common family name, but he shares it with a Latin grammarian of the era.

Four of the five were ordinary legionaries, and the fifth, Coelius, was a junior officer. He was a *signifer,* or standard bearer. His job was to carry the ensign of his unit, which consisted of a plaque with a metal hand on top, attached to a metal pole, covered with circular emblems and a laurel wreath. He wore a bearskin on his helmet, with the paws tied on his chest. As standard bearer, Coelius had to stand in a visible and dangerous position on deck during battle. On land, at any rate, the standard bearer carried a smaller shield than ordinary legionaries.

Cleopatra's ships probably held some Roman legionaries, but her forces surely consisted mainly of Ptolemaic soldiers. Judging from a mosaic illustration, those soldiers would have been splendidly attired in various helmets and linen armor, carrying either round Macedonian shields or oblong body shields, both decorated boldly. They were armed with pikes and swords.

None of the rowers at Actium is known by name. Ancient rowers rarely are, as they tended to be poor and unable to pay for epitaphs commemorating their careers. Some were surely slaves, as many of Sextus Pompey's rowers had been. Many of Antony's rowers had been forced into service unwillingly.

The rowers sat below deck in cramped and confined quarters. Their biggest fear was being rammed by the enemy, but their second biggest fear might have been the damage caused by the shock of ramming the enemy themselves. No one wanted to be trapped below deck with water rushing in. Having a ship boarded and captured was probably not as dangerous, as rowers were too valuable to kill: they could sell their services to one side as well as to another.

Warships carried special troops as well. Gun crews on deck worked the catapult. Portable wooden towers could be put up at both prow and stern of a big warship, from which slingers and archers would attack.

Every ship also contained a crew of sailors and specialists. By far the most important person was the helmsman, who had to work the heavy double rudder in the stern and steer the boat. There was also, finally, a captain. With luck, he would be a seasoned professional.

Action

And so, the two fleets waited, each hoping that the other would do something rash. Finally, around noon, the sea breeze began to blow. Antony had to time things just right. If he left too soon, the wind wouldn't have swung enough to the north or have strengthened enough to speed his ships on their way south. But if he waited too long, the wind would be too strong for his ships to row northwestward out to sea. So, Antony's line began to advance, beginning with the left (southern) wing, which had the farthest to go in order to get free of the obstacle of the island of Leucas. Opposite them, Octavian's right wing began to back water, still hoping to fight out to sea.

On the northern end of the battlespace, Agrippa began to extend his line in an attempt to outflank the enemy. Publicola, on Antony's right wing, followed suit. This was the correct choice, but it opened a gap between Antony's right and center squadrons. Antony's captains knew that they had to try to maintain a tight space between their ships within the squadron in order to prevent the enemy from sailing through, turning, and ramming their ships in the side or rear. Because of tight formations within each squadron, Antony's lieutenants were forced to allow gaps to open between the three squadrons. That was dangerous but not as dangerous as letting spaces develop within a squadron. In any case, Agrippa would certainly take advantage of the gaps between squadrons, so that it was no longer possible for Antony to avoid fighting.

Virgil set the scene in the *Aeneid*: "Moving they fight: with oars and forky prows/The froth is gather'd, and the water glows."

Although every battle is unique, they did have certain things in common. We can supplement the sketchy sources for Actium with information from better-documented naval battles of the era. One detail that those other sources emphasize is the sheer noise of naval battle.

At Actium, the stillness and quiet for the two hours when the fleets faced each other like a couple of gunslingers on the streets of Laredo, must have seemed eerie to any veteran of war at sea. Then came the clash and more familiar noises. An account of the battles of the Sicilian War in 36 BC reports the shouts of the rowers, the loud cries of the helmsmen, and the exhortations of the generals. As the soldiers leaped onto the deck of an enemy ship, they cried the watchword to their comrades in order to identify one another. Often, when they heard the enemy's watchword, they started crying it themselves in order to trick their opponent. There was the twang of arrows, the hissing of javelins, the detonation of catapults as they discharged their load, the whoosh of stones in the air, and the crash of their landing. Whenever a ship prepared to ram, the men on deck crouched and held on tight to keep from toppling off. A violent and rending *crash* of a ship's beak taking a bite out of the enemy accompanied each ramming. Oars cracked as they broke. A splash marked the sound of each man jumping into the sea to try to save his life. Meanwhile, the soldiers lining the shore watched and waited, trying without success to make sense of the distant fight but discerning nothing more than the alternate wailing of the men on each side. The men on shore at Actium shouted out orders to each side. Finally, when it was all over, hours after the battle had begun, the men on shipboard of the victorious side cheered, echoed by their comrades on shore. The losing side lamented.

The first stages of a battle, as the two lines of ships started toward each other, were marked by antipersonnel attacks—first, at a distance, via catapults, and then, once the fleets closed in on each other, by switching to bows and arrows and javelins. Occasionally someone might land a kill shot that took out an enemy helmsman or captain, but that would have been difficult to do indeed, especially from a moving boat.

If things had broken right for Antony, he would have been able to deliver a devastating prow-to-prow attack on the enemy. That attack never happened. The most likely reason is that Antony's men were too weak, tired, and few in number to deliver much of a blow after the milelong sprint needed to reach Octavian's fleet. It was predictable that Antony's biggest ships would have the greatest problems carrying out a sprint. Might the ships serve any useful military purpose?

Perhaps they represented a tactic of deception. Antony knew that the enemy would try to swarm each of his biggest ships with several smaller and faster ships of their own. The more he could tempt the enemy to do so, the better the chances that they would be too distracted to prevent other of his ships from escaping.

As the two lines drew close, they came to blows. Antony's vessels took advantage of their size and height to rain down missiles on the enemy. One of the tools they used was the "iron hand," a grappling iron with hooks. Agrippa's ships employed different tactics. They ganged up on Antony's vessels and rammed them amidships.

If they failed in their first attempt to ram an enemy ship, they would back water and try again. Both sides also engaged in deck fighting. Although the sources don't record Agrippa employing the catapult-launched grapnel that he had used to great effect off Sicily, we might imagine that he did so. This device, a grapple hook attached to a winch by a length of rope, harpooned the enemy ship and then pulled it alongside for boarding.

The battle raged, with neither side winning a distinct advantage. Suddenly everything changed.

Chapter 12

The Golden Ship with Purple Sails

Actium, September 2, 31 BC:
Approximately 2:00 to 3:00 P.M.

AS THE WIND PICKED UP OFF ACTIUM, ANY EARLIER haze disappeared from the sky. The sea breeze rose steadily, bringing relief to the hot September afternoon. The breeze started at a right angle to the shore. The surface of the water began to ripple. Then, as the wind intensified, and because of the rotation of the Earth, it shifted direction from west to northwest. Waves deepened, and the first hints of whitecaps appeared in the steel-blue sea. Locked in action, the two lines of warships might have seemed indifferent to marine or atmospheric conditions, but, in fact, they had been carefully following the wind all day—and probably no one more so than Cleopatra.

The Queen Leads the Way

As the wind picked up slowly, a gap widened increasingly in the center of Antony's line. It appears that he had planned this. He certainly had placed his most experienced admirals at either end of the line, as did the enemy. He might have expected that the fighting would be less intense in the center, thereby leaving an opening—just the place for a breakout. Cleopatra was the one to exploit it.

The queen waited for just the right moment, when it became clear that the two fleets were locked in battle. At that point, the fighting was too intense for the enemy to break off in pursuit. So, Cleopatra made her move. Her own squadron of sixty ships was held in reserve in the rear of Antony's armada. She ordered her ships to move. Their instructions were to row through the gap between the right wing and the center. Next, Cleopatra commanded her ship captains to raise their sails to catch the wind. "She called to the winds and let the swelling sails out more and more," as Virgil puts it. The time was between two and three in the afternoon, or so a plausible estimate has it.

Cleopatra's flagship, the *Antonias*, was no doubt splendid. The Ptolemies were not ones to spare expense on a royal vessel. Think of the barge on which Cleopatra had rowed upriver in Tarsus to meet Antony ten years earlier. When one source on Actium says that she signaled the breakout maneuver by raising the purple sail on her golden ship, it might not be an exaggeration. Purple was the color of royalty, and the ship might well have had gilded decorations.

In any event, it was a bold move. Prior to battle, the council of war had decided on a breakout strategy, and Cleopatra was executing it in an exemplary manner. The sources agree that she led the breakout. Indeed, she might have deserved a medal for leading her squadron to safety. Still, some of the ancient authors pour scorn on her. Flavius Josephus, writing a little more than a century after the battle, is the first to criticize her, asserting flatly that Cleopatra deserted Antony. But, then, the Jewish historian *always* criticizes Cleopatra, as he was a partisan of her rival King Herod. Cassius Dio, writing more than a century after Josephus, agrees. He says that she lost her nerve and fled, behaving—says Dio, in a combination of sexism and racism— just like a woman and an Egyptian.

Shakespeare follows the hostile tradition, having one of Antony's men say:

> *Yon ribrauded nag of Egypt,*
> *Whom leprosy o'ertake!—i' the midst o' the fight,*
> *When vantage like a pair of twins appear'd,*

> *Both as the same, or rather ours the elder,*
> *The breese upon her, like a cow in June,*
> *Hoists sails and flies.*

In fact, Antony's fleet was fighting a losing battle, and he knew it. Cleopatra wasn't "a cow in June" but rather a fox escaping from the hounds on a New Year's Day fox hunt.

Yet the flower of Roman manhood in the enemy fleet did nothing to stop Cleopatra. Why? Plutarch says that they were too amazed to do anything. He has a point. Romans were, in fact, generally sexist bigots. Most probably never imagined that a Greco-Egyptian squadron could have pulled off such a daring move, especially not when it was commanded by a woman. Having spent a lifetime being underestimated by men, Cleopatra knew how to take advantage of their mistake.

In any case, Cleopatra and her commanders executed their maneuver with speed and agility. The enemy admiral opposite her was Arruntius, who was in charge of the center of Octavian's fleet. In the thick of the fighting, Arruntius would have found it hard to get his ships to break off in time to pursue, especially if he lacked resolution or experience. He might have been surprised by Cleopatra's action, and surprise is a force multiplier.

Antony, however, was not surprised, and he soon followed Cleopatra. Again, this was probably according to plan, but that doesn't stop some of the ancient sources from saying otherwise. Josephus implies that by treacherously deserting Antony, the queen forced him to follow. The upshot was that Antony lost both his army and his empire. Velleius Paterculus, by contrast, puts the blame squarely on Antony, who made his own choice, the writer says, to accompany the queen instead of his own men. Rather than punish deserters from his army, as he should have, Antony deserted his army. Plutarch has it both ways. After writing that Antony was moved not by the reasoning of a commander or a man or even of himself, the Greek historian concludes that it was as if Antony's soul belonged to the body of the woman he loved. As soon as he saw Cleopatra's ship sailing off, Antony fled, abandoning and ultimately betraying the men who were fighting and dying for him. Cassius Dio, on the other hand, gives Antony a break. He says that when Antony saw Cleopatra's squadron fleeing, he blamed it not on the queen but on her men's fear that they had been defeated. And so, he decided to follow. In short, says Dio, Antony was moved by a rational calculation and not by a lover's passion.

Contrary to romance, Antony, like Cleopatra, moved with a precision and decisiveness that suggests a prearranged plan. His flagship was a big ship, possibly a ten, and too heavy for a quick escape. He transferred to a five, which was a compromise choice: though not the fastest of ships, it was heavy enough to fight off an enemy attack. When he reached Cleopatra, she recognized him and raised a signal; he approached her ship and was taken on board.

Predictably, enemy propaganda put out a tale to make Antony's well-executed escape look ridiculous. The story went that Antony had been forced to abandon his flagship and board Cleopatra's vessel only because his ship had become immobilized by a fish known as the *echeneïs,* or "ship detainer," which could become entangled in the rudder cables. *Echeneïs* are a type of remora, a fish that attaches itself to sharks and ships. By a happy accident, a common name for the fish in English gives away the propaganda game against Antony: "sucker fish."

Granted that Antony and Cleopatra fled according to a prearranged plan, why did the two of them take an Egyptian squadron rather than a Roman one? Was Cleopatra pushing Antony around? Hardly. Antony trusted the Roman squadrons more than the Egyptians to do the actual fighting. Better to keep the Egyptians in reserve, from which position they could lead the retreat if necessary. Besides, their destination was Egypt, which would welcome Egyptian warships more warmly than Roman ones. Most important, Cleopatra had the treasure on her ships, and she did not trust anyone but her own men. Hence, the flight of the Egyptian ships made good sense.

Many if not most of Antony's ships tried to follow him. In order to lighten their loads and escape more rapidly, they raised their sails and threw their towers into the sea. Yet most of them were unable to make it to safety. We don't know how many of his ships broke out. Estimates range as high as forty and as low as "a few." Somewhere between ten and twenty escapees is a reasonable guess. Add them to the sixty ships in Cleopatra's squadron, and the total is seventy to eighty warships that managed to break out of Actium.

Antony and Cleopatra began the battle with 230 warships, which means that about one-third escaped. That was not a bad total. Naval history has known more successful breakouts, although not without losses, but Antony and Cleopatra's achievement was nonetheless considerable, given that they were outnumbered, hungry, ill, and beset with tricky winds. True enough, it is a monument to mismanagement that they found themselves in this situation in the first place. Yet had they not planned and executed the battle as well as they did, they might have escaped with fewer ships or with none at all. Assuming that a few more ships stationed around the Peloponnese or the Greek islands joined the escapees, Antony and Cleopatra arguably left Greece with, at most, about ninety warships.

As they headed south from the battle zone on the lusty breeze, they weren't quite free. Some liburnians, the fastest warships in Octavian and Agrippa's fleet, chased the escapees. Antony ordered his ship to turn and face them. That scared off all of the pursuers except one Eurycles of Sparta. Earlier that spring, probably soon after the fall of Methone, Eurycles had defected from Antony to Octavian. Now he was proving his value to his new patron by chasing Octavian's rival.

Eurycles brandished a spear on deck and aimed it threateningly at Antony. When Antony asked him to identify himself, he replied proudly that he was Eurycles, son of Lachares, and thanks to "the fortune of Caesar," he was there to avenge his father's death. A prominent man in Sparta, Lachares had been beheaded by Antony on a charge of piracy. So spoke Eurycles—or at least that is what he claimed later.

His little comedy doesn't bear up, however. Eurycles's story of avenging his murdered father, Lachares, sounds suspiciously like Octavian's story of avenging his murdered (adoptive) father, Julius Caesar. Eurycles might have invented his speech and threatening behavior in a later report to the victor of Actium.

Although Eurycles did not harm Antony, he did ram another flagship that had escaped—possibly from Antony's center squadron—and captured both it and another ship carrying some of the royal equipment. With this one last set of trophies, the pursuit of Antony and Cleopatra came to an end.

Flames over Actium

The battle was not over with Antony and Cleopatra's departure; in fact, it continued for what seemed like a long time. Some historians have doubted that report in the sources, arguing that Antony's men more likely surrendered at once, but the bulk of the evidence suggests that they struggled on for another hour or two. The ancient sources agree that was the case, although some scholars dismiss that as propaganda to make Octavian look like a hero who won a hard-fought battle. Yet, practical considerations tend to confirm that the fight continued. Both casualty figures for Antony's men and captured ship totals claimed by Octavian indicate that several dozens of Antony's ships were sunk in the battle that ensued.

More on the figures presently, but first, consider the likely course of events after Antony and Cleopatra fled. Antony's men did not give up. Some tossed their towers and their heavy catapults overboard, then tried to flee but failed. A few managed to escape. Most attempted to fight their way through. Motives surely varied. Some believed in the cause of the republic, while others followed Antony personally. Most probably put more trust in receiving land and money from Antony and his rich Egyptian woman than from stingy, broke Octavian, if he even accepted their surrender. Besides, if Plutarch is right, most of Antony's men didn't even know that their leader had fled. Velleius adds that Octavian repeatedly shouted out the truth to the enemy in an attempt to get them to surrender, but in vain. That sounds like an ex post facto self-justification from Augustus's *Memoirs*.

They fought hard. In spite of all their advantages, Agrippa and Octavian had not yet won the battle. Antony's fleet was so strong that even as a rump at Actium, it still fought the enemy to a standstill until Agrippa resorted to a last-ditch tool: fire. It was unusual but not unprecedented for Romans to use fire as a weapon at sea. Ahenobarbus had used fire arrows successfully to defeat a relief force of ships on its way to help Antony and Octavian at Philippi. Perhaps, upon his defection, Ahenobarbus was debriefed about this experience by Agrippa and Octavian. In any case, the use of fire at Actium is a tribute to Agrippa's versatility.

Every admiral's goal was to capture the enemy's fleet, not to destroy it. Captured ships could be repurposed for your own use, but burned ships sank to the bottom. Agrippa and Octavian would not have put Antony's ships to the flame unless they had to. They didn't even consider using it while Cleopatra's treasure was still in reach; that, it was understood, was the most valuable prize of all.

And yet it must be conceded that fire achieved two positive goals. Fire killed a large number of enemy sailors and deck soldiers while reducing the risk to one's own men. Fire also sent a message to the surviving enemy: surrender or die. Like the execution of Bogud at Methone, the flames of Actium proclaimed Agrippa's deadly earnest. The loss of a few dozen enemy ships was a price worth paying to speed the surrender of a hundred thousand men on other ships and on shore.

Several ancient accounts mention the use of fire weapons in the battle, but only Dio provides details. His narrative, while sensational, offers a number of points that ring true, based on other descriptions of ancient incendiaries. If Dio is right, Octavian, or more likely Agrippa, realized that without the use of fire, they might not win. And so, they pressed their advantage.

The attackers approached Antony's ships from many directions at once. They shot blazing missiles, hurled spears with torches attached to them, and used catapults to shoot pots filled with charcoal and pitch. Roman warships were liberally coated with pitch, inside and out, and the charcoal pots added to the combustibility. The defenders tried to ward off the missiles, presumably with their shields, but some got past, and the ships caught on fire. First, they used drinking water on board to put it out, then they used buckets to draw up seawater. But pitch-coated ships made good firewood, especially after having been sitting in the hot sun of a Greek summer: the flames kept burning. Next, the men used their thick woolen mantles, and, if a sensationalist detail is true, they even used corpses, to try to check the flames. But then a strong wind blew up—presumably the same westerly or northwesterly wind that sped Antony and Cleopatra's escape—and it turned the clothing and dead bodies into fuel.

Dio notes an intriguing vignette of this ghastly scene. He claims that when the defenders poured full buckets of saltwater on the fires, the water doused the flames. In fact, the water probably just turned to steam in the heat of the blaze. According to Dio, when the defenders brought up buckets only half full and so poured only small amounts on the fire, they increased the flames, because small quantities of saltwater actually make a fire burn vigorously. That, of course, is not true. What is true, however, is that saltwater makes a fire flare up with a yellow flame—a common effect when a pot of salted water boils over on a gas stove, for example. Saltwater poured onto burning pitch might make some observers think that a fire was burning better. Hence, Dio might be reporting, however erroneously, an actual eyewitness account.

Some men retreated into the still-sound portion of their ship. They even tried to go on the offense and use grappling irons to drag the enemy into the flames, but the enemy kept his distance. Then came death by various unpleasant ways: by the flames, by smoke inhalation, by enemy arrows after the defenders had thrown off their armor in preparation for escaping into the sea, or by drowning. Some were struck in the water by their opponents wielding, say, a broken oar or a spear. And some allegedly were eaten alive by denizens of the deep. Sharks are no longer common in the Mediterranean, but they were in ancient times, and they attacked humans. Only those men who killed one another or took their own lives aboard the hopelessly burning ships found a happy death, claims Dio. Melodrama, to be sure, but even a sober narrator might stop and consider the gulf between the men's hopes that morning and their sorry end in a killing zone.

Dio adds that Agrippa's men waited until it was clear that the enemy could no longer do them any harm, and then they approached the burning ships in haste, hoping both to put out the fires and salvage the ships but also to loot any money on board. The result was that quite a few fell victim to the flames and their own greed.

Victory

Antony's men began to surrender around four in the afternoon, when the wind was blowing heavily and the high seas were battering their surviving ships. They did so reluctantly, the sources report. The flames of their ships might have burned for hours. The winds began to die down as the day faded. Sunset at Actium is 8:05 p.m. on September 2. Even then, the situation was sufficiently uncertain that Octavian did not go ashore. Apparently, some of Antony's warships had retreated into the Ambracian Gulf, and they could still make trouble. Octavian spent the night on his liburnian.

If September 3 was a typical late-summer morning at Actium, first light broke over the ridge of mountains in the east. With mist rising over the hills and valleys, the ghostly outlines of the warships became visible. Eventually the sun rose and cast a golden glow if one looked eastward over the water of the Ambracian Gulf. Agrippa and Octavian might have imagined an accompanying victory song as they surveyed the scene that morning. Until then, the full extent of their victory had been unclear.

They learned that they were in possession of most of what was
left of Antony's fleet. The threat of an invasion of Italy was no more.
Octavian and Agrippa had either captured or sunk about 140 enemy
galleys. The haul was even greater if one looks at the campaign as a
whole.

Octavian claimed later to have captured 300 warships from the
enemy, a figure that surely refers to the entire Actium War, beginning
at Methone in March, and that probably excludes ships smaller than a
three. If the thirty-five rams displayed in the Actium Victory Monument represent a tithe of the total, as was common in ancient dedica-
tions, then that figure should be rounded up to about 350.

Body counts were of less value to ancient commanders—especially
in a civil war, when many of those killed were fellow citizens—and,
so, were nothing to brag about. Plutarch reports five thousand deaths
in Antony's fleet, a total that comes directly from Augustus's memoirs. Writing centuries afterward, Orosius puts the number of deaths
at twelve thousand, and six thousand wounded, with a thousand
dying later. It has been suggested that Plutarch's figure refers only to
legionaries, while Orosius's figures include sailors and crew members,
but we don't know. Perhaps it is enough to think of Sextus Propertius
(born ca. 50 BC), the Latin poet who refers to Roman corpses floating
in the sea at Actium.

One source claims that after the battle you could see the vast
wreckage of Antony's great fleet. The wind and waves "continually
yielded up the purple and gold-bespangled spoils of the Arabians and
Sabaeans and a thousand other Asiatic peoples." An exaggerated description, pitting alleged eastern decadence against western propriety,
and yet the signs of defeat no doubt floated on the waters of the battle
zone and washed up on the shore.

After the battle, Octavian's men hailed him as imperator. It was
the sixth time he had received this recognition. The sources don't offer
a record of either Octavian's or Agrippa's words or thoughts as they
surveyed the scene of their success. However pleased the two men felt,

they probably did not crow. Caesar had left a model of the combination of vindication and regret with which a good Roman should treat his fallen foe in a civil war. Upon surveying the corpses of his defeated enemies on the field after the Battle of Pharsalus, Caesar remarked: "They wanted this" (*hoc voluerunt*).

The sources offer hints that Octavian put forth a similar public persona. He regretted the spilling of Roman blood, offered mercy to the surviving enemy soldiers, and placed the blame squarely on the shoulders of his opponents. Whether or not he said that Antony and Cleopatra "wanted this," Octavian made sure to point out to Antony's men that their imperator had abandoned them. After Antony and Cleopatra fled, and while the naval battle still raged, Octavian is supposed to have addressed the men on Antony's ships energetically, with shouted criticism of their absconded commander and promises of life and pardon. The aim was to talk them into surrendering, and they finally did. The lower enemy casualty figures in Augustus's *Memoirs*—his five thousand to Orosius's twelve thousand—might represent a strategy to downplay the number of Romans whom he had killed. Many if not most of the dead were, after all, citizens, not foreign enemies. For all their propaganda about war on Cleopatra, Octavian surely knew that.

One other sentiment that Octavian surely expressed after the battle was piety. No Roman would neglect to thank the gods in victory, and certainly not a Roman as politic as Octavian. His patron was Apollo, and Actium held a famous Temple of Apollo. Octavian probably thanked the god loudly and visibly. Virgil might well be giving the official version of the divinely inspired victory over foreign foes in this passage about the battle from the *Aeneid*:

> *Apollo, from his Actian height,*
> *Pours down his arrows; at whose winged flight*
> *The trembling Indians and Egyptians yield,*
> *And soft Sabaeans quit the wat'ry field.*

It was a great victory, but not a total one. Antony and Cleopatra had escaped with about a third of their war fleet and all of their treasury. The latter was a resource that could be used to buy troops and build new warships. Meanwhile, Antony's legions were still at large in Greece. And what of Antony and Cleopatra themselves?

The Man Who Fled

The attempt to break out at Actium had been brave, risky, but necessary. Although not as successful as might have been hoped, it achieved its primary aim of saving the leadership, a portion of the ships and men, and a fortune. Yet this sip of glory did not make up for the bitter cup of failure.

As they headed south, Antony and Cleopatra's ships passed their former bases in reverse. First came the white cliffs of the island of Leucas, which Agrippa had snatched practically before Antony's eyes; then they swept past the channel that led eastward to Patrae, their winter headquarters and another prize taken by Agrippa; then the emerald waters of Sosius's former base on the island of Zacynthus; then, as they rounded the southwestern tip of the Peloponnese, the islets that guarded the harbor of Methone, where Agrippa had launched his coup in March, killing King Bogud and starting the chain reaction that led to the fleet's deprivation at Actium. With such sights in the distance—even invisible, one knew they were there—it might have been hard to stay focused on the positive. The journey took three days.

Antony had not behaved according to what was expected of a Roman, a noble, and an imperator. A Roman would have expected him to stay with his legions. Yet he could hardly have believed that the fifty thousand or so sick and starving men whom he had left ashore would put up serious resistance to Octavian. To stay with the legions would have been, in effect, to decide to commit suicide. To that, a severe Roman might have responded: so be it. Since Cassius, Brutus, and Cato the Younger, Caesar's most diehard enemy, had done just that, Antony should follow in their footsteps.

Antony's response might have been something along these lines: as a patriotic Roman, it remained his responsibility to resist Octavian's tyranny, and he could still do so using Alexandria as a base. Egypt had strong natural defenses. Antony had four legions in Cyrenaica, and he might have been able to scrape together a fifth from the soldiers who had escaped with him from Actium plus those who made their way to him from his bases at Taenarum, Crete, and Corinth. Furthermore, Cleopatra had troops of her own. With her treasure, they could hire new soldiers. Meanwhile, Octavian's need to settle his own veterans as well as Antony's would impose severe political and financial pressure on Octavian. His support might even crack.

If he was unable to hold Egypt, Antony might have continued, there was plenty of time to commit suicide later. Perhaps it was even thinkable that Antony might head eastward to Parthia. After all, Quintus Labienus, the son of Caesar's dogged enemy Titus Labienus, had thrown in his lot with Parthia after the defeat of the republican army at Philippi. Passions ran high in times of civil war. Quintus went so far as to invade Rome's eastern provinces at the side of a Parthian prince. After conquering Syria and much of Asia Minor, and after killing a provincial governor, Quintus allowed himself to be acclaimed Parthicus Imperator, "Victorious in Parthia." Not long afterward, he fell to a counteroffensive by one of Antony's commanders and was executed. Might Antony have contemplated such a fate as a glorious way to die against a tyrant?

So, the imperator who abandoned his legions might have justified himself. But would he have believed it? The entire campaign of 31 BC was not merely a defeat but also a humiliation. After Philippi, Antony had been the greatest general of his day. The Median "disaster" featured a heroic retreat and a second act that yielded the conquest of Armenia and the wrenching away of Media from the Parthian orbit, including a political alliance and a royal betrothal. There was even the prospect of a renewed and victorious war against Parthia. But Actium was different. With the exception perhaps of a local victory on land against Octavian near his camp, the war had been one failure after another. Antony had simply been outclassed by the enemy's skill and experience at sea. And he had been unprepared for the enemy's boldness.

Plutarch reports a story that Antony sat depressed alone on the prow of the *Antonias* as it cut a course toward Taenarum. Supposedly he didn't even speak to Cleopatra for the entire three-day voyage. Readers can decide for themselves whether to believe the anecdote or not.

As for the Egyptian queen, the sources don't comment on her mood. Virgil imagines her leaving Actium pale, as if in an omen of her future death. Indomitable as she was, the real Cleopatra was probably ruddy with activity, eager to make her next move. First, though, she had to deal with Antony.

The commander and the queen were reconciled, the story goes, only when they put in at Taenarum. This was a harbor at the southern tip of the central peninsula of the Peloponnese, a few miles away from the same-named cape (today's Cape Matapan). It was a bare and rugged spot, famous for winds, pirates, and caves, one of which was considered the entrance to the underworld. Taenarum lay on the maritime route eastward to Crete, Cyrene, and Alexandria. Unlike most of Antony's bases in Greece, it had not fallen to Agrippa's warships. At Taenarum, Cleopatra's maids patched up the quarrel between the imperator and the queen. They resumed eating and sleeping together.

Antony had reason to be depressed, and not only due to the magnitude of his loss. Having been saved by Cleopatra, Antony now was in her power. He was about to become a Roman in Egypt without a mighty military force to back him up. Cleopatra was not likely to abandon Antony, her consort and father of three of her children, but monarchs sometimes make harsh decisions to save their thrones. Yet Antony was a man of action, and he didn't sit still while at Taenarum. Heavy transport ships arrived, either having escaped from Actium or, perhaps more likely, sailing from some other Greek harbor that had remained in friendly hands. Some of Antony's friends also reached him. They confirmed the worst about the destruction of the fleet at Actium, but they continued to have hope in the escape of the legions.

Antony sent word to Canidius, the commander of the legions, to march the army as fast as he could through Macedonia to Asia. But Antony did not offer to rejoin his men. Instead, he prepared to sail to Africa. Although he wasn't doing a good Roman's duty to his legions, he did behave in an approved manner with his closest associates by offering them support. He chose a transport vessel carrying coined money as well as gold and silver royal utensils and offered it to his friends. They refused, but Antony comforted them with great kindness and warmth. He also took another practical step to help them.

Antony wrote a letter to Theophilus, his procurator—that is, his financial administrator, a servant that every elite Roman would have had in his employ. *Servant* is the right word, because procurators were often freedmen, as Theophilus was. He was in Corinth at the time. Antony asked Theophilus to keep Antony's closest associates safely hidden until they made their peace with Octavian. No more is heard of these men, but they surely behaved like Theophilus's son, Hipparchus: he was the first of Antony's freedmen to go over to Octavian. Hipparchus had prospered under Antony and profited under the proscriptions, yet Octavian accepted him as an ally.

The point is that Antony understood that once he left Greece, his friends there would have to make a deal with the enemy. The army was no different. By not rejoining them in person, he demonstrated how little hope he had in that struggling and much-diminished force.

Not everyone around the defeated couple at Taenarum was trustworthy. Suspecting some of those there of treachery, Antony and Cleopatra sent them away. Some of the allies they wanted to keep left on their own, thinking it prudent to distance themselves.

Mark Antony. The inscription on this gold aureus coin from 40 BC identifies Antony and records his offices as imperator (victorious general) and triumvir.

Octavian. A silver denarius coin of 29–27 BC showing a youthful Octavian in profile. The reverse depicts a victory arch topped by a four-horse chariot on which Octavian stands. The arch is inscribed, "Octavian Imperator [victorious general]."

4

Cleopatra. This marble bust has been identified by most scholars as Cleopatra. Her hair is carefully coiffed. She wears a broad diadem, that is, a ribbon denoting royalty.

5

Antony and Cleopatra coin. This silver tetradrachm, issued by Mark Antony in the Eastern Mediterranean, 37–31 BC, depicts the two powerful rulers. Cleopatra looks mature and monarchical, while Antony appears massive.

Octavia. In 39 BC Mark Antony issued this gold coin that shows his new wife, Octavia, sister of his then ally—and later rival—Octavian.

Cleopatra and Caesarion. This sculpted relief on the wall of the Temple of Hathor, Dendera, Egypt, depicts the queen and her son, allegedly fathered by Julius Caesar. With their Egyptian audience in mind, the two are shown in Egyptian garb, rather than in the Greek style used for Greek and Roman audiences.

8

Alexander Helios. This bronze statuette, found in Egypt, has been identified by some as the older son of Antony and Cleopatra. He wears trousers and a pyramidal hat, both unusual in Greece and Rome but not in Armenia, where the boy was named a prince.

9

Antony, Legionary Coin. This silver denarius of Mark Antony, dated 32–31 BC, celebrates his third legion and shows one of his warships on the reverse. Antony is identified as augur and triumvir.

The Fort at Methone. This Venetian-Ottoman fort was built on the site of the ancient fortifications. The view here looks toward the island of Sapientza.

View from Octavian's Headquarters. Looking south toward Cape Actium from Michalitsi, above Nicopolis, the location of the later Victory Monument.

Roman Warship. This galley from the Temple of Fortuna at Praeneste (modern Palestrina), Italy, illustrates the sort of armed men and fighting tower that might have been found on one of the ships at Actium. It has been variously dated from the late first century BC to the second half of the first century AD.

Death of Mark Antony in Cleopatra's Arms. This 1819 etching on paper by Bartolomeo Pinelli depicts Antony's death in the arms of his lover after he had stabbed himself.

Dignitaries Marching in the Actium Triumph. Wearing togas and victory wreaths, these men, presumably Roman senators, march behind Octavian's chariot. The image is part of a sculpted relief depicting the Actium Triumph in Rome, which was part of the Victory Monument at Michalitsi, in the hills above Nicopolis.

Ram Socket in the Actium Victory Monument. An empty socket on the podium wall of Octavian's Victory Monument as it appears today. The socket once held one of Antony's massive bronze rams.

Ram Terrace, Actium Victory Monument. A reconstruction of the podium of Octavian's Victory Monument showing the line of warship rams attached to a long retaining wall.

Augustus. A gold aureus coin of Augustus, 20–19 BC. The reverse shows a golden shield of virtue flanked by laurel branches, with SPQR—the Senate and People of Rome—and the name Caesar Augustus. Augustus's wreath and shield were awarded to him by the Senate.

As for the legions marching under Canidius, the sources say how loyal the troops remained to Antony, and how much they yearned for him to return and lead them—and, one might add, to pay them. Supposedly they held together for a full seven days. According to the pro-Octavian tradition, they surrendered only after Canidius and other leading Roman and allied commanders abandoned the army and ran away. More likely, the leaders fled once they realized that the troops were about to make a deal with Octavian—and that no such deal awaited them.

Dealing was Octavian's forte. He had a well-established record as a negotiator. For example, he began his career in 44 BC by weaning away two legions from Antony. On that occasion, he offered them a generous raise and soothed the anger stoked by the executions of both legionaries and centurions with which Antony had enforced discipline. They defected and joined Octavian.

Octavian also knew that, more than once during Rome's various civil wars, the legions had shown that they preferred negotiating to fighting. Now, in the aftermath of Actium, all signs pointed to parleying with representatives of Antony's legions. They held out for good terms, and Octavian proposed a generous settlement. Antony had gathered nineteen legions at Actium. Despite battle losses and escapees, most of those legions were probably still intact. Octavian allowed at least four of the legions, and probably more, to maintain their names and numbers; the soldiers in the other legions were used to fill up gaps in Octavian's rank's. Promises of land upon demobilization were made, and they were eventually kept, but with settlement outside of Italy. Octavian's veterans were settled in Italy.

What Went Wrong?

That is the question that Antony and Cleopatra might have asked themselves at Taenarum. An honest answer would have been something along the following lines:

The allied fleet was splendid, and its resources were misspent. Its comparative advantage was the ability to smash into the ports of southern Italy and open up the road to Rome, thereby allowing Antony to fight and win his kind of war: a land war. In such an effort, the allied fleet would be unmatched.

When it came to war at sea, the allied fleet stood at a disadvantage. To be sure, it had certain strengths: in particular the reinforced prows that could be devastating in head-to-head ramming and the catapult towers that could barrage the enemy with missiles. Its admirals included the experienced Ahenobarbus, who had achieved victory at sea.

But these were not war winners when deployed against the greatest admiral of the era, Agrippa, and against the fleet that had defeated the most dynamic seafarer of the age, Sextus Pompey, especially not when they also had the cunning and ruthless leadership of Octavian.

Risky as an invasion of Italy was, Antony and Cleopatra's armada had a real chance of pulling it off. But if victory depended on command of the sea off the waters of western Greece, then the advantage passed to Agrippa and Octavian. Antony and Cleopatra might still win, but only if they were prepared to make a supreme effort of alertness and audacity. They were not.

Nor can we leave out of the equation the political differences and infighting that beset the alliance. Republicans distrusted Cleopatra, and she returned the compliment. Ahenobarbus was a major loss because of his naval experience; he might have made a difference at Actium if he had stayed loyal and healthy. Eastern princes chafed under Cleopatra's ambition for empire at their expense. Herod, who stayed home from Actium and sent troops rather than clash with the queen, was an extreme case, but he was not the only one. In spite of the notional division of the empire, Octavian made friends and contacts in the Roman East, supposedly Antony's realm. To be sure, Antony made similar approaches in Italy, but once the defeats began to pile up, his advances there fell on deaf ears.

Antony and Cleopatra had made the correct strategic choice of taking the war westward. Standing on the defensive in Egypt was not an option, because it would have conceded the rest of the Roman East to the enemy and led to massive allied defections— if not a coup or collapse in Egypt itself. Their mistake was not going to Actium but staying there when they should have invaded Italy, and, having decided to stay there, not securing their vulnerable rear bases.

Leadership was key. Had Antony deployed his resources with skill, aggressiveness, and efficiency, he could have won, even had he stayed on the defensive in western Greece. Instead, he showed himself to be unprepared, reactive, and inept. Antony and Cleopatra offered an example of a rift in the leadership. Their enemy was united. Octavian and Agrippa were a twin foe; Antony and Cleopatra, a house divided. No wonder the defections went from their camp to Octavian's.

For neither the first or last time in history, the side with more money and better technology opted for the wrong strategy. Having done so, they failed also to execute their chosen strategy correctly. And so, they lost the war.

Chapter 13

"I Preferred to Save Rather Than to Destroy"

Actium-Asia Minor, September 3, 31, to Spring 30 BC

Wars, both civil and foreign, I undertook throughout the world, on sea and land, and when victorious, I spared all citizens who sued for pardon. The foreign nations which could with safety be pardoned, I preferred to save rather than to destroy.

—*THE DEEDS OF THE DEIFIED AUGUSTUS* (AD 14)

LOOKING BACK FROM TWO CENTURIES LATER, THE historian Cassius Dio dated the beginning of Octavian's "sole possession of all power" from the date of Actium. That was true only in retrospect. At the time, things seemed less settled.

Victory at Actium did not end the war, but it brought a good outcome for Octavian much nearer. On the eve of his thirty-second birthday, September 23, 31 BC, he could imagine fulfilling the audacious vow that he had sworn at the age of nineteen: to have all the honors that had belonged to his adoptive father, Julius Caesar. That meant, of course, controlling the entire Roman Empire and not just the western half of it. The eastern part of the empire was wealthier, more populous, more urbanized, and more cultured than the West. No one of Octavian's ambition could do without it.

But what of the one great country on the Mediterranean that did not lie under Roman rule: What of Egypt? At a minimum, Octavian would have insisted on extracting its wealth, as Caesar had done. Yet surely he wanted more.

Octavian could dare to dream of obtaining the great, glittering, golden prize on the Nile. It was the wealthiest country in the Mediterranean. It was the site of one of his adoptive father's great exploits. And it contained the solution to his financial troubles: Cleopatra's treasure—or rather her treasure plus whatever else Antony had taken in the East by taxation, extortion, or plunder. These were the riches, of course, that had slipped out of his grasp at Actium. Octavian needed the money badly to pay his soldiers, to settle the discontent in Italy that followed the war tax he had been forced to levy, and to help fund the new regime that he planned for Rome.

Egypt, however, was not yet his for the asking. Octavian had to win it. It might look as if after Actium, everything would be easy. Octavian surely knew better.

Octavian understood that Antony had lost a battle, but it was commonplace that Romans were more spirited in defeat than in victory. Past history showed that a vanquished foe could continue to make serious trouble. Julius Caesar, for example, had defeated his Roman enemies' armies in Italy, Spain, Greece, and North Africa. He had seen his leading opponents die. And yet the sons of Pompey were still able to stir up a rebellion in Spain that presented Caesar with his greatest battlefield challenge, at Munda in 45 BC. Octavian, who had received his first taste of war when he joined his great-uncle in the mop-up after Munda, would hardly forget the lesson. Nor would he fail to recall how Ahenobarbus raided the coasts of Italy with his fleet even after his allies had suffered defeat at Philippi in 42 BC and then committed suicide. Nor, finally, could he overlook the case of Sextus, whose challenge required a herculean effort to overcome. Octavian knew, therefore, that as long as Antony and Cleopatra were alive and at large, they were not yet conquered.

In sum, Antony and Cleopatra continued to have resources and followers. If they dug in, they could put up a good defense in Egypt, as the country had strong natural defenses, with inhospitable terrain and powerful fortresses both on the east and the west that blocked entry to invading armies.

What loomed in the aftermath of Actium was a struggle for Egypt. We may regard it as the final campaign of the Actium War, but the Romans considered Egypt to be a separate war altogether. They called it the Alexandrian War.

There was talk of Antony and Cleopatra going to Hispania, which, as various enemies of Rome had shown—in particular Sertorius and the Pompey brothers—made fertile country for armed resistance. Hispania had mountainous terrain, still-hostile indigenous peoples, and silver mines, too, should Antony and Cleopatra's ample funds run out. And, as later history would bear out, Spain was the homeland of *la guerrilla*, Spanish for "small war," describing the unconventional tactics it used against Emperor Napoléon I of France from 1808 to 1814 and giving us our term for guerrilla warfare. It's no accident that around the time following Actium, Octavian fortified positions on the coast of Hispania, thereby adding a layer of protection from invasion. Consequently, Antony and Cleopatra looked to another possible refuge in the East.

Their money and connections gave the imperator and the queen a long reach. Octavian was well aware of how an assassin's dagger could change the world in a flash. One source claims that Antony and Cleopatra were looking for ways to use envoys and bribery either to deceive Octavian or to murder him. Short of that, there was the danger of rebellion in the rear, in Italy, while Octavian was pursuing the war in the East—a rebellion that the two of them might help stir up.

What Octavian Wanted

After defeating Sextus Pompey in 36 BC, Octavian and his advisors began to think about how they wanted to govern Rome. Or, as they might have put it, how to "renovate the republic." The phrase *res publica restituta* would become a watchword of the new regime that emerged in Rome after Actium. Usually translated as "the republic has been restored," it could also mean "the republic has been renovated" or the even more general "the commonwealth has been renovated." Although Octavian still had to work out the details of the new regime, he was certain of one thing: there was no going back to the old republic. That was the government that had killed Julius Caesar, and Caesar's son would have none of it.

If Octavian had his way, the new regime would be one in which his family would occupy center stage. His building program made that clear. In the late 30s BC, before Actium, he began building his tomb. He was only about thirty, but the timing was political, probably shortly after he denounced Antony for allegedly planning to be buried in Alexandria. Octavian took a different path: he would be buried in Rome. But there was nothing of republican austerity in the tomb he planned.

A grandiose dynastic tomb for Octavian and his extended family, it was the tallest building in the city. Religion prohibited burial inside the city walls, so the monument was located just outside them, in the rapidly urbanizing area of the Campus Martius. The tomb consisted of an artificial hill sitting on a white marble foundation and covered with evergreens, eventually to be crowned by a bronze statue of Octavian. The exterior was decorated with the loot of battle, rendering it a war memorial and trophy as well as a tomb. The massive ruins are still visible today in the Campo Marzio neighborhood of central Rome. The monument was reminiscent of Etruscan or Macedonian tombs, and perhaps of Alexander's tomb in Alexandria, although we can only guess at what that looked like. It certainly recalled the original mausoleum, the tomb of King Mausolus of Halicarnassus (in today's Turkey), and so it was eventually called the mausoleum of Augustus.

The new regime would continue to be called *res publica*: our "republic." Literally "public thing," *res publica* for the Romans was the opposite of *res privata*, a "private thing" or monarchy. No government in which the ruler had an enormous, monumental tomb dominating the skyline could be considered a true republic. Especially when that person had all of Italy take an oath of loyalty to him. And especially when he called himself Caesar. Even so, Octavian carefully distinguished himself from the eastern and allegedly decadent monarchical ways of Cleopatra and her supposed love slave Antony.

Yet Octavian had learned from the example of Caesar to be strategic about how he flaunted his power. In the last months of his life, Caesar had taken on monarchical airs. He dressed like one of the kings who had ruled Rome centuries earlier, before they were driven out by an armed rebellion that created the republic. He allowed himself to be worshipped as a god. He sat through a public ceremony in which he was offered the crown and then ostentatiously turned it down in a way that boosted his own ego—"Let it be recorded in the *fasti* [official records] that Caesar turned down the crown"—instead of bristling indignantly at the idea, as a republican of the old stamp might have. Finally, and most provocative of all, he accepted the title of *dictator perpetuo:* "dictator in perpetuity." It was a new title, and one that put the seal on the direction that he had been taking of extending the dictatorship, originally a short-term office, into something that lasted longer: a year, then ten years, and then "in perpetuity." Only about a month later, a conspiracy of republican senators stabbed Caesar to death in a Senate meeting.

Conveniently for Octavian, the office of dictator had been abolished shortly afterward and, ironically, as per the proposal of Antony. Octavian, therefore, did not have to consider taking the hated title of dictator. Instead, he was triumvir, consul, imperator, and, of course, Caesar. The constitutional details could be worked out in due course.

"Make Haste Slowly"

Another commander might have forged ahead after Actium and followed Antony and Cleopatra to Egypt, the way Caesar hastened after Pompey when the latter escaped from his defeat at Pharsalus in 48 BC. Both battles took place in Greece, and both sets of vanquished leaders fled to Egypt. Not Octavian. Instead, he followed, perhaps instinctively, one of his favorite maxims: *Speuda bradeos*, Greek for "make haste slowly." He knew that the situation called for careful and deliberate preparation, not precipitate action.

Octavian needed his army and navy to secure the final defeat of Antony and Cleopatra. But his political skills could make their task much easier. The more he was able to convince his opponents that he would reconcile with them and pardon them, the quicker and more easily they would surrender. Octavian could stymie Anthony and Cleopatra by killing their potential allies with kindness. And that is what he proceeded to do. No longer was he the bloody killer of the proscriptions, no longer the callous victor who commanded the phrase "It's time to die" as the executions of his defeated opponents were carried out. The new Octavian increasingly resembled the man he celebrated, years later, in his testament, "The Deeds of the Deified Augustus," better known as the *Res gestae divi Augusti,* or simply as *Res gestae*. He had this carefully worded document displayed in front of his tomb in Rome as well as in public places around the empire. In the East, it appeared in Greek as well as in Latin, to be more comprehensible to the locals. The most complete surviving text, in both languages, is found in Ankara, Turkey, on the wall of the Temple of Augustus and Rome.

In this document, Octavian claimed to have offered pardon to Roman citizens who asked for it and to foreign nations who could be pardoned with safety—that is, without harm to Rome's or his security. In both cases, he uses words that imply the sort of pardon that was given to criminals who had repented. It was a limited and almost legalistic claim, inferring both generosity and its limits.

So, one needs to take with a grain of salt historian Velleius Paterculus's gushing over Octavian's mildness: *"Victoria vero fuit clementissima"*—"It was a very merciful victory"—he wrote in early first century of our era. Cassius Dio, writing two centuries later, first says there were many executions and few pardons, but then states more blandly that Octavian punished some and pardoned others. His second statement seems more accurate.

There were no proscriptions, no mass killing. That simply wouldn't have suited Octavian's purpose of stabilizing the empire under his rule. Still, some were executed. To make the point that a new boss was in charge, he had to clean house. Besides, some men were simply too close to Antony or Cleopatra to be allowed to continue.

The names of seven high-profile victims have survived, although surely there were others. They are Canidius, Antony's loyal marshal and the commander of his legions at Actium; Publius Turullius and Cassius of Parma, the last two surviving assassins of Julius Caesar; and one Quintus Ovinius, a Roman senator who managed Cleopatra's textile industry. What a pity that we know nothing about Ovinius, because he might have had good tales to tell. A good story—maybe too good to be true—survives about the two other victims, the Aquilii Flori, father and son in a senatorial family. They were given the choice of drawing lots as to who would die. When the son gave himself to the executioner, foregoing the lottery, the father, in despair, is supposed to have committed suicide on the son's body.

The most evocative name among the executed is Gaius Scribonius Curio. His father was a brash and silver-tongued tribune who died fighting for Caesar in the civil war. The more relevant person, however, was his mother. She was none other than Fulvia, who'd married Antony after her husband Curio's death and who later raised an army to fight Octavian. Like mother, like son? The child of the steely warmonger of Perusia might well have refused to beg Octavian for mercy.

When it came to foreign princes, Octavian generally chose shrewdly. He punished rulers of small and insignificant states for their support of Antony but forgave the rulers of larger powers. He wanted to make the point that there was a new master, but he didn't want to shake the equilibrium of the region. Besides, Antony had selected well, and it would not have been easy to find good replacements. Then, too, it helped to save a throne if a ruler showed that he was ready to assist Octavian with money or manpower or both.

Herod of Judea is the best-known case. In spring 30 BC he sailed to the island of Rhodes to meet Octavian. Before going into their conversation, Herod took off his diadem—the ribbon of royalty, ancient equivalent of a crown—as well, perhaps, as his royal robes. It may be true that, as he said later, Herod spoke to Octavian man to man, even priding himself on all he had done for his friend Antony. The point was to show that Herod knew how to be a good client of a powerful Roman. No less important, the king had done his homework. Before the meeting, he had sent a military force to help the Roman governor of Syria by containing a contingent of gladiators en route to Egypt to assist Antony. The governor wrote Octavian to let him know of Herod's action. Having demonstrated that he would deliver for Octavian, Herod had reason to be optimistic about his chances. Indeed, Octavian gave Herod back his diadem, a sign that he could keep his throne.

The Pardoner

The names of four Roman beneficiaries of Octavian's pardon have survived. The most prominent was Antony's admiral Gaius Sosius. After fighting for Antony at Actium, where he commanded the left wing of the fleet, Sosius went into hiding. Small wonder, because he'd been a consul in 32 BC and had condemned Octavian in the Senate. The story goes that Octavian resisted the idea of granting Sosius clemency, but an admiral of his own at Actium, Arruntius, changed his mind. Roman society worked on connections so, in all likelihood, Arruntius and Sosius had some personal tie, now unknown. Or maybe they'd bonded over shared suffering. Condemned during the proscriptions in 43, Arruntius had fled Rome disguised as a centurion with an armed group of slaves for protection, then made his way to Sextus in Sicily. After the exiles were pardoned a few years later, Arruntius returned to Rome and joined Octavian. Now, supposedly it was Arruntius's reputation as a man of old-fashioned gravitas that persuaded Octavian to pardon Sosius after Arruntius vouched for him. Surely it also occurred to Octavian that he could use a man of Sosius's talent and reputation.

If Octavian granted pardon only to those who asked for it, as he claimed later, then it must have hurt Sosius to have to ask, judging by his previous record. A few years earlier, the admiral had defeated the pretender to the throne of Judea, Antigonus II. He threw himself at Sosius's feet, begging for mercy. Sosius laughed at Antigonus uproariously, called him a girl, "Antigone." Then he shackled him in chains and imprisoned him. Fortunately, Sosius received better treatment after Actium than he had dished out in Judea. After being pardoned, Sosius was able to return to Rome, where he completed a restoration of a Temple of Apollo that he had begun earlier. Sosius seems never to have held high military or political office again, but, a dozen years later, he held a prestigious if relatively powerless priesthood that planned a major festival for Augustus—as Octavian was called by then.

Another of Octavian's pardons of an Antony supporter was the talk of Rome: Marcus Aemilius Scaurus. He came of famous parents. Scaurus's like-named father had been notorious for his over-the-top townhouse and his country villa, both financed by his corruption in office, which eventually forced him into exile for the rest of his life. But the senior Scaurus was also known for a rift with his patron, Gnaeus Pompey. The trouble was that Scaurus married Pompey's divorced wife, Mucia Tertia, which Pompey took badly. She eventually bore Scaurus the son whom Octavian pardoned. If more details had survived, Mucia could be the subject of a book in her own right. A former lover of Julius Caesar's, she was a political power. One of her children with Pompey was Sextus Pompey. Mucia served as a go-between between Sextus and Octavian, leading to the treaty of 39 BC. Their agreement didn't last, of course, and Sextus was dead. Mucia now turned her negotiating skills on Octavian to save her only surviving son. She succeeded.

Victory Tour

As Octavian traveled through Greek lands, he retraced Antony's steps. It's unclear whether both men simply stopped at the likeliest places or if Octavian was engaging in a calculated insult to his rival, on the reasonable assumption that the news would get back to him. After leaving Actium, Octavian sailed to Athens. Antony had lived at least two lives in Athens, one with Octavia and one with Cleopatra. Now Octavian made Athens his base for a time. The city historically had close ties with the Ptolemies, so one would expect a fair amount of fence-mending and outreach. Octavian "made friends with the Greeks," writes Plutarch, himself a Greek; more likely, the Greeks made friends with Octavian. Some were punished for supporting Antony, but most received generous treatment. He distributed the army's leftover grain to Athenians and other Greeks whose supply had been depleted to feed Antony's troops. No less important, Octavian announced a general forgiveness of debts. The locals gave him their highest religious honor by initiating him into the cult of the Mysteries of Demeter; it is possible that they had done the same for Antony a decade earlier.

After Athens, Octavian crossed the Aegean and stopped at the island of Samos, which was precisely the place where Antony and Cleopatra had stopped in spring 32 BC. There they had held a festival and administered an oath of loyalty to their allies. Now Octavian used it as his winter headquarters. Indeed, he entered into his fifth consulship there on January 1, 30. From Samos, it was a short hop across a narrow strait to the mainland city of Ephesus, which had once hailed Antony ecstatically as the new Dionysus. In Ephesus the imperator and the queen had met and organized their fleet in March 32. True, Ephesus was the largest city in Asia Minor and a likely place for Octavian to visit, but, still, one wonders if the itinerary was chosen to dispirit Antony and Cleopatra. By visiting the sites of their former triumphs, it was as if Octavian was rubbing defeat in their eyes.

Various eastern cities now abandoned their former support for Antony and sent ambassadors and gifts to the victor. One lucky city was Rhosus (modern Arsuz, Turkey), a small seaport about seventy-five miles from the great metropolis of Antioch. They sent Octavian at Ephesus a golden crown, but the messenger was even more valuable. One Seleucus, he had served Octavian at sea at Actium. Their association went back earlier, possibly even to Philippi, and Octavian had made Seleucus and his family members Roman citizens and exempted them from taxation. In a letter from late 31 BC Octavian expressed the hope to visit Rhosus and repay the city for Seleucus's services to him. No record survives of whether Octavian ever made it there, but, if not, he surely sent an agent to grant further benefits to the little town.

Across the Wintry Waves

In early 30 BC Octavian had to hurry back to Italy from Samos, where he had gone into winter quarters. The issue was the veterans. After Actium, veterans who had served their time were demobilized and sent back to Italy. These included both Octavian's men and Antony's. They were all promised money and land, but Octavian had yet to raise the money. They would not like that, and they could cause trouble, as they had done in the past. Anticipating that, Octavian sent Agrippa back to Italy after Actium in order to manage the troops, but Agrippa kept writing to Octavian that matters were slipping out of control. He had to get back to Italy and soon.

A sea journey in winter was not to be taken lightly. That Octavian would make it indicates the seriousness of the threat. The trip would take an estimated eight days, including the time needed to have his ships carried across the Isthmus of Corinth, a necessary step to avoid the longer and stormier route around the southern Peloponnese. He traveled with a small entourage of galleys, as there were, after all, still enemies at large.

As Octavian's ships came out of the Corinthian Gulf and headed northward, they encountered a storm, and some of the vessels went down. A few days later, off the rugged mountains on the mainland north of Corcyra, the survivors met a second storm. Once again, ships were lost. On one of the two occasions, the rigging of the ship on which Octavian was sailing was swept away and its rudder broken. One wonders how things might have turned out differently for Antony and Cleopatra had Octavian, too, gone down in the tempest. He must have been relieved when, in another day or two, his ships covered the final part of their journey and reached Brundisium.

If the sources can be believed (and they probably go back to his memoirs), Octavian was greeted by the cream of Rome's political elite: both senators and equestrians, as well as "the greater part of the populace and still others." Presumably his wife, Livia, was part of the throng. One wonders if the welcoming committee also included Octavia, come to greet her beloved brother. How might she have responded to news of the defeat of her ex-husband and his mistress?

Whether Octavia met Octavian in person or not, the two of them surely corresponded. Octavian had delicate business ahead to try to convince Antony to surrender. Few knew Antony as intimately as his ex-wife, and the shrewd Octavian would certainly have wanted to consult her. Octavian might well have welcomed Antony's suicide, but it would have been indiscreet to say so. Perhaps Octavia felt the same way, at least in her steelier moments.

The angry veterans had come to Brundisium as well. Octavian met with them and made generous promises of land and money. He dealt with another aggrieved group as well: freedmen. To finance the war, in 32 BC Octavian had levied a 25 percent income tax on all free people in Italy and presumably the West. Freedmen had to pay an additional 12.5 percent tax on their property, in four installments. Their protests had included riots, murder, and arson. Fearing renewed trouble, Octavian now forgave them the final installment.

Then Octavian made a grand gesture. He put up his own property for auction along with that of his close comrades. It was a bluff; no one dared buy anything. But so was his promise of paying the soldiers, with a tax cut to boot. Everything depended on raising money in the East, and that meant, above all, getting his hands on Cleopatra's treasure.

Octavian spent only twenty-seven days in Brundisium before turning around and making another winter journey back eastward. There are no reports of any trouble on the trip this time. It all happened so quickly that, it was said, Antony and Cleopatra learned of Octavian's departure and return at the same time.

Sometime after Octavian's arrival back in the East, a plot on his life was foiled. A few years earlier, Octavian had forced Lepidus, the former triumvir, to live in internal exile in an isolated spot on the Italian coast. His son, Marcus Aemilius Lepidus the Younger, was accused of conspiring to assassinate Octavian. Young Lepidus was arrested on a charge of high treason and sent east to Octavian, where he was presumably executed. His mother was arrested, too, on the grounds of having knowledge of the crime, but her husband still had enough influence to get her released. Young Lepidus's wife, Servilia, committed suicide, supposedly by swallowing hot coals. The sources make no mention of Antony's involvement in the plot. Yet he had once been close to his fellow triumvir Lepidus, and they shared an enemy in Octavian. It surely occurred to Octavian that Antony might have been involved.

What to Do with Antony and Cleopatra?

Taking Egypt was easier in a way than deciding what to do with the Egyptians—that is to say, with Antony, Cleopatra, and their children.

Inconveniently, Antony was Octavian's former brother-in-law, the ex-husband of his sister, and the father of two of his nieces. It would not be easy for Octavian to have him killed. By far the most convenient fate would be to have Antony commit suicide. Octavian might have been willing to let him live, preferably in an isolated country spot under armed guard, as he had done with the triumvir Lepidus. But Lepidus had never been a serious threat, whereas Antony had practically stormed the gates of Italy. One suspects that any internal exile would have ended in poison for Antony.

Cleopatra was easier. Since the Roman state had declared war on her, she would have to surrender. In principle, Octavian could permit her to keep her throne, as Rome had done with other defeated monarchs. In practice, he was more likely to see the queen as a dangerous threat. Cleopatra was much too clever and much too resilient to stay out of trouble. Her knowledge of Julius Caesar might also have seemed threatening. She would have to be destroyed, just as an earlier generation of Romans had concluded that "Carthage must be destroyed," even though Roman arms had reduced that country from a great power to a minor state. Either suicide, execution, or severe mistreatment after being forced to march in a triumphal parade in Rome lay in the queen's future, if Octavian were to have his way.

Nor could her eldest son, Caesarion, be allowed to live, much less to rule Egypt, as he endangered Octavian's claim to be the only legitimate heir to the name of Caesar.

That left Antony and Cleopatra's three children as potential successors to their mother on the throne of Egypt. If Octavian toyed with the idea in order to keep Egypt nominally independent but for practical purposes subservient to Rome—and a cash cow—it is hard to imagine him allowing his enemies' son or daughter to rule the wealthiest country in the Mediterranean.

First, however, he had to win the war.

Part 4

THE ENDGAME

September 31 to January 27 BC

Chapter 14

Passage to India

Alexandria, September 31 to August 30 BC

ANTONY AND CLEOPATRA SAILED FROM CAPE TAE-
narum, at the southern tip of the Peloponnese, to the island of Crete
and then to the coast of Africa—a journey of about six days. Cleopatra continued to Alexandria. Antony landed at Paraetonium (the
modern Marsa Matruh, Egypt), about 180 miles west of Alexandria,
in the Roman province of Cyrene.

With its turquoise-blue waters and sandy beaches, Paraetonium
resembles a resort. But it was a historic town; one of those out-of-the-
way hinges of an empire that dot the Mediterranean. A nearby temple
of Rameses II recalled Egypt's grandiose, pharaonic past. There was a
whiff of Alexander the Great, because Paraetonium was the jumping-
off point for Alexander's famous visit to the desert oracle, where he
was first addressed as a god. For Antony, Paraetonium was a military
powerhouse with a Ptolemaic naval harbor. It guarded the western
approach to Egypt. Because the desert was treacherous, an invader
had to take the coastal road, and so he could not bypass the town; he
would have to take the fort or give up. If he had a fleet, he would have
to face the warships that could come rushing out of Paraetonium's
harbor.

In autumn 31 BC Paraetonium was Antony's most important remaining military base. At the start of the Actium campaign, he had
posted four legions there to protect Egypt. They were commanded by

Lucius Pinarius Scarpus. A trusted associate, Pinarius had served as Antony's legate at Philippi. He was also an heir of Julius Caesar and Octavian's cousin.

Antony wanted to take charge of Pinarius's legions, but Pinarius had another idea. Clearly, the news of Actium had reached him, perhaps along with a well-timed message from his cousin. Antony had sent some men ahead to Paraetonium in order to prepare for his arrival. Pinarius responded like a gangland kingpin: he had them killed, and when some men under his command objected, he had them killed too. He refused to allow Antony entrance to the camp. It was a well-executed coup, and it paid off for the perpetrator. After later turning over the legions to Octavian's agent, Pinarius was rewarded by being allowed to keep his position as provincial governor for at least four more years.

Earlier in 31 BC, Pinarius had issued coins celebrating Antony, whom he hailed as imperator. By year's end, he was issuing coins commemorating Octavian, whom he called "Caesar, the son of a god."

Antony had the company of two close friends. One of them, Lucilius, had also been at Philippi, but on the other side. Like Herod, Lucilius proved his worth by his loyalty—in his case, loyalty to Brutus. In fact, after the fighting at Philippi, Lucilius actually pretended to be Brutus and surrendered himself to Antony's men so that Brutus could later escape. Antony might have been angry, but, as a Roman, he respected loyalty, so he took on Lucilius as an associate. Now, according to Plutarch, Lucilius repaid the favor. Brutus had committed suicide after losing at Philippi. Now it was Antony who wanted to commit suicide after the rebuff at Paraetonium. Lucilius and a Greek politician from the Peloponnese whom Antony favored, Marcus Antonius Aristocrates, talked Antony out of it and saved his life. He then headed for Alexandria.

Plutarch is full of talk of Antony's depression in the year after Actium. It's hard to know how seriously to take it. Antony had good reason for melancholy, as the ancients called it. He also had good reason to project a public image of melancholy, for it was a useful mask to put on if he wanted to ask Octavian for a pardon—which he did, because how dangerous could a depressed man be? Similarly, it might also have deterred assassins if they thought that Antony was out of commission, as it were. That might have explained, for example, why Antony built himself a refuge on a jetty in the harbor of Alexandria. He named it the Timoneion, after the legendary misanthrope Timon of Athens, later a subject for Shakespeare. Antony let it be known that, like Timon, he felt betrayed by his friends, but, more likely, perhaps he felt at risk from his enemies' daggers.

Depression might also have served as an excuse for why Antony had done the very un-Roman thing of abandoning his legions. In the meantime, the real Antony had not given up.

With Prows Garlanded for Victory

When Cleopatra returned to Alexandria, she sailed into the harbor with the prows of her ships garlanded with wreaths, as if to announce a victory. The men were chanting victory songs to the accompaniment of flute players. Cleopatra always did know how to put on a show. As the queen understood, it would be dangerous to tell her people the truth. She hadn't given up, so why should they? She had come home to a city that no one could bear the thought of losing.

Alexander the Great conquered an empire; then Ptolemy created Alexandria, the greatest city the world had ever known. Alexander spent five months in Egypt, but it's unclear if he planned anything more than a harbor fort on the site of the future city. Ptolemy I, Alexander's general, who was first governor of Egypt and then its king, attributed the city to Alexander as a sort of seal of approval, but Ptolemy and his son were its real founders. Ptolemy even hijacked Alexander's funeral procession, en route from Babylon to the royal burial grounds in Macedonia, and diverted it to Alexandria. He had Alexander's mummified corpse displayed in a splendid tomb in the heart of the city. What better way to inaugurate the new capital than with a heist?

Poised between the wine-dark sea and the desert, Alexandria exemplified paradox. It sat on the border of East and West, Africa and Asia, Greek and Egyptian, Gentile and Jew. Greek speakers flocked to the new city to make their fortune in Egypt. Immigrants from Judea made Alexandria the largest Jewish city in the world, with the Jewish community poised uneasily between a Greco-Macedonian ruling class and a colonized but recently assertive class of Egyptians. Everything about Alexandria was eclectic, even its artwork. A visitor could see an improbable alternation of Greek bronzes and Egyptian granite colossi; miniature Hellenistic terra-cotta female figurines and painted-and-gilded limestone hieroglyphic steles (upright stone slabs); hunting dogs depicted in Greek mosaics and Egyptian cats mummified in elegant bronze urns; and a symbolic cacophony of laurel wreaths, ankhs, and menorahs.

Alexandria stood midway between the divine eternity of the pyramids and the pure reason of the Parthenon in Athens, the temple that symbolized the glory of classical Greece. The city nourished the mind in the Museum and the Library, the greatest research institution in the world, a center of engineering, astronomy, mathematics, medicine, and literature. Alexandria tended to the soul in the great temple of Serapis, a newly invented Greco-Egyptian god who encouraged assimilation and practiced incest. It tended to the body there as well, since the Serapeum, as the temple was known, was also a center of healing, famous for its doctors. There was also the shrine of Isis, known as the goddess of a thousand names, the holy mother whose adoration swept the Mediterranean basin.

But Alexandria was also the capital of power, of pleasure, and of greed. Macedonian spears had won Egypt for the Ptolemies, and a faded but still potent army and navy stood guard over their rule. Guiding sailors into the harbor, the Pharos lighthouse towered over the horizon.

Egyptian agriculture was the most fertile in the ancient world. Royal monopolies directed an economy that was a cornucopia of wealth. Trade was the city's lifeblood. Indian pearls and Chinese silk were equally at home there, along with Greek wine and Nile Valley love charms.

The kings owned or taxed it all, and so controlled vast riches, and they weren't modest about showing it. The dynasty owned gold mines on the southern edge of its realm, staffed with convict labor. Gold coins, a rarity among the Greeks, were standard issue in the flush years of the early Ptolemies. Even the less wealthy later Ptolemies enjoyed gold rings and earrings, bracelets and necklaces, pendants and charms, and gilded goblets and water jugs, all exquisitely crafted.

Alexandrian literature preferred love to war, pastoral to odes, and wit to epic. Its one great epic, *The Argonautica,* which tells the myth of the voyage of Jason and the Argonauts, is antiheroic. "Big book, big bad," said an Alexandrian writer, as if life were too enjoyable for anything heavy. True, the Museum was full of literary scholars and grammarians, but no one paid attention to them outside its walls.

Alexandria's broad, main avenue, the Canopic Way, was lined with marble buildings and prostitutes at either end. Parades of tonsured Egyptian priests alternated with bands of Dionysian revelers, while clots of philosophers and their disciples made their way past street musicians. Royal processions were famous for their lavishness and for the giant phalluses that were carried. The royal palace, rising beside the sea, had a reputation for elegance, intrigue, and multicourse banquets.

The Alexandrians were known as fast-talking, witty, and vicious. Their tempers could rise as rapidly and unpredictably as a thunderstorm from the sea or a khamsin, the hot southerly wind that blows in from the desert. They loved music and gossip, and they could be whipped up into a mob. They were capable of starting a fire, lynching an ambassador or dragging an unpopular king from the palace and murdering him.

This was the city of Cleopatra.

There was, in fact, still plenty of support for her in Egypt, especially the farther away one got from the coast and the news from Actium. A carved sandstone stele, nearly three feet tall, offers an ironic commentary on the power of denial. The stele consists of a thirty-one-line text topped by images in relief. The text records a legal contract between priests and two manufacturers' guilds who supplied their temple. It comes from a place far south in the Nile Valley, about five hundred miles from Alexandria. The top of the stele, above the text, is decorated with images of the king making offerings to the gods. The inscription refers to "the female pharaoh, the bodily daughter of kings who were on their part kings born of kings, Cleopatra the beneficent father-loving goddess and pharaoh Ptolemy called Caesar, the father- and mother-loving god." The date is September 21, 31 BC, nineteen days after Actium. Cleopatra and her son sat uneasily on their thrones, but you wouldn't know it. Clearly, the news of defeat hadn't reached the Egyptian countryside. Yet, the hieroglyphics and traditional images of the relief give the impression that, even had the results of Actium been known, eternal Egypt and its gods would have shrugged off something so ephemeral as a mere military setback.

Once she was home safely, Cleopatra cleaned house. Unlike Antony, Cleopatra does not come off in the sources with even a hint of melancholy about her. She is all strength and strategy. In order to silence old enemies and confiscate their estates, she executed prominent Alexandrians. If it is not just enemy propaganda, she looted Egypt's temples, too. She made sure her soldiers were well armed. In search of allies abroad, she executed the former king of Armenia, who lived under arrest in Alexandria. She had his head sent to the king of Media Atropatene, whose daughter was the fiancée of her son by Antony, Alexander Helios. Perhaps she hoped that it could open the door to aid not just from Media but also from Parthia. But she had a much bigger project in mind.

In the winter of 31–30 BC, Cleopatra had a new fleet built in the

Gulf of Suez. Its ambitious purpose was to carry her, Antony, and their family to a safe exile abroad, perhaps as far away as India. Far-fetched as such an escape plan sounds, it had a serious basis. Egypt maintained trade relations with India. Cleopatra had gone into exile before, during the Ptolemaic civil wars of her youth. With the odds of defeating Octavian very low, it was audacious but not irrational to think of fleeing eastward. There was always a chance of being able to come back one day.

Egypt already had a fleet on the Red Sea to do business with India, but, in all likelihood, those ships had been sent off to the Actium campaign and were now lost, which is why Cleopatra invested in a new navy. It could have been a masterstroke, but it failed. An old enemy, Malchus, king of the Nabataean Arabs, got in the way. He wanted revenge on Cleopatra for past abuses, such as taking part of his territory and turning King Herod against him, and he wanted to ingratiate himself with Octavian. So, at the instigation of the governor of Syria, Malchus burned her ships. As at Actium, fire proved more potent than water. Once again, Cleopatra's dreams were lost at sea.

The Alexandria Duet

Now comes the most intensely complicated and mythologized part of the whole story: the endgame in Alexandria. Antony and Cleopatra's final moves made an irresistible subject for ancient writers. They had everything: love, death, betrayal, money, power, and even the ghost of Alexander, all set in the most glamorous city of the ancient Mediterranean. We know of three ancient accounts—one by Cleopatra's physician, an epic poem, and the relevant chapters of Augustus's memoirs—and possibly five others. There were oral narratives as well, and tales that had been passed down and no doubt embroidered to be told to future visitors to Alexandria such as Plutarch. As usual, none of these sources now exists except for brief sections or quotations.

It is not easy to reconstruct the truth out of such varied but problematic sources and against such a politically and romantically charged background. Every historian has to decide if the story of Antony and Cleopatra's last year is a romantic tragedy or a film noir. Was Cleopatra the devoted lover of Shakespeare's play, or was she a scheming femme fatale? Was she one of the many actresses who have played the female lead in *Antony and Cleopatra* or was she, say, Mary Astor duping Humphrey Bogart in *The Maltese Falcon*?

Cleopatra was a queen, and her first obligation was to her kingdom. Besides, if the issue is emotion, she was a mother as much as she was a lover. Cleopatra wasn't in it just for herself; she had a responsibility to her children and her forebears, and for everything that her dynasty had stood for during three centuries. She could not afford to give it all up for a romantic attachment. Forced to choose, she would have preferred her children to her man.

Nor was it out of the question that Antony would put his own safety before Cleopatra's. Unlike her, he did not have a kingdom or a king's ransom to bargain with, but he did have moral resources. He was the scion of the Antonii, one of the noblest houses of the leading country in the world (as Romans saw it), the victor of Philippi, and four times proclaimed imperator. In spite of Actium, he still had many friends and supporters in Rome. Having fallen on his sword, Antony would be just another victim of Octavian's rise to power; but, allowed to live in exile like Lepidus, he would be a credit to Octavian's claim to clemency. Antony was also the father of Octavian's nieces.

It is no surprise, then, that Antony and Cleopatra engaged in negotiations with Octavian separately as well as jointly. For his part, the victor of Actium was eager to oblige. "Divide and conquer," after all, was a maxim in which no Roman needed instruction.

The negotiations were conducted behind closed doors, and perhaps only Octavian's version survives, so the sources need to be taken with the usual grain of salt. Still, Plutarch and Cassius Dio are largely in agreement. Trying to cull the most plausible details from their accounts, it looks like there were three negotiating missions, as follows.

In the first, Cleopatra and Antony jointly offered peace to Octavian and money to his associates. Cleopatra then went behind Antony's back and sent a golden scepter, a golden crown, and the royal throne in exchange for mercy. She was demonstrating her willingness to resume her status as a loyal Roman ally. Octavian ignored Antony. He accepted Cleopatra's gifts and replied that she would have to give up her armed forces and her kingdom before he would even consider her case. That was his *official* response; he also sent a secret message saying that if she had Antony killed, she would receive a full pardon and could keep her kingdom.

In the second embassy, Cleopatra and Antony promised more money, and Antony offered to live as a private person in Egypt or, failing that, in Athens. He also surrendered Publius Turullius, the last surviving assassin of Julius Caesar, who was living with Antony. Octavian had Turullius executed, and answered Cleopatra as before—but he sent no response to Antony.

The third time, Antony sent his young son Antyllus as ambassador, carrying a substantial amount of gold. Octavian kept the gold but sent the boy back empty-handed. Meanwhile, he responded to Cleopatra as before. For good measure, he also sent a trusted freedman, Thyrsus, to her. Octavian was afraid that she and Antony would escape to Hispania or Gaul. Supposedly, he also feared that they might put up a good fight. That was not an idle thought, because Pelusium, on Egypt's eastern border, was a powerful fortress, and well defended. Dominating the road from the east, it had a circuit wall more than two miles long. The surrounding territory consisted of desert on one side and marsh on the other.

Octavian probably expected that, with the forces at his disposal, he would take Pelusium eventually. There was also the hope of negotiating surrender or suborning treason. The bigger issue was Cleopatra's treasury, which Octavian needed in order to finance his promises to his veterans. Cleopatra had gathered it in a new structure that she was building in Alexandria: a mausoleum. The treasure included gold, silver, emeralds, pearls, ebony, ivory, and cinnamon. Included in the building was a supply of kindling and firewood. None of this was a secret. In other words, Cleopatra threatened to take the treasury and, presumably, herself down in a final blaze. Afterward, it would be difficult and time-consuming to recover and restore what was salvageable.

So Octavian sent Thyrsus on a mission to Cleopatra. Thyrsus had an extended and private interview with the queen. He promised her mercy from Octavian if she had Antony killed. In one of the messages, Cleopatra begged for the throne for her children. Perhaps Thyrsus promised this too, although the sources don't mention it. They do claim that Thyrsus said that Octavian was in love with her, just like Antony and Caesar before him.

Cassius Dio emphasizes Cleopatra's treachery to Antony. This might be merely Octavian's propaganda, but it is plausible. The queen would never have survived the murderous familial infighting in her youth without mastering the dark arts. Besides, her first priority was her children.

Antony certainly suspected her. After her lengthy interview with Thyrsus, he had the man seized and whipped. It is chilling to think that in Rome, the law allowed a patron (that is, former master) to inflict corporal punishment on his freedmen. Octavian was Thyrsus's patron, so only Octavian had the legal right to whip him. Antony recognized this by sending Thyrsus back to Octavian with a written message allowing him to whip Hipparchus in exchange. A member of Octavian's entourage, Hipparchus was, technically, Antony's freedman; he was the first of Antony's freedmen to defect to Octavian. Antony's note allowed him to express his contempt of those who betrayed him.

If Cleopatra was planning to betray Antony, she did not show it, unless it was a case of "the lady doth protest too much." While stinting on her own birthday celebration, which was either in December or early January, she made a festive celebration of Antony's birthday on January 14. She helped talk him out of his retreat on a breakwater in the harbor and back to the palace for a round of parties. They dissolved their Society of the Inimitable Livers and replaced it with a new Society of Those Who Will Die Together, in which they spent hours in extravagant dinner parties with their friends. The name of the group probably comes from a romantic comedy that apparently revolved around two lovers who are snatched from the jaws of death. As they calculated the odds and nervously wondered which of their friends was going to defect next, or which was going to turn on the other, Antony and Cleopatra might have lost the comic feeling.

Octavian Marches

In spring 30 BC Octavian prepared to invade Egypt. He might have concluded that negotiations had softened up Cleopatra and opened a gap between her and Antony, but it was clear that diplomacy would not end the war on terms that Octavian considered acceptable. He wanted Antony dead, Cleopatra his prisoner, and her treasure his property. Only military force could achieve that.

Octavian marched his army south from Asia Minor through Syria. At Ptolemais (today, Acre or Akko, Israel), he was met by King Herod. The two men rode side by side in an inspection of the troops. Pause for a moment and consider the scene as the king of Judea and the son of a god—the man who called himself Caesar—reviewed tens of thousands of legionaries and allied soldiers. After next treating Octavian and his staff to a lavish banquet, Herod served as quartermaster. He put on a feast for the rest of the army and then supplied water and wine for the march through the desert to Egypt. He also gave Octavian a personal gift of two thousand talents of silver—weighing nearly fifteen thousand pounds. It was a dizzying example of the normalization of disloyalty, considering that Herod had not only been Antony's ally but also owed his throne to him.

By summer, Octavian was ready to launch his attack. It was sophisticated and coordinated and came from two directions. In the

West, he had sent Lucius Cornelius Gallus to Cyrene. There Gallus took charge of the four legions that Antony had failed to obtain at Paraetonium the previous autumn. Next, Gallus marched to the Egyptian border.

In Alexandria, it was said that Antony had wanted to sail to Syria and join the troupe of gladiators who supported him. Evidently, they made a formidable force, because they had compelled the governor to tolerate their staying together as a unit in a suburb of Antioch. A well-organized and disciplined unit of gladiators could pose a problem even to the legions: think only of Spartacus and his men. Only after Octavian had dealt with Antony and Cleopatra would he be able to devote the resources needed to crush the gladiators. In any case, Gallus's approach kept Antony in Egypt. He marched against Gallus with both infantry and a navy. He had the legions that he had brought with him aboard ship from Actium as well as any Egyptian troops. It is not likely to have been a large force.

Antony hoped to talk his former legions into rejoining him, as he had once persuaded hostile legions in Gaul into uniting with him during an earlier civil war. But, as the story goes, when he approached the walls of Paraetonium, Gallus drowned him out by ordering all his trumpeters to play at once. Next, Antony tried a sudden raid, but that failed, as did a naval attack. Gallus's response was ingenious: he lured Antony's ships into the harbor, then had the chains that he had hidden underwater hauled up by winches, and finally launched a fiery attack that burned some ships and sank others. It was a creative act worthy of the man who would go on to become a distinguished poet—indeed, Gallus turned into a love poet, of all things. How many generals in history have become love poets?

Before leaving Paraetonium, Antony received news that made him hurry back to Alexandria: Pelusium, the fortress guarding Egypt's eastern border, had fallen to Octavian. Augustan poets claim that he took it by storm. Cassius Dio is more persuasive when he writes that Pelusium fell through treachery from within. Plutarch refers more

circumspectly to a report that the fort was betrayed by its commanding officer, Seleucus, acting at Cleopatra's behest. Cassius Dio insists:
Cleopatra was behind it. He adds that she had realized that the military situation was hopeless and concluded that it was better to ingratiate herself with Octavian. Besides, he says much less convincingly,
she was taken in by Thyrsus's promise that Octavian was in love with
her. So cunning a player as Cleopatra would not be gulled easily. Afterward, Antony wanted revenge on Seleucus, and Cleopatra allowed
him to order the execution of the man's wife and children. That
hardly endeared Antony to other Egyptian troops.

The God Abandons Antony

By the end of July, Octavian and his forces were encamped at the hip-
podrome, just east of the gates of Alexandria. Having returned to the
city, Antony now sallied out with his cavalry and attacked. The audacious move succeeded. Antony's men routed the enemy cavalry and
chased them as far as their camp. Octavian was not bothered unduly,
though, writing it off to his men's exhaustion after the long march.

A thrilled Antony returned to town and went straight to Cleopatra
without even taking off his armor. In a scene out of the *Iliad*, where
an armed Hector goes back to Troy and sees his wife, Antony kissed
the queen. Role players as they each were, they might both have enjoyed the scene. He then presented her with one of his soldiers who
had fought most keenly. Cleopatra responded by giving him a prize
of valor: namely, a golden breastplate and helmet. The man accepted
them but then spoiled the heroic mood by deserting to Octavian that
very night.

Now, just as before Actium, Antony sent a message challenging
Octavian to single combat. At last, Octavian replied to a message
from his former brother-in-law, but only to say that there were many
ways to die. The exchange summed up the war in a nutshell. Antony
wanted a fair fight in a single defining battle. Octavian chose an in-

direct and cunning response. As at Actium, Antony decided to fight anyhow. The next day, he would lead his troops into a battle from which he was unlikely to return.

The evening of July 31, Antony hosted a dinner party. It was a macabre affair. He told the slaves to fill his cup and serve him lavishly because tomorrow they might have new masters, and he might be a mummy. When his friends began to weep, he assured them that he would spare them from the battle; his goal, he said, wasn't deliverance or victory; his goal was a glorious death.

In bringing up the subject of death, Antony might have had Julius Caesar in mind. On March 14, 44 BC, the eve of what, unbeknownst to him, was the day he would die, Caesar attended a dinner party in Rome. We do not know if Antony was among the guests that evening, as he might well have been, but he certainly knew about the famous comments that Caesar had made then. The dictator himself had brought up the evening's topic of conversation: the most desirable manner of death. Caesar's answer was the phrase "an unexpected death," according to one source; "a sudden death," according to another; and "a sudden and unexpected death," according to a third. Knowing what was likely to await him on the morrow, Antony might have engaged in an old habit of following in Caesar's footsteps.

The next scene is one of Plutarch's finest touches. As the story goes, around midnight, in a city quiet and fearful, a sudden sound was heard. It sounded like a throng of revelers in a tumultuous procession. They were shouting "*Euhoe!*" the characteristic Dionysiac cry, accompanied by a harmony of musical instruments. Although no one could see them, the sounds suggested that they marched through almost the center of town until they reached the gate facing Octavian's army. At that point, they supposedly grew loudest, and then they left town.

The ancients believed that every city had a patron god or goddess. Rome's was Jupiter, for example. They also believed that when a city was about to fall to an enemy, the patron deity left, being wise in advance. The Romans even had a prebattle ceremony, called *evocatio*, in which their army tried to coax the god to leave a city under siege. As Plutarch explains, observers concluded that the noisy procession meant that Dionysus, the god with whom Antony had always associated himself most closely, was leaving him. Antony would have to go into battle without the help of heaven.

Plutarch does not state how Antony reacted. The twentieth-century Greek poet C. P. Cavafy, himself an inhabitant of Alexandria, imagined what the imperator might have thought:

"The God Abandons Antony"

If suddenly, the hour midnight, you hear
A company pass by invisibly,
A troupe of splendid music, a troupe of voice—
Your fortune has slipped away, your work ended in
Misfortune, your plans for life all proven to be
Merely seductive: vanities, don't cry for them.
Muster your courage, and like a man prepared for years,
Bid Alexandria good-bye: she's gone.
Above all, don't be laughed at, don't say it was
A dream, or that your hearing was deceived.
You have got to scorn that sort of futile hope.
Muster your courage, like a man prepared for years,
Like a man who has the right to claim a city great as this,
Go toward the window with a steadfast walk
And listen with emotion, but without
A coward's supplication or complaints.
For one last time, take pleasure from the sounds,
The splendid instruments of the secret troupe,
And bid good-bye to her: you are losing Alexandria.

The next day, August 1, the imperator again led his troops into battle.

Chapter 15

The Bite of the Asp

Alexandria, August 1 to 10, 30 BC

IN THE PREDAWN HOURS OF AUGUST 1, ANTONY PUT on his armor and led his troops out of Alexandria. Once again, he was making a joint attack; an ambitious undertaking, with infantry and cavalry on land and warships at sea. He tried to soften up the enemy by having his troops attack Octavian's camp. They shot arrows wrapped with leaflets that promised to pay soldiers for defecting. Octavian took the threat seriously; Antony had inflicted a defeat on his men just days before. Octavian read the leaflets aloud personally to his soldiers. He wanted to use shame of dishonor and fear of his revenge to keep them in line. It worked. Antony's cavalry deserted him, and his infantry was defeated.

Meanwhile, at sea, Antony's crews rowed out to meet the enemy, but instead of charging, they raised their oars to salute them. As soon as the salute was returned by Octavian's ships, Antony's galleys joined the enemy. Now united, they rowed against the city. Antony looked on, perhaps as Cavafy recommended, with emotion but without complaint, and returned to Alexandria.

Historians disagree as to whether Cleopatra had ordered her ships and cavalry to desert. Cassius Dio states that she had, while Plutarch notes merely that Antony, upon returning to town, loudly accused her of it. For some, the charge is a slander put out by Octavian's propaganda. Yet it would have been the smart move for Cleopatra. By surrendering to Octavian, she was showing her willingness to serve as a loyal client queen. If it was too much to ask that she keep her throne, then perhaps her loyalty would work in favor of one of her children as her successor.

Octavian might have wanted her to kill Antony or to arrange for an "accident," but a Roman commander such as Antony had bodyguards and a taster. Besides, the resulting criticism would have been too great.

What the queen did do was to flee the palace to her nearby mausoleum and lock herself inside, behind the heavy gate, with a eunuch and two maidservants. She sent a messenger to tell Antony that she was dead, either because she was afraid of him and wanted to keep him away or because she had coolly decided to get rid of him, and she hoped to encourage his suicide.

Ave atque Vale/Death of a Commander

Antony believed the message from Cleopatra. He went into his private suite in the palace and prepared to die. Like his old enemy Cassius, who committed suicide at Philippi, Antony had prepared a slave for the job of killing him if needed. The slave's name was Eros, which points to a Greek origin. A word meaning "love," the name is almost too good to be true, given Antony's reputation as a ladies' man, not to mention his relationship with Cleopatra.

But Eros refused to kill his master. Instead, he turned away and killed himself. One can't help wondering whether the act was carried out due more to affection or desperation. The slave might have reasoned that he would not be pardoned for killing Antony. Perhaps he knew, too, that the freedman who had done his duty by killing his patron Cassius had disappeared afterward and was suspected of murder—which may be why Cassius's freedman fled, knowing what accusations would lie ahead.

Antony had no choice but to do the deed himself. He stabbed himself in the abdomen with his sword. The wound, however, did not kill him. Antony fell on his couch, bleeding but alive. Fact is, it's not easy to achieve an immediate death through abdominal stabbing, not unless the cut is deep enough to sever the descending aorta. In Japan, for example, a practitioner of the traditional samurai ritual of suicide through disembowelment usually enlisted the help of a second person to cut off his head after the victim had stabbed himself.

Antony now asked the others present—and apparently there were others present—to deliver the coup de grâce, but they ran away. Again, one doesn't know whether love or fear moved them. Antony's cries of agony were soon heard, when Diomedes, Cleopatra's secretary, came with orders to bring him to the queen. One might wonder how she knew what was going on, but it is hard to imagine that anything happened in the palace, if not the city, without Cleopatra's spies informing her. For what it's worth, Cassius Dio thought that she heard an uproar and figured out what had happened.

Antony was surprised to learn that Cleopatra was still alive. He had his servants carry him to her tomb. Cleopatra would not open the gate, but a crane or pulley system happened to be in place for hauling stone blocks to the top of the still-unfinished structure. The system was used to pull Antony up and into the mausoleum's upper story. Plutarch describes the bizarre scene:

> Never, as those who were present tell us, was there a more piteous sight. Smeared with blood and struggling with death, he was drawn up, stretching out his hands to her even as he dangled in the air. For the task was not an easy one for the women, and scarcely could Cleopatra, with clinging hands and strained face, pull up the rope, while those below called out encouragement to her and shared her agony.

Finally, they got Antony into the building and laid him down. Cleopatra engaged in a ritual lament. She tore her clothes, beat and gashed her breasts, and smeared herself with Antony's blood. She called him her master and husband and imperator. He told her to stop and asked for a drink of wine. One might dismiss this detail as a final smear against the "drunken" Antony by Octavian's propagandists, but it was a reasonable request by someone in agony. Plutarch seems to have consulted an eyewitness account—possibly the now-lost memoirs of Cleopatra's personal physician. As usual in ancient literature, however, Antony's last words are probably fiction. He is supposed to have advised Cleopatra to do whatever she needed to save herself, as long as it was without disgrace. He told her to trust only one person among Octavian's men: Gaius Proculeius. Finally, like a noble Roman, he told her not to lament his recent bad fortune. Instead, she should rejoice over all the good things that he had achieved and how he had become the most celebrated and powerful of men. Nor was it ignoble for him, a Roman, to be defeated by a Roman. And so Antony died. He was fifty-three.

Eulogy for an Imperator

Everybody loved Antony, it seemed sometimes, from the women who adored him to the men who stuck by him. He was a strong man who shared his soldiers' suffering and commanded their loyalty. Yet Antony had a marked taste for strong women. He was the first Roman to put a mortal woman's face on his coins.

He was the architect of victory over Caesar's assassins at the Battle of Philippi. As a general, however, he is best known for his retreats. By turns charismatic and punitive, he held together his army on the dangerous roads through rough country back from Mutina and Phraaspa. Perhaps he would have done the same after Actium if there had been the slightest chance of victory, but his sick and hungry legions were good for nothing but surrender. Instead, he managed to break out of the enemy's trap with nearly a third of what was left of his fleet, but most of the ships were his ally's, not his.

Antony was a great diplomat, forging a lasting settlement in the Roman East. Between Alexandria and the thrones that he planned to fill with his three children by Cleopatra, he built a base for an empire in the East—and one that might have allowed him the conquest of the West as well. He gathered enormous resources for fighting a war, including one of the most formidable navies the ancient world had ever seen. He just didn't know how to use those resources effectively. He failed both as a leader and as a strategist. Looking back at his one great victory, over Brutus and Cassius at Philippi, it's clear he owed success in large part to his enemy's mistakes. Antony did not have the same luxury against Octavian and Agrippa at Actium.

By then, however, he was no longer entirely a free agent. The moment Antony decided to rely on an ally's resources to wage a war, he lost a part of his independence. Cleopatra paid for his ships and his soldiers, and so she had a say in all his important decisions. Antony had to walk a fine line between being an imperator and an ancillary.

But was he also a fool for love? Given his financial needs, Antony would have been in an awkward position had he merely shared an alliance and not a bed with the Egyptian monarch. Yet even in the most mercenary marriage, emotions play a part. Surely their story would have been different had Antony and Cleopatra just been friends. Alas, the heart doesn't share its secrets with historians.

Antony fell in love with the East. He embraced his roles as the consort of a queen, the father of princes, and the founder of dynasties. He counted on his charm and his access to money and glamor to win over skeptical Roman republicans, on the one hand, and eastern princes, on the other hand. They were jealous of their own power and fearful of Cleopatra's. It might have worked had Antony backed it up by winning military victories.

Antony was a great man, but, living in an age of giants, it wasn't enough to keep him from meeting his match, and repeatedly. Had he found a more tractable mate than Cleopatra or faced a lesser foe than Octavian, he might have succeeded. But, to paraphrase another

Shakespeare play, *The Tragedy of Julius Caesar*, the fault was not in Antony's stars but in himself. Compared to most people, he was a colossus, but at the level on which he played, he was a subordinate or, as the Bard says, an underling. That was Antony's tragedy.

As a dying Antony was being carried to Cleopatra, one of his bodyguards grabbed Antony's bloody sword and brought it to Octavian's camp. Upon hearing the news, Octavian wept, but probably not very much. He soon called his friends into his tent, pulled out his correspondence with Antony, and read selections to show just how reasonably and fairly he had always written, only to receive rude and overbearing responses from Antony. So much for not speaking ill of the dead. It was said that, after entering Alexandria, Octavian personally viewed Antony's corpse. If that happened—and it seems plausible—one would give much to know what thoughts went through Octavian's mind. Did he feel anger? Satisfaction? Regret? Resignation at the thought that one day he too would be ashes and dust?

Requests are supposed to have come in from many kings and generals for the honor of burying Antony's body, although, in reality, few would have wanted to risk inciting Octavian's anger. It has been proposed that maybe Octavia requested it as well, but that is just an intriguing suggestion, without support in the sources. Instead, Octavian gave Cleopatra permission to have Antony's remains laid to rest in her mausoleum, where she could expect to follow one day. According to one source, Antony's corpse was embalmed, but since that process took seventy days, simple burial seems more likely. No doubt, it suited Octavian's narrative to fulfill the alleged provisions of the will that Octavian had "discovered" earlier, in which Antony supposedly requested burial in Alexandria beside Cleopatra. It would have been awkward for Octavian to give Antony's remains a proper funeral in Rome.

The death of Antony marked the end of Rome's civil war between the two remaining triumvirs. It was only the first day of the month, however. Even bigger and more historic changes lay ahead.

Capturing the Queen

Before entering Alexandria on August 1, Octavian sent a trusted associate on a crucial but delicate mission. It was his job to get into Cleopatra's mausoleum and gain control of both the queen and her treasury. He had to keep her from setting the place on fire and killing herself.

Octavian entrusted the mission to Gaius Proculeius. A Roman knight, Proculeius was one of Octavian's closest friends. Several years earlier, at a moment of desperation in the war against Sextus Pompey, when it looked like all was lost in an engagement at sea, Octavian had turned to Proculeius and asked him to take Octavian's life. This extravagant gesture turned out to be unnecessary, and Octavian escaped in a small boat and survived.

Somehow Proculeius had also earned the trust of Antony, which might be one of the reasons why Octavian chose him for the mission. Even though Antony had told Cleopatra she could trust Proculeius, she didn't. When he showed up at her mausoleum, shortly after Antony's death, she made him speak to her through the bars of the gate. She asked that her children be allowed to rule Egypt, and he replied that she should trust Octavian. She didn't.

Stymied, Proculeius sent word to Octavian, who sent Gallus to help. Gallus had recently defeated Antony at Paraetonium. Now he stood at the gate of the mausoleum and charmed the queen, and the soldier–love poet could be very charming. While she was distracted, Proculeius took a ladder to another part of the building and, accompanied by two servants, climbed into the second-floor window. It was the very opening through which Cleopatra's maids had recently hauled up poor, mortally wounded Antony. One of the women warned Cleopatra, and supposedly the queen pulled a dagger out of her girdle and tried to kill herself, but Proculeius stopped her in time. Just like that, Cleopatra had lost her freedom and her leverage: the treasure. Octavian now had Egypt's fortune and no longer had to worry about a revolt on the part of his troops demanding to be paid. It was, in its own way, as great a coup as his victory at Actium.

The queen still remained to be dealt with, but Octavian sent a freedman to keep a close eye on her to make sure she stayed alive. By the same token, the freedman was under orders to treat her well. Apparently, she was taken back to the palace.

Later that day, buoyed by the news of his great success, Octavian entered Alexandria.

Making alliances, settling scores, and arranging for murders, in short, all the work of taking over a conquered city, occupied Octavian's time. Besides, it was in his interest to wait and make Cleopatra worry about his intentions. The queen, in the meantime, was allowed to mourn and bury Antony.

Ancient societies took mourning seriously. It was not unusual for a woman to tear her clothes, beat or bare her breasts, and scratch her cheeks. According to the memoir by Cleopatra's physician, Olympus, her breasts grew inflamed from the blows she inflicted. She developed a fever and used it as an excuse to stop eating and so commit suicide. The story goes that Octavian got wind of this and threatened to harm her children if she didn't start eating again. The queen complied. Whatever really happened—and this tale seems suspect—Cleopatra's real intent was to force a meeting with Octavian. In a week, she got her wish.

Octavian and Cleopatra

Octavian came to see Cleopatra on August 8 in the royal palace.

Ancient literature recounts several one-on-one meetings between enemies, such as Scipio Africanus and Hannibal meeting in the latter's tent before the Battle of Zama. The meeting of Octavian and Cleopatra ranks as one of history's more dramatic personal encounters.

He was the victor; she, the vanquished. The Egyptian queen had threatened to invade Italy but had been invaded and defeated instead. He had declared war on her and not on Antony. Octavian and Cleopatra were rivals for the legacy of Julius Caesar. Octavian denied Caesar's paternity of Caesarion and claimed that he, Octavian, was the only son of Caesar. He and Cleopatra were ruthless, ambitious, violent. Neither was to be trusted.

History does not record whether they had met before. Given the amount of time that Cleopatra had spent in Rome, they probably had, but then, Octavian had been a boy. Now he was the ruler of the Roman world. He had fulfilled the vow made as a nineteen-year-old: to achieve all of Caesar's honors.

Antony and Caesar had each been older than Cleopatra, whereas Octavian was six years younger. It must have been a challenge for her to deal with a Roman who seemed impervious to her sexual allure, as Octavian did, but Cleopatra relished challenges.

Did the two of them speak Greek or Latin? Octavian's Greek was imperfect. No source states that Cleopatra was able to speak Latin, but, given her fluency in languages and her intimate relations with both Caesar and Antony, she probably did. Whatever else Cleopatra was, she was a great performer. If she judged the odds better of persuading Octavian by speaking Latin, she would have poured out phrases polished enough to have pleased Cicero. But if she thought it better to proceed in Greek and to flatter Octavian on his mastery of the language, no matter how flawed, then she would have toned down her Hellenic diction to make him feel at ease.

We'll never know what they each really said. Octavian probably published his version in his memoirs, and perhaps Cleopatra told her version to her physician or another intimate who later published a secondhand account. At least one servant was present, or was close enough in the next room to be within listening range. Other contemporaries might simply have invented versions to win an audience or flatter Octavian. Writing much later, Plutarch and Cassius Dio each provides a detailed account, but with significant differences between them. Although they agree that Cleopatra turned on the charm, Dio's Cleopatra tries to seduce Octavian, while Plutarch's queen is more restrained.

In Plutarch, Octavian comes to Cleopatra; in Cassius Dio, the queen requests the meeting. Both authors agree that she played up the scene for his arrival, but they disagree about her plan of attack. Plutarch has Cleopatra lying wretchedly on a straw bed and dressed only in a tunic. As he entered, she got up and threw herself at his feet. Although the self-inflicted wounds to her face and body were obvious, nonetheless her charm and beauty shone through.

Cassius Dio has Cleopatra emphasize the luxury of her apartment and describes her in flattering mourning clothes. Dio says that she had artfully arranged images of Julius Caesar in the room and that she was carrying his handwritten letters to her in her bosom. She proceeded to read aloud excerpts from the letters to demonstrate Caesar's love for her. Meanwhile, with meaningful glances and sweet words, she tried to seduce Octavian. It was all in vain, however, because Octavian merely looked down at the ground and assured Cleopatra that she would be safe. As another Roman writer put it, "her beauty was unable to prevail over his self-control." A frustrated queen fell to her knees and begged the privilege of dying and being buried with Antony. A noncommittal Octavian told her to be of good cheer and left. He put measures in place to make sure she would stay alive in order to take part in his triumph in Rome. This sounds like the official version in Augustus's memoirs or as told by one of his flatterers.

Plutarch is more subtle, but more vicious. He has Octavian generously tell Cleopatra to lie back down on her bed while he sits beside her. She starts to justify her behavior by blaming it all on Antony, but Octavian isn't having any of it. She changes her tune and begs for pity. She then hands him a full list of her treasures, but one of her stewards intervenes and reveals that she has left out certain valuables. Cleopatra leaps up and starts to beat the man, but Octavian stops her. She then concedes the point: she was saving some jewelry for his sister, Octavia, and his wife, Livia. It is such a nice turnabout that one suspects that Cleopatra had arranged the steward's "betrayal." In any case, the scene worked. Octavian planned to bring Cleopatra to Rome and humiliate her by marching her in his triumph, an indignity usually followed by execution. Convinced that she wanted to live and that suicide wasn't a danger, he went off and let down his guard. He thought that he had tricked her, writes Plutarch, but he was the one who had been tricked.

Cassius Dio and Plutarch emphasize the lurid details of the meeting. But more important is its purpose as each of the two participants saw it. One question was key: whether or not Cleopatra would march in Octavian's triumph in Rome. Octavian greatly wanted her to do so; Cleopatra wanted with equal vigor to avoid that humiliation. One source reports that while she was held in captivity by Octavian—and treated generously—Cleopatra said more than once, "I will not be shown in a triumph"—"*ou thriambeusomai,*" is the resonant sound in Greek. The only way out was suicide.

For Cleopatra, the goal of the meeting was to get Octavian to lower his guard so that she could smuggle in the means to commit suicide. For Octavian, it was to get Cleopatra to relax enough that she would go on living and could be brought to Rome.

That, at any rate, was how things seemed on the surface. Yet neither of these two master manipulators was superficial. Perhaps each had a deeper intention. Perhaps the real point of the interview was to agree upon the terms of Cleopatra's death. Did Octavian really want to march Cleopatra in his triumph in Rome? He might have had second thoughts. Octavian surely had in mind executing Cleopatra, but as he knew, not every captured ruler was put to death. One exception in particular must have caught his attention. Julius Caesar had marched Cleopatra's sister, Arsinoe, in his triumph of 46 BC. Her pitiful state so moved the Roman crowd that they forced Caesar to let her live; he sent her into exile in Ephesus. What if the crowd did the same with Cleopatra, who would have known how to play up her misery? What if they prevented her execution? Octavian could not have faced such a possibility with happiness. As long as she lived, Cleopatra could stir up trouble.

By the same token, Octavian could not simply execute Cleopatra. Killing Egypt's popular queen in Alexandria might have stirred up a revolt. Nor do national leaders execute their counterparts without nervously fingering their own necks. That Cleopatra was a woman only made Octavian's position more awkward. He might have concluded that Cleopatra's suicide was the best solution, especially if he arranged things so that he seemed blameless.

Astute Cleopatra surely realized that herself. She didn't shrink before the possibility of death, but she had no intention of gratifying Octavian without getting something in return. Although no source mentions it, what she wanted most of all was the safety of her children—in particular her three children by Antony. By sending Caesarion away, she tacitly admitted that Octavian would not tolerate her son by Caesar.

Perhaps the thought of her children is why Cleopatra mentioned Livia and Octavia. The two sacrosanct women of Octavian's household were both mothers. Octavia was already raising Antony's younger son by Fulvia. Cleopatra knew that it would probably fall to Octavia and Livia to raise her children. So, if Cleopatra brought up those two Roman ladies, then her message to Octavian was probably along these lines: promise me that my household will continue, and I'll promise you to exit gracefully.

Could Cleopatra trust a promise by Octavian? Perhaps not, but a Roman did not give his word lightly, and Cleopatra would have known how to remind him of a Roman's obligations. Nor would she have any difficulty reading his body language, however hard he tried to hide his real intentions. Finally, the presence of her steward supplied a witness who could tell others.

All speculation, but when it comes to Octavian and Cleopatra, it is unwise to rule out a secret bargain—both knew how to play negotiation hardball.

The Queen Departs

Few things about Cleopatra are more famous than her death by the bite of an asp. Octavian portrayed the scene with a float in his triumphal procession in Rome. Shakespeare dramatized it. The Italian Renaissance artist Michelangelo depicted it. Yet we will never know if it really happened. For once, the two main sources share a common humility about how Cleopatra died. "No one knows the truth," writes Plutarch. "No one knows for certain," writes Cassius Dio. Perhaps that in and of itself speaks to Cleopatra's success, for it left her the center of attention even in the manner of her death.

One thing is certain: the queen committed suicide. Perhaps Octavian welcomed it or even connived in bringing it on. Cleopatra staged her own exit, and she left like royalty.

According to Plutarch, the process began with a message from a young officer in Octavian's retinue named Cornelius Dolabella. Supposedly, he was fond of Cleopatra and she knew it, so she sent him a message to which he replied secretly. He warned her that Octavian was planning to leave Alexandria soon; in fact, he intended to send her and her children off within three days. The story is suspicious, from the gullible young man to the ease of transmitting messages. Perhaps Dolabella was actually working at Octavian's behest. Yet Cleopatra could be seductive, and young men can be seduced, and the tale just might be true. In any case, it began her final act.

Cleopatra asked for and received permission to mourn at Antony's tomb. Then she returned to the palace, took a bath, and prepared an elaborate meal. At that point, a man from the country arrived with a large basket. The guards asked to have a look, and the man removed the leaves to show some large and especially nice figs. The man offered some to the admiring guards, which put them at ease, and they let him through. Cleopatra proceeded to enjoy her meal. The room had windows with a view of the sea. Perhaps, looking out, she thought of Actium and of what might have been. If so, the thought probably did not occupy her for long, because Cleopatra was a pragmatist. Upon finishing her meal, she sent a sealed tablet to Octavian that had already been written upon, sent away everyone except her most faithful maidservants, Iras and Charmion, and closed the doors.

Octavian received the message and began reading it. Cleopatra begged him to let her be buried beside Antony. Immediately suspecting the worst, Octavian sent messengers to investigate. They came on the run, but it was too late. Thrusting open the doors of Cleopatra's chamber, they found a gruesome sight. She was lying dead on a golden couch, dressed in her royal robes. Iras was lying at her feet. Charmion was dying and trying to rearrange the queen's diadem. One of the messengers supposedly said, "A fine deed, this, Charmion!" She supposedly replied, "It is most fine, indeed, and it befits one descended from so many kings." Then she fell and died.

It was August 10, 30 BC. Cleopatra was thirty-nine years old.

What killed Cleopatra? Plutarch and Cassius Dio talk of the possibility that Cleopatra was killed by an asp. *Asp* is not a technical term but a generic word for a venomous snake. In the Egyptian context, *asp* probably refers to a cobra. The standard story goes that the cobra was hidden under the figs. Another version says the cobra was carefully kept shut up in a water jar, and Cleopatra stirred it up with a golden distaff until it bit her arm. A third version says she hid the asp in some flowers. The earliest sources speak of two snakes.

It has been objected that the Egyptian cobra grows to six feet long, and in some cases nearly ten feet long, and so would have been hard to hide in a basket of figs. One cobra could not be relied on to kill three people, and it is difficult to imagine two snakes being smuggled in. Nor is death by a cobra bite necessarily painless. Note also that the double snake was a symbol of Egyptian royalty, and Cleopatra's death was nothing if not symbolic. All the more reason for Octavian to claim the wearer of the cobra crown was undone by a cobra.

That is not the end of the story, however. A baby Egyptian cobra is sufficiently venomous and aggressive enough to kill an adult human. Only sixteen to eighteen inches long, a baby cobra could easily have been hidden in a basket of figs or a water jar. In fact, it would not have been difficult to smuggle in three such snakes. It is not difficult to get a cobra to bite.

Perhaps Iras and Charmion each chose the less dramatic route of taking poison. Perhaps Cleopatra did so as well. There was plenty of precedent for committing suicide by poison, from the philosopher Socrates drinking a cup of hemlock, to the Athenian statesman Demosthenes sucking poison hidden in a pen, to Ptolemy of Cyprus, who, in 58 BC, took poison to end his life as a king rather than submit to Rome and give up his throne. He was Cleopatra's uncle.

Plutarch mentions a report that Cleopatra had kept the poison in a hollow comb hidden in her hair, while Cassius Dio says she had the poison in a hairpin. Supposedly Cleopatra had used the period of Octavian's approach to Alexandria in order to experiment with various deadly poisons and venomous animals on condemned prisoners, to see which ones brought the quickest and most painless deaths. Alexandria was the medical capital of the ancient world, and Cleopatra had access to its best doctors.

Yet the sources insist there was no proof of poison. There were no blisters or other signs of it on her body. Nor was there any proof of a snakebite, although some said that slight punctures were visible on Cleopatra's arm. No snake was seen in the death chamber, although some claimed to have seen its trail nearby, close to the sea. That Cleopatra's body was not disfigured, and that she died within the day are all consistent with a cobra bite, although they certainly don't prove it.

Octavian claimed that he tried to revive Cleopatra, both by the use of drugs and by sending for experts at sucking out snake venom.

It appears that he at least suspected a snakebite. If so, neither effort availed. We are left with the verdict of our sources: nobody really knows how Cleopatra killed herself.

Octavian ordered that she be buried with full royal honors and laid to rest beside Antony, presumably in her mausoleum. The standard treatment for fallen foes, this graciousness also suited Octavian's propaganda, since he had claimed that Antony had disgraced himself and insisted on burial beside Cleopatra in Alexandria, rather than lying in the family tomb outside Rome.

Eulogy for a Queen

Cleopatra was one of history's greatest female statesmen. After two centuries of decline and defeat, she turned around her country's fate. At home, she presided over prosperity. The first monarch in three centuries of her dynasty to speak Egyptian, and possibly part Egyptian herself, she won great popularity among her people. Abroad, she reclaimed most of the lost territories of the Ptolemaic Empire. She raised Egypt to a position of power and influence that it had not held for generations. She was the greatest Macedonian ruler since Alexander and the greatest Egyptian queen since Hatshepsut.

Cleopatra could not have achieved success without forming alliances with the two most powerful Romans of her day, Julius Caesar and Mark Antony. One of the tools she used was sex. Whether or not Cleopatra was beautiful, she was indisputably charming and attractive. She probably bore Caesar's son and definitely bore two sons and a daughter by Mark Antony. Highly strategic in her choice of partners, she might also have loved them. So we would like to think: she was only human, after all.

Through her partnership with Antony, she came close to winning control of Rome itself and thereby securing the long-term independence of her kingdom. Cleopatra's ships and treasure brought Antony to the gates of Italy, but she might well have been the force that held him back. The decision to stay on the western Greek coast and wait for the enemy was a fatal mistake.

She showed resolution in defeat. Less than loyal as a lover—it appears that she sacrificed Antony—she was indomitable as a mother. She tried to save Caesarion and succeeded in preserving the lives of her three other children. When she finally met her enemy Octavian, Cleopatra was unable to repeat her earlier great entrances: with Caesar, smuggled into his presence in a bedroll; with Antony, dazzling him by arriving on a golden barge. But she was able to recap and perhaps even better her smooth and sudden escape from Actium. She left life on her own terms, at a time and place of her own choosing and not her foe's, and dressed in the royal robes of a queen.

Horace, one of the poets in Octavian's retinue, wrote admiringly of Cleopatra's end. In the now-famous Poem 37 in his first book of Odes, sometimes known as the "Cleopatra Ode," he acknowledges that Octavian had wanted to parade her in chains through Rome in his triumph, but "she sought to die / More nobly." Horace writes:

> *Amid her ruin'd halls she stood*
> *Unblench'd, and fearless to the end*
> *Grasp'd the fell snakes, that all her blood*
> *Might with the cold black venom blend,*
> *Death's purpose flushing in her face;*
> *Nor to our ships the glory gave,*
> *That she, no vulgar dame, should grace*
> *A triumph, crownless, and a slave.*

Chapter 16

"I Wanted to See a King"

Alexandria, 30 BC

ON AUGUST 1, WITH CLEOPATRA AND HER TREA-
sure in his hands, the victor had entered Alexandria. Octavian rode
into town in a carriage not with a fierce legionary but with his former
tutor, Arius Didymus, a native of Alexandria. Like most of the local
elite, Arius was Greek in language and culture. Octavian went so far
as to give Arius his right hand, a gesture of respect that was meant
to reassure the local inhabitants. Octavian entered the most beautiful
public building in the city, the Gymnasium, the very symbol of Greek
civilization. It was the same place where, four years earlier, Antony
and Cleopatra had celebrated the triumph over Armenia and presented their children to the Alexandrians as future monarchs.

In the Gymnasium, Octavian stood up on a tribunal and addressed the people. He must have looked a strange sight. He was
short and slight, unlike the martial and well-built Antony. Octavian
was dressed like a Roman, without any hint of Dionysus or eastern
ways. Yet when he spoke to the assembly, Octavian used not Latin but
Greek. Knowing that his mastery of the language was limited, Octavian had written out his speech first in Latin and then had it translated, perhaps by Arius.

The crowd was no doubt terrified in spite of Arius's presence. "The
people," writes Plutarch, "were beside themselves with fear and pros-
trated themselves before him [Octavian]." Rome's reputation as a con-

queror proceeded him, written in the blood of Carthage and Corinth, among other places. But Octavian told his listeners to get up. He then announced to a relieved audience that he meant to be merciful. He said that he would spare the people of Alexandria for three reasons: in memory of Alexander the Great, in recognition of the size and beauty of the city, and as a favor to his teacher. The speech became celebrated and was quoted often. The combination of royalty, culture, and cronyism was classic Octavian. Leniency toward a city of perhaps a half million people was incidental.

Octavian treated Alexandria's inhabitants generously. A politician of his caliber didn't need to be told that it was better to have friendly natives than hostile ones. He even pardoned Philostratus, a sort of court philosopher who had enlivened Cleopatra's entertainments with his flair for speaking without preparation. Philostratus made such a public spectacle of begging Arius for help that Octavian finally gave in. It would have been bad for business to kill an old man with a long, white beard.

Antony had died on August 1; Cleopatra on August 10. But what of their children: two by other spouses, three together? What, in particular, of Octavian's adoptive brother, Caesarion?

The Last Pharaoh

Of all the faces of the ancient world that stare out at us in silence, his is the most eloquent. We know so much about him that we could almost write a book, but at the end of the day, we know nothing. We have words but no music. We have nothing written by him and precious little written about him. Gossip, jokes, and images swirl around his memory, but we cannot penetrate to the real being.

"In history, only a few lines are found about you," wrote the poet Cavafy, addressing himself to a Caesarion whose appearance the poet imagines. In fact, we can do better. Two statues in the Greco-Egyptian style have been plausibly identified as Caesarion, and they preserve his face, at least as royal propaganda presented him to the public. In each, he wears the striped headcloth traditionally worn by the pharaoh, but Greek-style locks of hair peek out below and fall on his forehead. He has pleasant, regular, youthful features. His face is flat, in one case, and rounded in the other. One statue shows a small nose and well-defined eyes. The other is less well preserved—it was fished out of the Alexandria harbor—but it shows, like its counterpart, a full mouth, with downturned lips, and a distinct chin. These are all conventional features of first-century BC Ptolemaic portraits, so they do not present the real Caesarion. Much less do the traditional, pharaonic-style reliefs showing Caesarion in profile, complete with false beard, thick eyebrows, and the tall double crown of the Upper and Lower Nile perched on his head.

"He Resembled Caesar in Appearance and Gait"

According to the biographer of the emperors, Gaius Suetonius Tranquillus, "several of the Greeks relate that he resembled Caesar in appearance and gait." The sources agree that Caesar was tall and had a fair complexion, with lively, dark eyes. He was either well built or lean—portrait busts and coins suggest the latter. The sources also suggest a broad mouth, and both a prominent nose and Adam's apple, although they were perhaps less visible in a younger, healthier Caesar. If Caesarion indeed resembled Caesar, then he had some of these features.

The Romans set great store by a person's gait. Noble families hired actors to observe their distinguished members so that an actor could impersonate a great man at his funeral, down to his way of walking. Either Caesarion naturally walked like Caesar or he had been taught to walk like him. The physical resemblance, however, was probably natural.

He was, in all likelihood, the product of a union between two of the most talented, ambitious, visionary, ruthless, and violent statesmen in the ancient world. Of his mother, there is no doubt. As for his father: once one dispenses with Octavian's propaganda about Cleopatra being a loose woman, what's left is a shrewd and calculating monarch. The queen had every reason to be cautious about her bed partners. For once, the official story is probably true: that she slept with only two men, Julius Caesar and Mark Antony. It was hardly an accident that she chose the two most powerful Romans of the day as her mates.

That Caesar was Caesarion's birth father was widely believed, if vociferously denied by Antony and Cleopatra's enemies. Above all, we know that Octavian hated and feared the association. He was determined to be rid of Caesarion.

Progress of a Prince

The little we know of Caesarion's life records the progress of a prince. He was probably born in 47 BC. Cleopatra might have brought the baby with her when she visited Rome in 46 BC or on her second trip there in 45 BC, the better to win Caesar's favor. While she was in Rome, he gave her permission to call the child by his name.

Back in Egypt, in 44 BC, Caesarion's uncle, Ptolemy XIV, who was Cleopatra's brother and coruler, died. After this convenient—and, therefore, suspicious—death, Cleopatra named Caesarion as her coruler. Like all Ptolemaic rulers, he was both a Greek king and an Egyptian pharaoh. He had traditional pharaonic titles: "Heir of the God That Saves, Chosen of Ptah, Carrying out the Rule of Re, Living image of Amun." Like his parents, Caesarion was declared a god. He was given the title of the Father- and Mother-Loving God, the former a reference to Caesar. Later, when he was thirteen, he received the grandiose appellation of king of kings.

He was raised in the luxury of the palace and no doubt wanted for nothing. One imagines him wearing at times a broad-brimmed Macedonian hat and at other times wearing a royal diadem or the double crown of Egypt. Depending on the occasion, he might be dressed in a traditional Egyptian kilt or a Greek mantle, surely dyed purple and gold.

Young Caesarion no doubt received an excellent education. Nicolaus of Damascus, for instance, who taught his half siblings, is indicative of the caliber of the tutors at the royal court. Intellectual, diplomat, and writer, Nicolaus later served both Herod and Augustus in turn. Latin was surely among the subjects that Caesarion learned, since a knowledge of that language would help him deal with Rome. And the boy was, after all, supposed to be a son of the most famous Roman of the age.

Cleopatra was not subtle about celebrating Caesarion and his father. In Alexandria, she built a huge temple to Caesar, the Caesareum. This was a Greek-style structure built on a huge scale and with no expense spared, known for its art works, libraries, and statues in gold and silver. In the Nile Valley, she had an Egyptian-style temple built to celebrate the birth of Caesarion. She had a huge relief of herself and her son making offerings to the gods carved on the rear wall of the massive temple of the goddess Hathor, also in the Nile Valley.

The temple celebrating Caesarion's birth identified the young prince with the god Horus. In Egyptian mythology, Horus avenged the murder of his father, Osiris. That suggested that Caesarion would one day avenge the murder of his father, Caesar. Yet Octavian claimed to be Caesar's avenging son, so this was potentially uncomfortable for Octavian.

Caesarion reached an important milestone sometime in the months after Actium. It was then that Cleopatra had him enrolled in the ephebate, the organization of young men approaching military age. He was sixteen. This was a rite of manhood. The purpose was to get her subjects used to the idea that Caesarion was ready to rule alone as king, should anything happen to her. No doubt Cleopatra considered putting off this step, since, if Caesarion could still be considered a boy, he might receive more merciful treatment from Octavian. At sixteen, however, Caesarion was no child, so Cleopatra might have concluded that, on balance, it was better to have him declared of age. Whether he was ready to rule is another matter. He surely knew his way around the royal court, but it is hard to imagine him leading an army that put down a revolt and founding a city, as Alexander the Great did at sixteen. In any case, Caesarion's coming-of-age ceremony was celebrated with a round of banquets and a distribution of gifts to the populace.

Caesarion was born and groomed for greatness. He might have grown into a monarch like his mother or a warrior and writer as well as a statesman like his father. His heritage was epic, but instead, he suffered tragedy.

Flight into Exile

As Octavian closed in on Alexandria in the summer of 30 BC, Caesarion ran for safety. To be sure, each of his parents had beat a prudent retreat early in his or her career: Caesar, by taking to the hills in fear of the dictator Sulla, and Cleopatra, when she was driven out of Egypt by her brother. Caesar and Cleopatra each bounced back, and Caesarion might have dreamt of a similar comeback.

When Caesar fled Sulla, however, he left of his own accord. Caesarion was sent to safety by his mother. She sent him down the Nile Valley to make his way to a port on the Red Sea coast, with part of the royal treasure to grease palms along the way. His ultimate destination was India. Perhaps the plan was to find refuge in one of the kingdoms on the west coast of the subcontinent, with whose ruler Cleopatra had no doubt been in contact. He could establish himself there and perhaps one day come back to Egypt.

Presumably Caesarion left Alexandria before Octavian entered the city on August 1. One wonders if Cleopatra gave him a tearful good-bye. Early August is the hottest time of the year in Egypt. Caesarion had to leave the ocean breezes of Alexandria for the scorching heat of the South, but there was no choice.

Caesarion never reached his destination. The sources disagree as to just what went wrong. According to some, he was captured by Octavian's men on the road and brought back to Alexandria. Plutarch weaves a more pathetic tale. He says that Caesarion's tutor, one Rhodon, convinced him to go back to Alexandria on the grounds that Octavian had decided to make him king. One supposes that Octavian had sent a message to this effect in order to lure Caesarion back. Whether Rhodon believed it or whether he had decided to betray his pupil in exchange for a reward is unknown. But if Caesarion really allowed himself to be talked into returning to the tender mercies of his "brother" Octavian—officially Gaius Julius Caesar—then, the young man would have disappointed his parents by his naïveté. One doesn't imagine young Caesar needing a tutor or young Cleopatra listening to one.

Antyllus

Recognizing Caesarion as king was the last thing Octavian planned to do. He had in mind, instead, the fate that he visited upon Caesarion's stepbrother and Antony's older son by Fulvia. That lad was Marcus Antonius, whose nickname was Antyllus. He had lived with his father in Alexandria; his younger brother was in Rome. When Caesarion was enrolled as an ephebe several months earlier, Antyllus put on the "toga of manhood" (*toga virilis*). He was probably fifteen at the time. Several days of banquets and parties in Alexandria marked this Roman coming-of-age ceremony. They were premature. Octavian used Antyllus's manhood as an excuse to have him executed. Antyllus had once been betrothed to Octavian's daughter, Julia, when they were both still children, but that match had surely been dissolved long before.

Octavian had several reasons for harshness. Antyllus had served as a go-between in the negotiations meant to maintain Antony's power after Actium. He delivered a large bribe to Octavian, who, as mentioned earlier, kept the money but sent Antyllus back to his father without any agreement. Having made his career as the avenger of his adopted father, Octavian might have looked warily at Antyllus's status as his father's heir under Roman law, and so he might have wanted to avenge Antony. And there was the fact that Antyllus was, technically, a man. So, by the brutal calculus of civil war, execution made sense.

Antyllus, like Caesarion, was betrayed by his tutor. In his case, Antyllus is said to have taken refuge in Alexandria, either in a shrine of Antony that Cleopatra had built or beside a statue of Julius Caesar. The teenager pleaded for his life but in vain. After he was decapitated by Octavian's henchman, his tutor supposedly stole the very precious stone that Antyllus had worn around his neck and sewed it into his girdle for safekeeping. The man came under suspicion, denied the theft, was convicted, and was either crucified or impaled.

Too Many Caesars

Just how Caesarion was executed is not recorded. What is written down is the savage pun that smoothed his way to slaughter. Octavian needed no advice to kill Caesarion; in fact, his entire career had been about killing Caesarion. Only that would render him secure as Caesar's son. It served Octavian's purpose, however, to be able to say that the deed was someone else's idea. And who better than an Alexandrian Greek? And not just any Greek, but a philosopher. And not just any philosopher, but Arius, who played so big a role in Octavian's entry into Alexandria. Yes, Arius was just the man for the job.

It was he, they said, who advised the execution of Caesarion and who did so with an elegant irony that even those connoisseurs of humor, the Alexandrians, might have admired—had the victim not been their king. Arius referred to the *Iliad*, a work known to all educated Greeks. In that epic, the wise Odysseus warns rebels in his army that "it is not good to have too many kings (*Ouk agathon polukoira-niē*)." The philosopher Arius advised Octavian that "it is not good to have too many Caesars (*Ouk agathon polukaisariē*)," with a change of only two letters in Greek. And so, with Homer himself seeming to bless the act, the last Greek king of Egypt was killed. Not to put too fine a point on it, but as the son of Julius Caesar, he was also Egypt's first Roman king.

Cleopatra died on August 10. For eighteen days, if an ancient source can be believed, Caesarion had ruled Egypt as sole king. Then, on August 29, Octavian announced the annexation of Egypt. Henceforth, it would belong to Rome or, more precisely, to Octavian, because he claimed the country as his personal estate.

It wouldn't be surprising if Octavian permitted Caesarion a royal burial, since Caesarion had been pharaoh, and Octavian was always careful not to insult the sensibilities of the Egyptians, especially not their elite priesthood.

After Caesarion's death, the priests of Egypt represented Octavian as pharaoh, but he himself never claimed the title, nor did his successors as Roman emperors. Egypt had been ruled by kings for three millennia. It seems appropriate, somehow, that the last man to sit on the throne of Khufu, Thutmose, and Rameses would be the son of Julius Caesar.

Antony and Cleopatra's three children were spared. Octavian brought them with him back to Rome.

Alexander's Tomb

If Alexandria was a city of kings, then Alexander's Tomb was its most royal place. There was a palace, of course, but the tomb was, in effect, a hero shrine and a holy site. Just as Alexander himself had visited Achilles' Tomb (or so it was identified) when he passed through Troy, so Octavian visited Alexander's Tomb while in Alexandria. He used it as a teaching moment to show that empire had a new hero.

Octavian showed his respect to Alexander's mummy by placing a golden crown on his head and strewing the corpse with flowers. Yet, the story goes, Octavian not only viewed Alexander's mummy but also touched it. It is said that when he did so, a piece of the mummy's nose broke off. Would Sigmund Freud himself have dared to tell such a tale? Just short of his thirty-third birthday, Octavian was precisely the age that Alexander had been when he died. By accidentally breaking off a piece of the nose of the Mediterranean's most legendary conqueror, Octavian was saying, in effect, that he was greater. It is such a powerful symbol that there was a new king in town that it is hard to believe it really happened.

There was, however, more. Octavian's hosts wanted to show him the remains of the Ptolemaic kings, who lay at rest near Alexander. Only Alexander had been mummified; his successors had been cremated and placed in urns. Octavian declined the invitation. It was beneath his dignity as a Roman consul—an office he held for the fourth time in 30 BC—and imperator to pay his respects to a group that he had considered his inferiors. Indeed, some of the Ptolemies had been clients of Rome.

Octavian replied archly, "I wanted to see a king, not corpses." He made a similar response when asked to go see Apis. This was a sacred bull worshipped in the city of Memphis, the ancient capital located upriver on the Nile, slightly south of the Great Pyramids. Apis was thought to be divine; a sort of representative of the god of creation. Once again Octavian turned down the request, saying that he worshipped gods, not cattle.

We want the grand opening of the Roman Empire to come in Rome. It is after all, the Eternal City, and was already known as such in antiquity. And the founding of Imperial Rome was the first step in the birth of modern Europe. But, in fact, the transfer of empire took place in Alexandria. Today the second city of Egypt, overshadowed by Cairo, and long a part of the Islamic world—Arab armies conquered the city in AD 641—Alexandria seems remote from the West, which Rome still represents. Yet Alexandria was a pivotal place in the ancient Mediterranean. It was the Mediterranean's cultural capital.

Unbeknownst to those at the time, the city was about to enter a new phase as the crucible of Christianity. Here much of early Christian theology would be worked out. As the place that spread the notion of Christian monasticism, which was invented in Egypt, the city would play as big a role in the formation of Western culture as did Rome or Jerusalem. In short, therefore, Alexandria was a splendid stage on which to turn over the keys to the kingdom.

August 30 BC was one of the most consequential months in the history of the world. It began, on the very first day, with the death of Antony and Octavian's entry into Alexandria. On the tenth, Cleopatra committed suicide. Then, on some day before nearly the end of the month, Caesarion was murdered. On August 29 Octavian announced the annexation of Egypt. August 29 happened to be New Year's Day, according to the Egyptian calendar, thereby neatly allowing Octavian to commence his rule with a new year and a fresh start. In Rome, the Senate backdated the annexation to his entry into the city on August 1. They declared the day a holiday, because Octavian had "delivered the republic from a most severe danger."

Octavian's annexation of Egypt was the end of the three-hundred-year-old Ptolemaic dynasty. It was also the end of something even grander: the three-thousand-year-old history of Egyptian kings.

It was the beginning of Imperial Rome and, with it, the foundations of the modern West. Roman provinces were traditionally governed by senators, but Egypt was different. To keep the Senate's hands off, Octavian put Egypt under the control of a Roman knight. He chose, as the first governor, Gallus, the poet and general who had proved so effective in the campaign to conquer Egypt, having defeated Antony with arms and Cleopatra with lies.

Shortly after his announcement, Octavian left Egypt and headed back toward Italy. His trip home took him across the sea. Every people around the ancient Mediterranean had their own name for the sea.

To the Phoenicians, it was the Great Sea. To the Egyptians, it was the Great Green. To the Greeks, it was the Sea in the Middle of the Land, the literal meaning of Mediterranean, which is how we know it today. To the Jews, it was the Hinder (or Hind) Sea, because it was behind a person facing east. To the Carthaginians, it was the Syrian Sea. From 30 BC on and for the next five centuries, until the fall of the Roman Empire in the West, the Mediterranean would become simply Mare Nostrum: "Our Sea." Few expressions better express the arrogance of an empire that considered the world to be its own.

Chapter 17

The Triumph of Augustus

Rome, August 29 to January 27 BC

ON THE NIGHT OF AUGUST 12, 29 BC, ANTICIPATION gripped Rome. After two and a half years away, Octavian was about to come home. He and thousands of his soldiers were gathered outside the city's walls. The next morning, they would march through the streets of town and its cheering crowds, go past the Circus Maximus, and then head through the Forum along the Sacred Way. Finally, they would climb the Capitoline Hill and sacrifice to Jupiter the Best and the Greatest. The procession, the famous Roman triumph, was a ritual marking the end of a victorious military campaign. Only the most successful generals received the privilege of celebrating a triumph, an honor granted by vote of the Senate. Octavian had been honored with not one but three triumphs, a rare distinction, which he celebrated in an unprecedented way, by back-to-back, three-day ceremonies. The first day would be a triumph for the Illyrian War of 35 to 33 BC. The second day would be a triumph for the Actium War of 32 to 31 BC. And the third day would be a triumph for the Alexandrian War of 30 BC.

There were multiple reasons for the triumphs. Octavian wanted to show that he was a great victor; that he had won a civil war; that he was the first man in Rome; that he had added new domains to the empire; and that he was now the master of the world. He also wanted to handle his victory over Antony diplomatically, since it would not do to trumpet his victory over fellow Romans. He solved the problem by leaving Antony unmentioned, by bookending the triumph of Actium between Illyria and Alexandria, and by displaying booty from Alexandria on all three days. He had no intention, though, of letting anyone forget the magnitude of his achievement in the Actium War.

As careful scholarship has shown, it is difficult to reconstruct a typical triumph or even to be sure if there was any such thing as "typical." Evidence for the order of events on each day in 29 BC survives both in literary sources and, more vividly, in a frieze illustrating the triumph. The frieze decorated the altar at Augustus's Victory Monument in Nicopolis, constructed between 29 and 27 BC. It is probably an idealized representation and should be taken with a grain of salt. According to the frieze, the procession started with musicians, followed by a ship on wheels—presumably a galley captured from the enemy. That was followed, in turn, by bulls destined for sacrifice. Then came attendants bearing shoulder-high portable stretchers carrying trophies, war booty, prisoners of war, and paintings of scenes of the conflict. Another sculpted relief from this era, this one from a temple in Rome, is thought also to show a scene from one day of the triple triumph. It depicts two prisoners sitting barefoot on the floor of a stretcher with downcast looks, dressed in tunics, their hands tied behind their backs. A display of captured armor looms above them.

Next came the lictors, or attendants of the consul (a title that Octavian held in 29 BC), wearing laurel wreaths and carrying fasces, the bundles of rods symbolizing the power of a Roman magistrate. Finally, there was Octavian. It is possible that he entered the city only once, on the last of the three days of triumphs. When Octavian did take part in the parade, he stood on a four-horse-drawn chariot, decorated with illustrations of acanthus-leaf vines and Corinthian columns, and perhaps laced with gold and ivory. He was dressed in the fringed tunic and purple toga of a triumphator. His face was painted red. Octavian carried a laurel branch in one hand and a scepter in the other, and his head was ringed with a laurel wreath. There is no sign in the sources of another person who supposedly took part in a triumph, a public slave who held a golden wreath above the triumphator's head. The slave supposedly had the job of whispering into the victor's ear from time to time, "Remember, you are mortal."

Literary sources state that Octavian was accompanied by two young men of his family. Riding a horse to his left was Tiberius, the older son of his wife, Livia, from her earlier marriage. On the right horse sat Marcellus, the son of his sister, Octavia, from her first marriage. Two younger children stood beside Octavian in the chariot: arguably, they were Julia, Octavian's daughter by his first marriage; and Drusus, Livia's younger son from her earlier marriage.

Behind Octavian came the other consul, the magistrates, and the senators who had participated in the victory, certainly including Agrippa. Although it was customary for the consul and the magistrates to lead the procession, in this case they followed the triumphator. It was probably more a gesture of recognition than an insult because so many senators (including some magistrates) had taken part in the Actium campaign; to be sure, Octavian had forced them to do so. In either case, the order of the march symbolized the new power relations in Rome: Octavian came first. Laurel-wreathed soldiers brought up the rear, marching and shouting "Hurrah for the triumph!" They also sang mocking and often obscene songs about their commander.

On the first day, Octavian celebrated victories in the Illyrian War. It is not known what captives or booty he displayed. The second day marked victories in the Actium campaign. In order to avoid the stain of civil war, he did not represent Antony or any other Roman enemies. Nor did he show an image of Cleopatra, which he was saving for the third day. Instead, he paraded two minor allied kings; Octavian had pardoned the major ones. The first, Adiatorix, the ruler of a small kingdom in northern Asia Minor on the Euxine Sea, was forced to march with his wife and two sons. Shortly before the Battle of Actium, Adiatorix had led a successful night raid on Octavian's camp that killed a number of Octavian's men. Adiatorix tried to blame Antony, but Octavian wasn't persuaded and ordered the execution of both Adiatorix and one of his sons after the triumph. The second king was Alexander of Emesa (Homs, Syria). Before Actium, Alexander had informed Antony that his brother, then-king Iamblichus, was planning to defect. Antony had Iamblichus tortured and killed, and gave his throne to Alexander. Now Octavian marched Alexander in his triumph and had him executed afterward as well.

Yet in spite of the absence of any image of Antony, the triumphal procession was not subtle about the results of the naval battle in which he had taken part. The Nicopolis frieze shows a captured warship on wheels being displayed in the triumph, as mentioned. A Roman poet claims that captured ships' beaks (rostra) were displayed, but that might be a figure of speech for whole ships. Afterward, the beaks were attached to the front of the Temple of the Deified Julius, at the Senate's command.

The triumphs made a splendid spectacle. Virgil commemorated them in the *Aeneid,* writing:

> *The victor to the gods his thanks express'd,*
> *And Rome, triumphant, with his presence bless'd.*
> *Three hundred temples in the town he plac'd;*
> *With spoils and altars ev'ry temple grac'd.*
> *Three shining nights, and three succeeding days,*
> *The fields resound with shouts, the streets with praise,*
> *The domes with songs, the theaters with plays.*
> *All altars flame: before each altar lies,*
> *Drench'd in his gore, the destin'd sacrifice.*

Nothing was grander than the third and climactic day of the triumph: the victory in Alexandria. Displays of Egyptian wealth and a vivid representation of the Nile competed for the public's admiration with the rare spectacle of rhinoceroses and hippopotami parading down the Sacred Way. The most impressive sight of all was the Ptolemaic royal family.

The two older children of Antony and Cleopatra appeared before the victor's chariot: eleven-year-old Alexander Helios and Cleopatra Selene. Whether they marched or were carried on stretchers is not known. Nothing is recorded about their brother, seven-year-old Ptolemy Philadelphus. Perhaps he is mistakenly omitted by the sources or perhaps he was spared because of his youth or perhaps he was dead, having succumbed to the ordeal of exile and captivity.

Their mother was not forgotten. She had died almost exactly a year before, an anniversary that might have occurred to her sorrowing children. Although not present at the triumph herself, Cleopatra's image was, either as a painted placard or an effigy. No longer the virago of Octavian's wartime propaganda, she was shown in defeat: committing suicide, with two asps on her arms. There is no record of Caesarion being represented, but Octavian would surely just as soon have had people forget his rival for the name of Caesar's son.

The triple triumph was a great moment for Octavian. It marked not only his victories but also the end of the civil wars. For the first time in fifteen years, since the assassination of Julius Caesar in 44 BC, Rome feared no violence. Earlier in 30 BC, the Senate had voted to close the gates of the shrine of the god Janus in the Roman Forum, but the actual act might have been postponed until the triumphs. The gates were open during wartime, which is to say, most of the time, and closed only to mark peace, a rare event.

The triumphs offered another message as well. At the end of the civil wars stood Octavian. He led the magistrates of Rome and not vice versa. His was the face on every coin. His was the mausoleum rising in oversized majesty outside the city walls on the Campus Martius. He was the only living son of Caesar, the deified man whose name he bore.

Octavian allowed his veterans to call themselves Actians (*Actiaci*), but they were settled in northern Italy, far from the capital. He constructed a magnificent victory monument to Actium but in Nicopolis, Greece, and not in Rome. In Rome, he raised a more modest tribute: a triumphal arch to Actium on the outskirts of the Forum, although even that is not certain, and some question whether the arch really existed. In any case, if Octavian did build it, he overhauled the arch a decade later and changed the subject.

In 2 BC Octavian put on a mock sea battle in Rome, in a basin constructed across the Tiber, to celebrate the dedication of a temple. The battle in question, however, was the Battle of Salamis, between the Greeks and Persians in 480 BC, not the Battle of Actium. Since the mock battle took place almost thirty years later, an observer might conclude that Actium remained a sensitive subject.

Cleopatra's statue continued to stand in the precinct of the Temple of Venus Genetrix (Venus the Ancestral Mother), where Julius Caesar had erected it. Antony's images were largely destroyed. When he was remembered, it was usually in unfavorable terms. His birthday, January 14, for example, was included among those days each year when neither the courts nor assemblies were allowed to meet, although all other business continued as usual. The public considered such days to be ill-omened. But the victory celebrations eclipsed all negative thoughts.

Returning to the events of August 29 BC: Octavian continued the pageantry after the third triumph. Before the end of the month, he dedicated Rome's new Senate House, the Curia Julia, named after the family of Julius Caesar, and the Temple of the Deified Julius, an event followed by days of spectacular public games and banquets. He gave the Senate House an altar and statue of Victoria—a winged goddess personifying victory—decorated with Egyptian spoils. It was as if to say, writes Cassius Dio, that Octavian had received his political authority from a military victory.

Perhaps one of the Egyptian objects in the temple was a masterpiece of Greek painting showing Venus—Caesar's patron goddess and alleged ancestor—emerging from the ocean. In addition to the temple proper, the structure consisted of a rectangular platform that

was decorated with the prows of ships captured at Actium. They symbolized divine approval of the new order.

The victories at Actium and Alexandria did not create Imperial
Rome in and of themselves, but they gave Octavian the time and
money to do so. Even before Actium, he had been thinking about the
kind of government that he wanted. Now he worked out the details.
It was a long-term process, and one of trial and error.

Becoming Augustus

Having defeated Antony and Cleopatra, Octavian faced another great
challenge of a different sort—stabilizing Rome's political system after
a century of war and revolution. And he had to do so in a way that
would leave him in charge without exposing himself to the daggers
that brought down Caesar. The system that Octavian worked out
was, in name, a republic led by its first citizen, but, in fact, it was a
monarchy.

Octavian adapted traditional Roman constitutional procedures
to new circumstances. The Senate continued to exist, but it became
a sounding board and recruiting ground for reliable officers rather
than the ruling body of Rome. Magistrates continued to hold office
but were chosen by Octavian, not by popular election. Rome was governed by the rule of law, but Octavian was, for practical purposes,
above the law.

A year or so later, he decided to adopt a new dignity. On January
16, 27 BC, the Senate voted Octavian a new name. He already called
himself Gaius Julius Caesar, with the added titles of imperator and
son of a god. Now he received an additional honorific: revered one,
or Augustus. It is, of course, the name by which he is usually referred
to today, at least for his long reign from 27 BC to AD 14. At the time,
Augustus represented a novelty, not to say a shock. No Roman had
ever had such an appellation before.

The senator who proposed the motion was a man who knew

his way around titles: none other than Lucius Munatius Plancus. In 32 BC Plancus had defected to Octavian with news of Antony's will. He had been Antony's man before then, and a leading reveler at the court of Cleopatra in Alexandria. Now older and more sober, Plancus surely had received Octavian's approval for his motion.

Three days earlier, on January 13, Octavian had announced that he was stepping down from power, but everyone knew that was a mere show. He was only thirty-five and had many more years of rule in him. But the careful stage managing hints at how Augustus, as we will now call him, broke the cycle of war and violence.

Augustus asked the Senate to grant him the powers of a tribune—that is, the powers to propose legislation and exercise a veto. He also asked for supreme military power in both Rome and the provinces. The Senate agreed, as no doubt it had to, but it put Augustus's rule on a legal footing.

Augustus gained various political and military powers, but his standing in Rome never rested solely on his legal capacity. It was also a function of his authority—what the Romans called *auctoritas*, which meant not just authority but also prestige, respect, and the ability to inspire awe. Augustus had the fingertip feel for power that was typically Roman. He understood that successful regimes don't merely crush the opposition but coopt it. Accordingly, Augustus granted senators a degree of influence and honor. He and his successors, however, turned increasingly to a wealthy group that were just below the senators in authority, Roman knights, to serve as commanders and administrators. This did not please the Senate.

Nor did Augustus stay in the city of Rome. After returning from the civil wars in 29 BC, he spent another decade outside Italy on a series of military and political trips around the empire—logging more time abroad than any other emperor until Hadrian, who ruled AD 117 to 138. Although Augustus did visit the East, he never set foot in Egypt again. He was shrewd enough not to push his luck in a country that had, after all, preferred his enemies.

In theory, Rome was still a republic. Augustus was just a public official exercising enhanced powers at the request of SPQR: Senatus Populusque Romanus, the Senate and the Roman people. In practice, Augustus was a monarch, but the founder of the Roman Empire never called himself king, much less emperor, at least not in Rome. In the Greek-speaking East, Augustus was often called king, but he did not permit that appellation in the capital. Instead, in Rome he called himself by a variety of other titles, of which the most important were Caesar, Augustus, and Princeps, or First Man.

Our word *emperor* comes from the Latin *imperator*, meaning "victorious general." Augustus knew that the spirit of republican liberty still survived. So, having won supreme power, he masked it.

Augustus lived in a house on Rome's Palatine Hill. His successors would build splendid palaces there, but he lived in relatively modest circumstances—but only relatively so, as his estate did include such features as a Temple of Apollo. Previously a neighborhood for wealthy families, the Palatine was on its way to an imperial takeover. It became an exclusive site for the emperor and his courtiers. Still, when Augustus went down from the Palatine to the Forum to attend Senate meetings, he made sure to greet every member by name, without a prompter, and he didn't make them get up from their seats in his presence.

Augustus had achieved the ambitious agenda that he had set himself at age nineteen. He had all of the power and glory of Julius Caesar. But it took fifteen years to get it, and it came at a heavy price in blood and treasure. At least Augustus learned something in the process: how to build a lasting and stable peace.

He chose his advisors wisely. None did more to execute Augustus's vision than his old friend Marcus Agrippa. The architect of naval victories, Agrippa showed himself to be just as able a politician and diplomat. Both at home and abroad, he was a troubleshooter, a manager, a builder, and, when need be, an enforcer. He negotiated with senators and kings and sponsored major infrastructure programs.

Agrippa did not lack personal ambition, but he always put loyalty to Augustus first. The poet Horace called Agrippa "a cunning fox imitating a noble lion," a reference both to Agrippa's craftiness and his social climbing.

The Augustan Peace

Roman civil wars had a well-established pattern: first came the bloodshed, then came the settlement. But it was easier to win the war than to forge the peace, since few generals were as good at making peace as they were at waging war. Augustus was the exception. The cold-blooded killer grew with the job.

From 44 to 30 BC, he had fought, lied, cheated, and trampled on the law. It is estimated that he killed more than a hundred senators. Then, after defeating all his domestic enemies, Augustus dedicated himself to peace at home and limited military expansion against foreign—and never Roman—enemies. Still, however gentle he became, Augustus always remembered that his rule depended on his soldiers.

Victory at Actium meant peace. Augustus demobilized about half his legions. Egyptian wealth allowed him to buy land in Italy and around the empire for new colonies to settle his veterans. Then, when that wealth began to run out, after the year AD 6, he began to tax the rich. There were no more property confiscations to settle former soldiers, as there had been in 46, 45, and 41 BC. Augustus managed to resolve one of Rome's biggest causes of conflict: real estate. He reduced the size of the army from more than sixty legions to twenty-eight, yielding a total military, including light infantry and cavalry, of about three hundred thousand men.

He ended a century of civil war and laid the foundations of two hundred years of peace and prosperity: the famous Pax Romana, or "Roman Peace." Trade flourished in the Augustan peace. The cheapest way to transport goods was by sea. Thanks to Agrippa's victories, Rome ruled the waves, and piracy virtually disappeared. Rome represented a huge market for grain imports, but many other goods were traded as well. Stability and the security of Roman law encouraged money lending. A military drawdown took pressure off taxes. In short, conditions were ripe for good times.

No one knew then, but Actium was the last major naval battle fought in the Mediterranean for 350 years. Not until the Battle of the Hellespont in AD 324, which helped win control of the East for the western Roman emperor, Constantine I, was there another naval clash. Purists might point out that the Hellespont is a narrow strait off the Mediterranean, and so might postpone the date of the first major naval battle in that sea after Actium to AD 468. In that year, a Vandal fleet destroyed an eastern Roman armada in the Battle of Cape Bon (off the coast of Tunisia), thereby hastening the end of the western Roman Empire.

Augustus did not stop expansion—far from it. Romans expected their leaders to conquer new territory and thereby demonstrate the favor of the gods. Augustus carried out this responsibility with enthusiasm. As his favored poet, Virgil, wrote, Rome had a duty to achieve "empire without end." So, Augustus won new lands in Hispania and the northern Balkans, as well as annexing Egypt. A huge effort to conquer Germany as far east as the Elbe River ended in a military disaster late in Augustus's life, although the Romans were able to hold on to the left bank of the Rhine.

The Parthians Again

Before he accepted the challenge of war with Octavian in 32 BC, Antony had tried and failed to win a victory over Parthia. In the back of Antony's mind was the ambition of fulfilling Julius Caesar's unfinished agenda. Before he was assassinated, Caesar had planned to go to war against Parthia to avenge the massive defeat that the Romans suffered under Parthian hands in 53 BC.

Augustus had no intention of following in Antony's footsteps and risking failure on the Parthian front. Instead, he negotiated, although not without a show of force. Annexed by Antony, Armenia had used the chaos of the Actium War to regain its independence. Rome and Parthia competed for control of the kingdom. Augustus sent a Roman army into Armenia to place Rome's favored candidate on the throne of that border state. The Parthians had a candidate of their own, but they backed down. Rome succeeded in Armenia without bloodshed. Augustus probably agreed, in return, to withdraw support for a pretender to the Parthian throne who lived in exile in Rome.

There was one more part of the deal. In 20 BC Parthia agreed to return the multiple Roman legionary eagles and battle standards that had been captured in 53 BC, in the 41–40 BC invasion of the Roman East, and in 36 BC against Antony. The Parthians returned as well Roman prisoners of war, some of whom had spent more than thirty years in exile.

It was a great coup for Augustus. The Senate showered him with honors, most of which Augustus declined. He did, however, build a triumphal arch. It was either a new one or, if he, in fact, had erected an arch to commemorate Actium, a modification of that existing arch. The arch, which stood beside the Temple of the Deified Julius, had three bays, making it the first triple arch in Rome. On top stood a chariot carrying Augustus, the triumphator. On either side of him stood a Parthian, holding the restored standards.

Augustus, who had a sense of humor, might have imagined his former fellow triumvir and brother-in-law agonizing in the underworld, getting the news of the victory over Parthia. A decade after Antony's death, Octavian had finally carried out Antony's task and brought the captured standards back to Rome. At long last, the stain of dishonor had been erased. It was as if the books had finally been closed on one last piece of business from the bad old days of the triumvirs.

Augustus went further. Prophecies held that victory over the Parthians was a precondition for the establishment of a golden age. Now that success had been declared, Augustus held a magnificent celebration of a new age in 17 BC. The Ludi Saeculares, or Games Marking the Age, were a magnificent, two-week-long series of events, presided over by Augustus and Agrippa. The poet Horace wrote a hymn sung by a mixed choir of boys and girls. It was the kind of spectacular that might have elicited admiration even in Ptolemaic Alexandria.

August

In 8 BC the Senate and the people decided on a new honor for Augustus: they chose to name a month after him. In this, he followed in his adoptive father's footsteps, as Julius Caesar was the only other Roman to have a month renamed in his honor: the former Quintilis became Julius—our July. Now a similar distinction was given to his heir.

The assemblies of the Roman people and the tribunes who presided, once real powers in the state, were now largely ceremonial. Still, they let it be known that they wanted the month of September to be renamed Augustus, in honor of their ruler's birthday on September 23. Augustus himself, however, preferred the preceding month, the late-summer month of Sextilis. He noted that he had first been elected consul then and had won many brilliant victories in Sextilis. Anyone can have a birthday, he might have reasoned, but his civil and military achievements were unique. Besides, he might have preferred to place "his" month as close as possible to his father's month, in order to emphasize his own legitimacy. Finally, it might have occurred to Augustus that, in the heat of summer, people tend to work less and hence might pay more attention to a public occasion such as the name of the month. By September, when it starts to cool down, people return to their own occupations. As usual, Augustus looked after his public image, and, as usual, he got his way: Sextilis it was.

And so it came to pass. The month in which Augustus entered Alexandria, in which his enemies Antony and Cleopatra and his rival Caesarion all died, in which he announced the annexation of Egypt, and in which he celebrated his triple triumph a year later—that month became Augustus—our August. The decree of the Senate has been preserved:

> Since Imperator Caesar Augustus entered into his first consulship in the month of Sextilis, and celebrated three triumphs in the City of Rome, and the legions on the Janiculum Hill [outside Rome] followed him and entrusted themselves to his auspices, and since Egypt was given into the power of the Roman people in this month, and since this month brought an end to the civil wars, on account of these causes the month is and has been most propitious to the empire, the Senate has resolved to name this month Augustus.

Sextus Pacubius, a tribune of the people, proposed the law by which the People's Assembly made the change official.

City of Marble

In summer of the year AD 14, Augustus lay dying. He was traveling in southern Italy when he grew sick and took to his bed. He lay in a villa in the small provincial city of Nola. It was, ironically, the very house—indeed, the same room—where his father, Gaius Octavius, had died some seventy years before. It was as if the near-demigod who ruled the Roman world had dropped the mask and become mortal again. Neither Caesar nor Augustus nor Octavian, he was simply Octavius.

Whatever his name, in AD 14 he was the last surviving principal of the Actium War. Nearly seventy-seven years old, he had outlived them all. Antony, Cleopatra, and Caesarion had all died in 30 BC. Agrippa died in 12 BC. Octavia followed a year or so later, around age fifty-eight.

Now, at the end of his days, Augustus might have remembered his sister with love and affection. He had given Octavia a state funeral, a rare honor for a woman. Augustus ordered that her body lie in state in the Temple of the Deified Julius, and there the funeral was held. The location reminded the public that Octavia was Caesar's niece and that she, like her brother, descended from one of the city's most distinguished families. Augustus himself gave a eulogy. When Agrippa died, Augustus eulogized him as a man whose virtues everyone acknowledged. His words about Octavia are not recorded, but Augustus might have praised his sister as a paragon of motherhood. It was a central theme in the policy of renewed family values that he pursued in the decades after Actium. Gone were the naughty ways of his youth.

And what a mother Octavia was! After the deaths of Antony and Cleopatra, she welcomed their three surviving offspring into her home. She raised five children of her own to adulthood, four daughters and one son, including the two Antonias whom she had borne Mark Antony. Octavia also raised four of Antony's children by other women: not just his son Iullus Antonius, Antony's son by his third wife, Fulvia, but also Antony and Cleopatra's three children: Alexander Helios, Ptolemy Philadelphus, and Cleopatra Selene II. The boys died: one perhaps before the triumphs of 29 BC, another at some unknown time later. Selene lived and prospered.

With as many as nine children under her roof at one time, and with four of them the progeny of her ex-husband—three the products of his love affair with a woman with whom he had cheated on her—Octavia was practically a world's record holder in maternity. The process engendered ironic results. Three of her descendants by Antony became Roman emperors: her great-grandson, Gaius (better known as Caligula, r. 37–41), her grandson, Claudius (r. 41–54), and Nero (r. 54–68). The latter was Octavia's great-grandson on his father's side and great-great-grandson on his mother's side. As students of Imperial Rome know, Caligula and Nero were two of the empire's more notorious rulers, and Claudius, although he provided good government, was humiliated by his first wife and outmaneuvered by his second—she, in turn, another descendant of Octavia and Antony. Meanwhile, Cleopatra Selene had a glittering career.

Augustus arranged for her marriage to Juba II, a North African prince. As a child, Juba too had been brought to Rome to take part in a triumph—Julius Caesar's triumph over his father, Juba I, who had committed suicide, like Cleopatra. Juba II was raised in Augustus's household, not far from Cleopatra Selene. Augustus had them marry in 20 BC. He gave Juba control of the kingdom of Mauretania, the realm once ruled by Bogud, the man who lost Methone. Juba and Cleopatra governed from the city they renamed Caesarea (modern Cherchell, Algeria), which honored Augustus, but they had a son named Ptolemy, a reference to the dynasty of Cleopatra Selene's mother. Like her parents, Cleopatra Selene displayed leadership skills. She sponsored a building program, imported intellectuals and scholars from Alexandria, and issued coins in her own name. It was almost as if the lively court of Ptolemaic Alexandria had been brought back to life.

Cleopatra Selene died probably in 5 BC. She and her husband, who survived until AD 23, shared a mausoleum that still stands. Even in death, they gave a nod to the realities of power. A circular structure topped by a cone or pyramid, the Mauretanian mausoleum resembles the more famous Mausoleum of Augustus in Rome.

It was in the latter monument that the remains of Octavia were laid to rest. She was entombed beside her son Marcellus. By chance, Octavia's inscribed-marble epitaph still exists. It labels her simply as

OCTAVIA C F SOROR AUGUSTI
OCTAVIA, DAUGHTER OF GAIUS, SISTER OF AUGUSTUS

Octavia had once been worshipped as a goddess in Athens. Now she had a simpler appellation, but one no less suggestive of influence. Octavia had been the wife of Mark Antony, the triumvir, the ruler of half of the Roman world. Now he was gone, and, if not forgotten, he was cursed—all but a nonperson in the city where his discarded wife was deeply mourned. The warships of Actium might have created a Roman-Egyptian empire. Instead, they gave birth to the Augustan Age. In her own quiet way, Octavia had been the new era's midwife.

As he lay dying, perhaps Augustus took comfort from the thought that his remains too would repose in the mausoleum that bore his name. It was the most spectacular structure that he had built in Rome, but it was by no means the only one. He had undertaken a monumental building program that gave the city at last a series of public spaces worthy of an imperial capital. Gone was republican modesty, replaced with dynastic swagger. Augustus practically rebranded Rome's cityscape with his name and that of his family. They built temples, aqueducts, baths, theaters, porticoes, and parks. Augustus completed the renovation of the Senate House begun by Caesar; built a new rostra, or speakers' platform; and laid out a new Forum of Augustus to compete with the Forum of Caesar. The new forum included an enormous marble statue of the Guardian Spirit of Augustus (Genius Augusti), which resembled him in appearance. It was as if to say that, although Augustus did not call himself a king, he had no less authority than any monarch.

He erected in 9 BC a stunning Altar of Augustan Peace. A white marble structure painted originally in bright colors, the altar featured a sculpted relief of Augustus's family marching in dignified procession. It recalled the sculpture of the victory monument at Nicopolis (around 29 BC) as well as the Parthenon frieze of classical Athens (fifth century BC). But it was not only Athens whose image Augustus summoned up: it was Alexandria.

Everywhere one turned in Rome, there were reminders of Augustus's conquest of Egypt. He adorned the city with obelisks and images of Isis. Booty brought back to Rome included paintings, statues, gold and silver plates and vessels, cameos and scarabs, amulets, rings, and other jewelry. Augustan artwork included Egyptian motifs such as sphinxes, lotus flowers, crocodiles, hippopotami, and a stylized cobra crown. One prominent friend of Augustus displayed a statue of the sacred Egyptian Apis Bull in the gardens of his urban villa, while one of Agrippa's associates built himself a pyramid-shaped tomb on the edge of town.

The Augustan makeover produced a new Rome. Now, for the first time, it began to be known as the Eternal City. It was enough to justify one of Augustus's most memorable remarks, made on his deathbed: "I found a Rome of bricks; I leave to you one of marble." Thanks to Augustus, Rome no longer suffered by comparison to the splendid cityscape of Alexandria. Augustus had won. Yet before he passed into eternity on August 19, AD 14, Augustus might have given a thought to the queen whose city inspired the image of urban grandeur. With his taste for irony, Augustus might even have considered this: in spite of the rams of Actium, in spite of the swords that took Alexandria, and in spite of the bite of the asp, in the end, Cleopatra had come to Rome after all.

Acknowledgments

Writing a history book is hard work. It is a joy, by contrast, to take stock of those who helped you along the way and to say thank you.

Friends, colleagues, and students at several institutions, on three continents, were kind enough to share their knowledge and proficiency on matters large and small. I thank: Annetta Alexandridis, Darius Arya, Caitlin Barrett, Elizabeth Bartman, Colin Behrens, Bettina Bergmann, Nikki Bonanni, Peter Campbell, Robert Coates-Stephens, Simon Cotton, Tristan Daedalus, Craig and Jad Davis, Philip de Souza, Ertürk Durmus, Jason Feulner, Michael Fontaine, Bernard Frischer, Mikel Gago, Harry W. Greene, Sandra Greene, Matthew Guillot, Martha Haynes, John Hyland, Barbara Kellum, Thomas Kerch, Jeffrey Kline, Eric Kondratieff, Arthur Kover, Lynne Lancaster, Olga Litvak, Tamara Loos, Thomas Lucas, Daniel Meegan, Sturt Manning, Brook Manville, Ann Michel, Jake Nabel, Gary Ohls, Carl Oros, John Pollini, Eric Rebillard, Jeffrey Rusten, Daniel Schwarz, Matthew Sears, Aaron Taylor, Kostas Vergos, Karl Walling, Kevin Weddle, Peter Yao, Theo Zemek.

I was fortunate to have friends and colleagues read all or part of the draft manuscript. Their comments improved it greatly. The flaws, of course, remain my own. I thank: Maia Aron, John Arquilla, Philippe Boström, Serhan Güngör, David Guaspari, Adrienne Mayor, Gordon McCormick, Adam Mogelonsky, and Josiah Ober. In particular I would like to express my gratitude to William M. Murray, one of the great scholars of Actium, its monuments, and Hellenistic naval warfare, for generously sharing his expertise. I would also like to thank

Konstantinos Zachos, whose excavations at Nicopolis are reshaping our knowledge of Actium and its impact on Roman culture.

I owe a debt of gratitude to five great academic institutions for making this book possible—that fact alone is testimony to my good fortune. At Cornell University, I owe great thanks to the support and help of many colleagues, both faculty and staff, and students there, particularly in the Departments of Classics and History, and to the John M. Olin Library for its superb bibliographical resources. I am grateful to Cornell for granting me sabbatical leave to work on this project.

I could not have written this book without the gift of an academic year as a Distinguished Visiting Professor in the Department of Defense Analysis at the Naval Postgraduate School in Monterey, California. By making a pest of myself, I hope I managed to learn something about how war is fought. I would like to express my gratitude to both my colleagues and my students there.

The Hoover Institution of Stanford University named me first Visiting Fellow and then Corliss Page Dean Fellow. Hoover offers a remarkable intellectual environment for the study of history and of military affairs. I would like to thank in particular Director and Senior Fellow Condoleezza Rice and Senior Fellow Victor Davis Hanson. Among my many colleagues in Hoover's Working Group on the Role of Military History in Contemporary Conflict, I would like to thank David Berkey and Hy Rothstein.

The American Academy in Rome generously hosted me as a visiting scholar again in summer 2019, thereby providing access to key sites in Rome and to even more important conversations with expert scholars. Many productive hours in the Arthur and Janet C. Ross Library have made me better able to understand Rome's inexhaustible riches.

The American School of Classical Studies at Athens granted me the Heinrich Schliemann Fellowship for 1978–79. The late Colin N. Edmonson, a great educator, who was then Mellon Professor of Classical Studies at the School, led the trip that brought me and my fellow students to the site of Nicopolis in autumn 1978. There my interest in Actium began.

At Simon & Schuster, that superb editor Bob Bender once again worked his magic on a refractory draft. Johanna Li, his assistant, is both efficient and caring. Marketing Director Stephen Bedford is generous and wise. Phil Metcalf and Philip Bashe provided careful copyediting. I thank them and the entire team at Simon & Schuster.

Angela Baggetta is an excellent publicist. As for my literary agent, Cathy Hemming, she makes everything happen.

My wife, Marcia Mogelonsky, offered insight, support, and advice on matters big and small. I'm confident that she understands Cleopatra better than I do, and she probably has Antony's number as well.

My mother passed away as I was writing this book. My father passed away some years ago. Devoted grandparents, Diane and Aaron Strauss loved sharing the lives of our children, Michael and Sylvie. They would have been thrilled to see them continue to blossom and grow to adulthood, as Marcia and I have been blessed to do. I dedicate this book to my parents' memory.

A Note on Sources

What follows is a list of the most relevant works that I have consulted, almost all in English, for readers who would like additional information.

ANCIENT SOURCES

The following works are all available in various translations. They all appear in the Loeb Classical Library, published by Harvard University Press, which offers the Greek and Latin originals as well as translations. Most of them are available in English on the internet on such sites as LacusCurtius: Into the Roman World, http://penelope.uchicago.edu/Thayer/E/Roman/Texts/home.html; Livius.org: Articles on Ancient History, https://www.livius.org/; and Perseus Digital Library, www.perseus.tufts.edu. Many of these works are available in readable and accurate translations published by, for example, Oxford University Press and Penguin. I include below certain useful historical commentaries.

Augustus. *Res Gestae.*
Augustus, and Alison Cooley. *Res Gestae Divi Augusti: Text, Translation, and Commentary.* Cambridge: Cambridge University Press, 2009.
Carmen de Bello Actiaco.
Courtney, E., ed. *The Fragmentary Latin Poets.* Oxford: Clarendon Press, 1993, 334–40.
Cassius Dio. *Roman History*, especially books 49–51.
Reinhold, Meyer. *From Republic to Principate: An Historical Commentary on Cassius Dio's Roman History Books 49–52 (36–29 B.C.).* Atlanta: Scholars Press, 1987.
Cicero. *Philippics.*
Florus. *Epitome of Roman History*
Horace. *Epodes* 1, 9; *Ode* 1.37 ("Cleopatra Ode").
Josephus. *Against Apion.*
———. *Antiquities of the Jews.*
Livy (Titus Livius). *History of Rome.*
———. *Periochae* (summaries).
Nicolaus of Damascus. *Autobiography.*
———. *Life of Augustus.*

————. *The Life of Augustus and the Autobiography*. Edited by Mark Toher. Cambridge: Cambridge University Press, 2016.

Orosius. *Against the Pagans*.

Pliny. *Natural History*.

Plutarch. *Life of Antony*.

Plutarch. *Life of Antony*. Edited by C. B. R. Pelling. Cambridge: Cambridge University Press, 1988.

Porphyry. *On Abstinence*.

Propertius, Sextus. *Elegies,* 2.15; 1; 3.11; 4.6.

Strabo. *Geography*.

Suetonius Tranquillus, C. *Life of Augustus*.

————. *Life of Augustus = Vita Divi Augusti*. Translated with introduction and historical commentary by D. Wardle. Oxford: Oxford University Press, 2014.

Velleius Paterculus. *The Roman History*.

————. *The Caesarian and Augustan Narrative (2.41–93)*. Edited by A. J. Woodman. Cambridge: Cambridge University Press, 1983.

Virgil. *Aeneid,* bk. 8.

————. *Eclogue* 6.

REFERENCE

Hornblower, Simon, Anthony Spawforth, and Esther Eidinow. *The Oxford Classical Dictionary*. 4th ed. Oxford: Oxford University Press, 2012.

Hubert Cancik and Helmut Schneider, eds.; English ed., Christine F. Salazar and David E. Orton, eds. *Brill's New Pauly: Encyclopaedia of the Ancient World*. Boston: Brill, 2002–2010. The publisher offers an excellent online edition.

"Mantis: A Numismatic Technologies Integration Service." This database, which includes ancient coins from the extensive collection of the American Numismatic Society, can be accessed online at http://numismatics.org/search/.

"Orbis: The Stanford Geospatial Network of the Ancient World." Stanford University Libraries. http://orbis.stanford.edu.

Talbert, Richard J. A., ed. *The Barrington Atlas of the Ancient Greco-Roman World*. Princeton, NJ: Princeton University Press, 2000. This book is also available as an app.

INTRODUCTORY

Green, Peter. *Alexander to Actium: An Essay on the Historical Evolution of the Hellenistic Age*. Berkeley: University of California Press, 1990.

Osgood, Josiah. *Caesar's Legacy: Civil War and the Emergence of the Roman Empire*. Cambridge: Cambridge University Press, 2006.

Pelling, Christopher. "The Triumviral Period." In *The Cambridge Ancient History,* 2nd ed., vol. X, The Augustan Empire, 43 B.C.–A.D. 69, edited by Alan K.

Bowman, Edward Champlin, and A. W. Lintott. Cambridge: Cambridge University Press, 1996: 1–69.

Strauss, Barry. *The Death of Caesar: the Story of History's Most Famous Assassination*. New York: Simon & Schuster, 2015.

Syme, Ronald. *The Roman Revolution*. Oxford: Oxford University Press, 2002. First published 1939 by Clarendon Press (Oxford, UK).

CLEOPATRA

Burstein, Stanley Mayer. *The Reign of Cleopatra*. Westport, CT: Greenwood Press, 2004.

Chauveau, M. *Egypt in the Age of Cleopatra*. Translated by David Lorton. Ithaca, NY: Cornell University Press, 2000.

Gentili, Giovanni. *Cleopatra: Roma e l'Incantesimo Dell'Egitto*. Milano, It. Skira, 2013.

Grant, Michael. *Cleopatra*. New York: Simon & Schuster, 1972.

Haley, Shelley P. "Black Feminist Thought and Classics: Re-membering, Re-claiming, Re-empowering." In *Feminist Theory and the Classics*, edited by Nancy Sorkin and Amy Richlin. New York: Routledge, 1993, 23–43.

Hughes-Hallett, Lucy. *Cleopatra: Histories, Dreams and Distortions*. New York: Harper & Row, 1990.

Jones, Prudence J. *Cleopatra: a Sourcebook*. Norman, OK: University of Oklahoma Press, 2006.

———. "Cleopatra's Cocktail," *Classical World* 103, no. 2 (2010): 207–20.

Kleiner, Diana E. E. *Cleopatra and Rome*. Cambridge, MA: Belknap Press of Harvard University Press, 2005.

Mayor, Adrienne. "Cleopatra & Antony Go Fishing." Wonders & Marvels. https://www.wondersandmarvels.com/2014/06/cleopatra-and-Antony-go-fishing.html.

Preston, Diana. *Cleopatra & Antony: Power, Love, and Politics in the Ancient World*. New York: Walker, 2009.

Roller, Duane W. *Cleopatra: A Biography*. Oxford: Oxford University Press, 2010.

Schiff, Stacy. *Cleopatra: A Life*. New York: Little, Brown, 2010.

Tarn, W. W., "Alexander Helios and the Golden Age." *Journal of Roman Studies* 22, no. 2 (1932): 135–60.

Tsoucalas, Gregory, and Marcos Sgantzos. "The Death of Cleopatra: Suicide by Snakebite or Poisoned by Her Enemies?" Chap. 2 in *Toxicology in Antiquity*. Vol. 1, edited by Philip Wexler. History of Toxicology and Environmental Health. Waltham, MA: Academic Press, 2014: 11–20.

Tyldesley, Joyce A. *Cleopatra: Last Queen of Egypt*. New York: Basic Books, 2008.

Walker, Susan, and Peter Higgs, eds. *Cleopatra of Egypt: From History to Myth*. London: British Museum, 2001.

ANTONY

Carbone, Lucia. "Mark Antony: Rogue with Monetary Insight." *ANS* online, no. 3 (2017): 7–19.

Fraser, P. M. "Mark Antony in Alexandria: A Note." *Journal of Roman Studies* 47, nos. 1/2 (1957): 71–73.

Goldsworthy, Adrian Keith. *Antony and Cleopatra.* New Haven, CT: Yale University Press, 2010.

Huzar, Eleanor Goltz. *Mark Antony, A Biography.* Minneapolis: University of Minnesota Press, 1978.

Jones, Kenneth R. "Marcus Antonius' Median War and the Dynastic Politics of the Near East." In *Arsacids, Romans, and Local Elites: Cross-Cultural Interactions of the Parthian Empire,* edited by Jason Schlude and Benjamin Rubin. Oxford: Oxbow Books, 2017, 51–63.

Duane W. Roller, "The Lost Building Program of Marcus Antonius," *L'Antiquité Classique* 76 (2007): 87–98.

Rossi, Ruggero F. *Marco Antonio Nella Lotta Politica Della Tarda Repubblica Romana.* Trieste, It., 1959.

Schieber, A. S. "Anthony and Parthia." *Rivista storica dell'Antichità* 9 (1979): 105–24.

Scott, Kenneth. "Octavian's Propaganda and Antony's De Sua Ebrietate." *Classical Philology* 24, no. 2 (1929): 133–41.

Southern, Pat. *Mark Antony: A Life.* Stroud, UK: Tempus, 1998.

Strauss, Barry S., and Josiah Ober. "Mark Antony: The Man Who Would Be Caesar," in *The Anatomy of Error: Ancient Military Disasters and Their Lessons for Modern Strategists.* New York: St. Martin's Press, 1990.

Weigall, Arthur E. P. Brome. *The Life and Times of Marc Antony.* Garden City, NY: Garden City, 1931.

OCTAVIA

Dixon, Suzanne. "A Family Business: Women's Role in Patronage and Politics at Rome: 80–44 B.C." *Classica et Mediaevalia* 34 (1983): 104.

García Vivas, Gustavo. *Octavia Contra Cleopatra. El Papel De La Mujer En La Propaganda Política Del Triunvirato. 44–30 A. C.* Madrid: Liceus Ediciones, 2013.

Kellum, Barbara. "Representations and Re-Presentations of the Battle of Actium." In *Citizens of Discord: Rome and Its Civil Wars,* edited by Brian Breed, Cynthia Damon, and Andreola Rossi. Oxford: Oxford University Press, 2010, 187–202.

Moore, Katrina. "Octavia Minor and the Transition from Republic to Empire." Master's thesis, Clemson University, 2017. https://tigerprint.clemson.edu/all_theses/2738.

Osgood, Josiah. *Turia: A Roman Woman's Civil War.* Oxford: Oxford University Press, 2014.

Raubitschek, Antony E. "Octavia's Deification at Athens." TAPhA 77 (1946): 146–50.

Singer, Mary White. "Octavia's Mediation at Tarentum." *Classical Journal* 43, no. 3 (1947): 173–78.

———. "The Problem of Octavia Minor and Octavia Maior." *Transactions of the American Philological Association* 79 (1948): 268–74.

Ziogas, Ioannis. "Singing for Octavia: Vergil's *Life* and Marcellus's Death." *Harvard Studies in Classical Philology* 109 (2018): 429–81.

OCTAVIAN

Bowersock, G. W. *Augustus and the Greek World.* Oxford: Clarendon Press, 1965.

Everitt, Anthony. *Augustus: The Life of Rome's First Emperor.* New York: Random House, 2006.

Gaddis, John Lewis. *On Grand Strategy.* New York: Penguin Press, 2018, 69–91.

Goldsworthy, Adrian Keith. *Augustus: First Emperor of Rome.* New Haven, CT: Yale University Press, 2014.

Galinsky, Karl. *Augustus: Introduction to the Life of an Emperor.* New York: Cambridge University Press, 2012.

Holmes, T. Rice. *The Architect of the Roman Empire.* Oxford: Clarendon Press, 1928.

Smith, Christopher John, Anton Powell, and Tim Cornell. *The Lost Memoirs of Augustus and the Development of Roman Autobiography.* Swansea, Wales: Classical Press of Wales, 2009.

Southern, Pat. *Augustus.* 2nd ed. Abingdon, UK: Routledge, 2014.

AGRIPPA

Powell, Lindsay. *Marcus Agrippa: Right-Hand Man of Caesar Augustus.* Barnsley, UK: Pen & Sword Books, 2015.

Reinhold, Meyer. *Marcus Agrippa: A Biography.* Ed. anastatica. Roma: "L'Erma" di Bretschneider, 1965.

Roddaz, Jean-Michel. *Marcus Agrippa.* Rome: École française de Rome, 1984.

Wright, F. A. *Marcus Agrippa: Organizer of Victory.* London: G. Routledge & Sons, 1937.

THE YEARS OF THE TRIUMVIRATE

Berdowski, P. *Res Gestae Neptuni Filii: Sextus Pompeius I Rzymskie Wojny Domowe.* Rzeszów, Pol.: Wydawnictwo Uniwersytetu Rzeszowskiego, 2015. English summary, 397–404.

Delia, Diana. "Fulvia Reconsidered." In *Women's History and Ancient History,* edited by Sarah B. Pomeroy. Chapel Hill: University of North Carolina Press, 1991, 197–217.

Lange, Carsten Hjort. "Civil War and the (Almost) Forgotten Pact of Brundisium." In *The Triumviral Period: Civil War, Political Crisis, and Socioeconomic Transformations,* edited by Francisco Pina Polo. Zaragoza, Spain: Prensas de la Universidad de Zaragoza, 2020, 139–41.

———. *Res Publica Constituta: Actium, Apollo, and the Accomplishment of the Triumviral Assignment.* Leiden, Neth.: Brill, 2009.

Osgood, Josiah. *Caesar's Legacy: Civil War and the Emergence of the Roman Empire.* Cambridge: Cambridge University Press, 2006.

———.*Turia: A Roman Woman's Civil War.* Oxford: Oxford University Press, 2014.

Powell, Anton, Kathryn Welch, and Alain M. Gowing. *Sextus Pompeius.* Swansea, Wales: Classical Press of Wales, 2002.

Rich, John. "Warlords and the Roman Republic." In *War, Warlords and Interstate Relations in the Ancient Mediterranean,* edited by T. Ñaco del Hoyo and F. López Sánchez. Boston: Brill, 2018, 284–86.

Scott, Kenneth. "The Political Propaganda of 44–30 B.C." *Memoirs of the American Academy in Rome* 11 (1933): 7–49.

Strauss, Barry. "Sextus Pompeius and the Strategy and Tactics of Ancient Sea Power." In *Rector maris. Sextus Pompeius und das Meer,* edited by Laura Kersten and Christian Wendt. Bonn, Ger.: Habelt (Antiquitas I, vol. 74), 2020: 121–40.

Welch, Kathryn. *Magnus Pompeius: Sextus Pompeius and the Transformation of the Roman Republic.* Swansea, Wales: Classical Press of Wales, 2012.

BOGUD AND METHONE

Andrews, Kevin. *Castles of the Morea.* Princeton, NJ: American School of Classical Studies at Athens, 1953.

Brizzi, Giovanni. "La Battaglia d'Azio." In Gentili, *Cleopatra*, 19–22.

Camps, G. "Bogud," *Encyclopédie berbère*, vol. 10. Aix-en-Provence, France: EDISUD, 1991: 1557–58.

Lawrence, A. W. *Greek Aims in Fortification.* Oxford: Clarendon Press, 1979.

Roller, Duane W. *The World of Juba II and Kleopatra Selene: Royal Scholarship on Rome's African Frontier.* New York: Routledge, 2003.

ACTIUM, THE BATTLE

Carter, John. *The Battle of Actium.* London: Hamish Hamilton, 1970.

Fratantuono, Lee. *The Battle of Actium 31 BC: War for the World.* Barnsley, UK: Pen & Sword Books, 2016.

Kromayer, J. "Actium: Ein Epilog." *Hermes* 68 (1933): 361–83.

———. "Kleine Forschungen zur Geschichte des Zweiten Triumvirats. VII. Der Feldzug von Actium und der sogenannte Verrath der Cleopatra." *Hermes* 34, no. 1 (1899): 1–54.

Lange, Carsten Hjorst. "The Battle of Actium: A Reconsideration." *Classical Quarterly* 61, no. 2 (2011): 608–23.

Leroux, J. "Les problems stratégiques de la bataille d'Actium." *Recherches de Philologie et de Linguistique* 2 (1968): 29–37, 55.

Murray, William M. "Reconsidering the Battle of Actium—Again." In *Oikistes: Studies in Constitutions, Colonies, and Military Power in the Ancient World. Offered in Honor of A. J. Graham,* edited by Vanessa B. Gorman and Eric W. Robinson. Leiden, Neth.: Brill, 2002, 339–60.

Richardson, G. W. "Actium." *Journal of Roman Studies* 27, no. 2 (1937): 153–64.

Sheppard, Si. *Actium 31 BC: Downfall of Antony and Cleopatra.* Oxford, UK: Osprey Publishing, 2009.

Tarn, W. W. "The Battle of Actium." *Journal of Roman Studies* 21 (1931): 173–99.

ACTIUM, THE SITE AND THE MONUMENTS

Murray, William M. "The Dedication Inscription." In Konstantinos Zachos, ed. *The Victory Monument of Augustus at Nicopolis.* Athens: Athens Archaeological Society, forthcoming.

—————. "The Rostral Display on the Podium's Façade." Ibid.

Murray, William M., and Photios M. Petsas. *Octavian's Campsite Memorial for the Actian War.* Philadelphia: American Philosophical Society, 1989.

Zachos, Konstantinos. *An Archaeological Guide to Nicopolis. Rambling Through the Historical, Sacred, and Civic Landscape.* Trans. Deborah Brown. Monuments of Nicopolis 10. Athens: DIPCA-Scientific Committee of Nicopolis, 2015.

—————. "Excavations at the Actian Tropaeum at Nicopolis, A Preliminary Report." In *Foundation and Destruction, Nikopolis and Northwestern Greece: the Archaeological Evidence for the City Destructions, the Foundation of Nikopolis and the Synoecism,* edited by Jacob Isager. Athens: Danish Institute at Athens, 2001, 29–41.

—————. *To Mnēmeio tou Oktavianou Augoustou stē Nikopolē—To Tropaio tēs Naumachias tou Aktiou.* Athens: Hypourgeio Politismou, 2001.

—————. "The *Tropaeum* of the Sea-Battle of Actium at Nikopolis: Interim Report." *Journal of Roman Archaeology* 16 (2003): 64–92.

ANCIENT SHIPS AND NAVAL WARFARE

Belfiglio, Valentine J. *A Study of Ancient Roman Amphibious and Offensive Sea-Ground Task Force Operations.* Lewiston, NY: Edward Mellen Press, 2001.

Beresford, James. *The Ancient Sailing Season.* Leiden, Neth.: Brill, 2013.

Callahan, Harold Augustin. *The Sky and the Sailor: A History of Celestial Navigation.* New York: Harper and Brothers, 1952, 10–18.

Casson, Lionel. *Ships and Seamanship in the Ancient World.* Princeton, NJ: Princeton University Press, 1971.

De Souza, Philip. *Piracy in the Graeco-Roman World.* Cambridge: Cambridge University Press, 1999.

Kromayer, J. "Die Entwickelung der römischen Flotte vom Seeräuberkriege des Pompeius bis zur Schlacht von Actium." *Philologus* 56.JG (December 1897): 458–466.

Morrison, J. F., and J. S. Coates. *Greek and Roman Oared Warships, 399–30 BC.* Oxford, UK: Oxbow Books, 2016. First published 1996 by Oxbow Books, Oxford: UK.

Morton, Jamie. *The Role of the Physical Environment in Ancient Greek Seafaring.* Leiden, Neth.: Brill, 2001.

Murray, William M. *The Age of Titans: the Rise and Fall of the Great Hellenistic Navies.* New York: Oxford University Press, 2012.

Pitassi, Michael. *The Navies of Rome.* Woodbridge, UK: Boydell, 2009.

Rodgers, William Ledyard. *Greek and Roman Naval Warfare: A Study of Strategy, Tactics, and Ship Design from Salamis (480 B.C.) to Actium (31 B.C.).* Annapolis, MD: United States Naval Institute, 1937.

Starr, Chester G. *The Influence of Seapower on Ancient History.* New York: Oxford University Press, 1989.

———. *The Roman Imperial Navy: 31 B.C.–A.D. 324.* Ithaca, NY: Cornell University Press, 1941.

Taylor, E. G. R. *The Haven-Finding Art: A History of Navigation from Odysseus to Captain Cook.* New York: Abelard-Schuman, 1957.

Thiel, J. H. *Studies on the History of Roman Sea-Power in Republican Times.* Amsterdam: North-Holland (N. v. Noord-hollandsche uitgevers mij.), 1946.

ROMAN ARMY

Austin, N. J. E., and N. B. Rankov. *Exploratio: Military and Political Intelligence in the Roman World.* New York: Routledge, 1995.

Gilliver, Catherine, Adrian Keith Goldsworthy, and Michael Whitby. *Rome at War.* Oxford, UK: Osprey, 2005.

Goldsworthy, Adrian Keith, and John Keegan. *Roman Warfare.* New York: Smithsonian Books/Collins, 2005.

Keppie, L. J. F. *Colonisation and Veteran Settlement in Italy, 47–14 B.C.* London: British School at Rome, 1983.

———. *The Making of the Roman Army: From Republic to Empire.* Totowa, NJ: Barnes & Noble Books, 1984.

———. "Mark Antony's Legions." In *Legions and Veterans: Roman Army Papers 1971–2000.* Stuttgart, Ger.: Franz Steiner Verlag, 2000, 74–96.

———. "A Note on the Title Actiacus." In *Legions and Veterans*, 97–98. [=*Classical Review* 21, no. 3 (1971): 329–30.]

Roth, Jonathan P. *The Logistics of the Roman Army at War (264 B.C.–A.D. 235).* Leiden, Neth.: Brill, 1999.

AFTER ACTIUM

Beard, Mary. *The Roman Triumph*. Cambridge, MA: Belknap Press of Harvard University Press, 2007.

Gray-Fow, Michael. "What to Do with Caesarion?," *Greece & Rome* 61, no. 1 (2014): 38–67.

Gurval, Robert Alan. *Actium and Augustus: The Politics and Emotions of Civil War.* Ann Arbor: University of Michigan Press, 1995.

Ober, Josiah. "Not by a Nose: The Triumph of Antony and Cleopatra at Actium, 31 B.C." In *What If 2: Eminent Historians Imagine What Might Have Been,* edited by Robert Cowley. New York: G. P. Putnam's Sons, 2001, 23–47.

Östenberg, Ida. *Staging the World: Spoils, Captives, and Representations in the Roman Triumphal Procession*. Oxford: Oxford University Press, 2009.

Zanker, Paul. *The Power of Images in the Age of Augustus.* Ann Arbor: University of Michigan Press, 1988.

Notes

Prologue

3 *The Victorious General [Imperator] Caesar*: William M. Murray, "The Dedication Inscription," in Konstantinos Zachos, ed. *The Victory Monument of Augustus at Nicopolis* (Athens: Athens Archaeological Society, forthcoming), esp. 21–22; William M. Murray and Photios M. Petsas, *Octavian's Campsite Memorial for the Actian War* (Philadelphia: American Philosophical Society, 1989), 62–76; Konstantinos Zachos, *An Archaeological Guide to Nicopolis. Rambling Through the Historical, Sacred, and Civic Landscape*, Monuments of Nicopolis 10, trans. Deborah Brown (Athens: DIPCA–Scientific Committee of Nicopolis, 2015), 65.

4 *He called it Victory City, or, in Greek, Nicopolis*: The official name was Actia Nicopolis—"Victory City of Actium"—a Greek-Latin hybrid name.

4 *"I propose to write that history myself"*: Winston S. Churchill, "Foreign Affairs" (debate in the House of Commons, January 23, 1948), transcript available at Hansard 1803–2005, accessed April 11, 2021, https://api.parliament .uk/historic-hansard/commons/1948/jan/23/foreign-affairs#S5CV0446P0 _19480123_HOC_99.

Chapter I: The Road to Philippi

12 *suffered a miscarriage*: Cicero, *Letters to Atticus*, 14.20.2; see, for comparison, Joyce Tyldesley, *Cleopatra: Last Queen of Egypt* (New York: Basic Books, 2008), 107–8.

17 *Antony who offered Caesar the crown*: Technically he offered him a diadem, or fillet—that is, a ribbon denoting royalty—rather than a crown, since, unlike modern monarchs, kings in the Greco-Roman world wore those ribbons and not crowns.

17 *At a Senate meeting on the Ides of March*: On the assassination of Julius Caesar, see my *The Death of Caesar: The Story of History's Most Famous Assassination* (New York: Simon & Schuster), 2015.

19 *his great-grandmother and grandmother, who together gave detailed evidence in court*: Possibly it was his great-aunt and not his grandmother who gave that testimony.

21 *a boy who owed everything to his name*: o puer, qui omnia nomini debes, Cicero, *Philippics,* 13.24.

22 *down to and including moderate drinking*: C. Suetonius Tranquillus, *Life of Augustus,* 77. See the commentary by D. Wardle in Suetonius, *Life of Augustus (Vita Divi Augusti),* ed. D. Wardle (Oxford: Oxford University Press, 2014), 468.

22 *suspicion has fallen on him for poisoning the consuls*: Suetonius, *Augustus*, 11.

24 *A "slight, unmeritable man," Shakespeare's Antony calls Lepidus*: William Shakespeare, *Julius Caesar,* act 4, scene 1, lines 12–13: "a slight, unmeritable man / Meet to be sent on errands."

24 *Gaius Asinius Pollio*: Velleius Paterculus, *The Roman History,* 2.86.3.

25 *Either they would free the Roman people, Brutus wrote*: Plutarch (Lucius Mestrius Plutarchus), *Brutus*, 29.9.

25 *a coin commemorating the assassination*: "Silver Denarius, Uncertain Value, 43 B.C.–42 B.C. 1944.100.4554," American Numismatic Society online, accessed April 11, 2021, http://numismatics.org/collection/1944.100.4554.

25 *One of the few gold versions sold in 2020*: "Julius Caesar 'Assassination Coin' Sets World Record of Nearly $4.2 Million," ArtDaily, accessed April 11, 2021, https://artdaily.cc/news/129649/Julius-Caesar--assassination-coin--sets -world-record-of-nearly--4-2-million.

26 *the noblest Roman of them all*: Shakespeare, *Julius Caesar,* act 5, scene 5, line 73.

Chapter 2: The Commander and the Queen

29 *verses that Octavian wrote later*: Martial (Marcus Valerius Martialis), *Epigrams*, 11.20.

30 *Pompey (Gnaeus Pompeius Magnus, that is, "Pompey the Great"), for example, modeled his African triumph of 79 BC on Dionysus's mythical Indian triumph*: Duane W. Roller, *Cleopatra: A Biography* (Oxford: Oxford University Press, 2010), 116.

31 *"The barge she sat in . . . And what they undid did"*: William Shakespeare, *Antony and Cleopatra,* act 1, scene 2, lines 196–210.

31 *Plutarch's* Antony: Plutarch, *Life of Antony*, 26.1–2; Plutarch (Lucius Mestrius Plutarchus), *Plutarch's Lives*, vol. 9, *Demetrius and Antony. Pyrrhus and Caius Marius,* trans. Bernadotte Perrin (London: W. Heinemann, 1920), 193–95.

31 *"Aphrodite had come to make merry with Dionysus for the good of Asia"*: Ibid., 26.5; ibid., 195, modified.

32 *She then turned down Antony's dinner invitation*: Plutarch, *Antony*, 26.3–4; see, for comparison, Shakespeare, *Antony and Cleopatra*, act 2, scene 2, lines 225–32.

32 *whether she was killed at Cleopatra's behest or Antony's is debatable*: Flavius Josephus, *Antiquities of the Jews*, 15.4.1, and *Against Apion*, 2.5; Appian of Alexandria, *Civil Wars,* 5.9; Lucius Cassius Dio, *Roman History*, 48.24.2. The sources contain contradictions and are biased against Cleopatra.

32 *ride a horse and hunt*: Plutarch, *Antony*, 29.1.

34 *"Age cannot wither her"*: Shakespeare, *Antony and Cleopatra*, act 2, scene 2, line 240.

35 *the combination of Cleopatra's voice, appearance, and character proved charming*: Plutarch, *Antony,* 27, see, for comparison, 25.4–5; Cassius Dio, *Roman History*, 42.34.4–6.

35 *on one coin of this era, a necklace is visible*: "Silver Tetradrachm of Cleopatra VII of Egypt/Mark Antony/Cleopatra VII of Egypt, Antioch, 36 BC. 1977.158.621," American Numismatic Society online, accessed April 11, 2021, http://numismatics.org/collection/1977.158.621.

35 *On some coins, she has rolls of fat on her neck*: "Bronze 80 drachm of Cleopatra VII of Egypt, Alexandreia, 51 BC–29 BC. 1941.131.1158," American Numismatic Society online, accessed April 11, 2021, http://numismatics.org /collection/1941.131.1158.

35 *This Cleopatra is generally attractive*: Bronze 80 drachm of Cleopatra VII of Egypt, Alexandreia, 51 BC–29 BC. 1944.100.75442," American Numismatic Society online, accessed April 11, 2021, http://numismatics.org/collection /1944.100.75442.

36 *the reverse of the coin illustrates an eagle*: Susan Walker and Peter Higgs, *Cleopatra of Egypt: From History to Myth* (London: British Museum, 2001), catalog no. 179, p. 177; silver coin: catalog no. 220, p. 234.

36 *this Cleopatra appears massive, stiff, and older*: "Silver Tetradrachm of Antony and Cleopatra, Antioch, 36 BC. 1967.152.567," American Numismatic Society online, accessed April 11, 2021, http://numismatics.org/collection/1967 .152.567.

36 *An inscription names her as "Cleopatra Thea"*: "Silver Tetradrachm of Antony and Cleopatra, Antioch, 36 BC. 1967.152.567," American Numismatic Society online, accessed April 11, 2021, http://numismatics.org/collection/1944 .100.65512.

37 *There is good reason to think Cleopatra's mother was half Egyptian*: Or she might be one quarter Egyptian, but that seems less likely, given (a) the degree to which Cleopatra emphasized the Egyptian language and culture and (b) the honor paid to an Egyptian priestly family by Cleopatra's daughter. For the complex and ingenious argument, see Roller, *Cleopatra,* 165–66. On Cleopatra's race, see also Shelley P. Haley, "Black Feminist Thought and Classics: Re-membering, Re-claiming, Re-empowering," in *Feminist Theory and the Classics*, ed. Nancy Sorkin Rabinowitz and Amy Richlin (New York: Routledge, 1993), 23–43.

37 *he rolled out the various Greco-Roman stereotypes of eastern decadence*: Horace, *Ode* 1.37.7, 9–10, 12,13,14. The poets Horace (Quintus Horatius Flaccus) and Sextus Propertius represent Octavian's interpretation of Antony's relationship with Cleopatra: Kenneth Scott, "The Political Propaganda of 44–30 B.C.," *Memoirs of the American Academy in Rome* 11 (1933): 49.

37 *He accused her of corrupting Antony*: Cassius Dio, *Roman History*, 50.1, 3, 5, 24–25; Horace, *Epode*, 9.11–16, and *Ode*, 1.37.7.12,13,14.

37   *Octavian called her Egyptian*: For example, see Ovid (Publius Ovidius Naso), *Metamorphoses,* 15.827; Cassius Dio, *Roman History*, 50.26.2.

37   *She enslaved him*: Horace, *Epodes*, 9.12.

37   *bewitched him*: Propertius, *Elegies,* 2.16.39–40, 4.6.21–22.

37   *softened him*: Horace, *Epodes*, 9.12.

37   *corrupted him with sensual passions*: Josephus, *Against Apion,* 2.59.

37   *and with foreign customs*: Cassius Dio, *Roman History,* 50.25.3.

37   *turned him against his fatherland and his friends*: Josephus, *Against Apion,* 2.59.

37   *disgraced his navy by her feminine presence*: Propertius, *Elegies,* 4.6.21–22.

37   *gave orders to his soldiers*: scholiast on Virgil (Publius Vergilius Maro), *Aeneid,* 8.696.

37   *and talked him into surrendering the Roman Empire*: Florus, *Epitome of Roman History*, 21.3.11.

38   *medieval Arab historians*: These include al-Masudi and (Agapius) Mahbub ibn Qustantin. See Okasha El- Daly, *Egyptology: The Missing Millennium, Ancient Egypt in Medieval Arabic Writings* (London: UCL Press, 2005), 121–23, 130–37.

38   *Greek tradition, too*: Philostratus (Lucius Flavius Philostratus), *Lives of the Sophists,* 1.5.

38   *seven languages*: Plutarch, *Antony,* 27.4–5.

39   *allowed Cleopatra to give his name to the child*: Suetonius, *Julius Caesar,* 52.1.

40   *We do not know if Caesar had illegitimate children*: See Ronald Syme, "No Son for Caesar?," *Historia: Zeitschrift für Alte Geschichte*, 29, no. 4 (1980): 422–37.

40   *published a pamphlet*: Arnaldo Momigliano, Theodore John Cadoux, and Ernst Badian, "Oppius," in Simon Hornblower, Anthony Spawforth, and Esther Eidinow, eds.,*The Oxford Classical Dictionary*, 4th ed. (Oxford: Oxford University Press, 2012).

40   *Plutarch expresses doubts about Oppius's reliability*: Plutarch, *Pompey*, 10.5.

40   *Other ancient writers also denied Caesar's paternity*: Nicolaus of Damascus, *Life of Augustus*, 68; Cassius Dio, *Roman History,* 47.31.5.

40   *Antony got up before the Senate in Rome and affirmed*: Suetonius, *Caesar*, 52.2.

41   *"Imperator, hand over your fishing rod"*: Plutarch, *Antony*, 29.5–7; Adrienne Mayor, "Cleopatra & Antony Go Fishing," Wonders & Marvels, accessed April, 11, 2021, http://www.wondersandmarvels.com/2014/06/cleopatra-and-Antony-go-fishing.html.

41   *Cleopatra once bet him that she could put on the most expensive banquet ever*: Pliny the Elder, *Natural History,* 9.119–21.

41   *Modern experiments show*: Prudence J. Jones, "Cleopatra's Cocktail," *Classical World* 103, no. 2 (2010): 207–20.

42   *He regales his readers with gossip*: Plutarch, *Antony*, 29.

43   *"It's time to die:"* Suetonius, *Augustus*, 15.1.

43   *"Make haste slowly"*: Ibid., 25.4.

Chapter 3: Three Treaties and a Marriage

46 *Judging by his coin image, Ahenobarbus was a hard man*: Reference "Filters," American Numismatic Society online, accessed April 11, 2021, http://numismatics.org/search/results?q=year_num%3A%5B-50+TO+-30%5D+AND+domitius+ahenobarbus+AND+department_facet%3A%22Roman%22&lang=en.

47 *Octavian, who had a reputation for playing dice*: Suetonius, *Augustus* 70.2; Plutarch, *Antony,* 33.2–3.

49 *the information that Antony was a widower probably reached Octavia later*: Appian, *Civil Wars*, 5.59.

50 *Marcellus remained with his faction after the dictator's assassination in 44 BC*: Nicolaus, *Life of Augustus,* 28; see Nicolaus, *The Life of Augustus and the Autobiography*, ed. Mark Toher (Cambridge: Cambridge University Press, 2016), 214–15.

50 *Octavia and her mother were in Rome*: Appian, *Civil Wars*, 3.91–92.

50 *career advice from his mother*: Ibid., 3.14; Nicolaus, *Augustus*, 52–54.

51 *excessively fond of his sister*: Plutarch, *Antony*, 31.2.

51 *Octavia involved in two mediation efforts*: Appian, *Civil Wars,* 4.32–34.

51 *many people felt that Octavia would be a good influence*: Plutarch, *Antony,* 31.4–5.

51 *"a treacherous connection"*: Publius Cornelius Tacitus, *Annals,* 1.10, subdolae adfinitatis, translated Tacitus, Cornelius, John Yardley, and Anthony Barrett, *The Annals: the Reigns of Tiberius, Claudius, and Nero* (Oxford: Oxford University Press, 2008), 9.

51 *Octavia was certainly pretty, to judge by coin portraits*: "Silver Cistophorus of Marc Antony, Ephesus, 39 BC. 1944.100.7032," American Numanistic Society online, accessed April 11, 2021, http://numismatics.org/collection/1944.100.7032?lang=en.

51 *her naturally attractive hair*: Priscian (Priscianus), *Institutio de arte grammatica*, X.47 (ed. H. Keil II, 536 [Leipzig, Ger., 1855]), cited in Emily A. Hemelrijk, *Matrona Docta: Educated Women in the Roman Élite from Cornelia to Julia Domna* (New York: Routledge, 1999), 107, 293n43.

52 *a statue of Concordia, the goddess of marital and societal harmony*: Cassius Dio, *Roman History*, 48.31.2; Degrassi, Attilio, *Inscriptiones Latinae Liberae Rei Publicae,* 2. Ed., aucta et emendata (Florence: La nuova Italia, 1972), 562a = Hermann Dessau, *Inscriptiones Latinae Selectae* (Berolini: Weidmann, 1892) 3784; Josiah Osgood, *Caesar's Legacy: Civil War and the Emergence of the Roman Empire* (Cambridge: Cambridge University Press, 2006), 193.

52 *the gold coin that Antony issued with his head on the obverse*: "Gold Aureus, Uncertain Value, 38 B.C. 1976.10.1," American Numismatic Society online, accessed April 11, 2021, http://numismatics.org/collection/1976.10.1?lang=en.

52 *If the identification is correct, the first was Fulvia*: Jackie Butler, "Fulvia: The Power Behind the Lion?," *Coins at Warwick* (blog), August 1, 2018, https://blogs.warwick.ac.uk/numismatics/entry/fulvia_the_power/ . Antony left Octavia's name off the coins, but she is easily identified by her marked family resemblance to contemporary images of Octavian.

53 *Only do thou, at the boy's birth in whom*: Virgil, *Eclogues*, trans. J. B. Greenough (Boston: Ginn, 1895), lines 8–12, http://www.perseus.tufts.edu/hopper/text ?doc=Perseus%3Atext%3A1999.02.0057%3Apoem%3D4.

53 *it is possible to interpret the poem as hope for a child born to Antony and Octavia*: See the discussion in Osgood, *Caesar's Legacy*, 193–201.

53 *they received from the Senate the right to celebrate an ovation*: Attilio Degrassi, *Inscriptiones Italiae*, vol. 13.1: *Fasti Triumphales et Consulares* (Rome: Libreria dello Stato, 1947), 86–87, 568, see, for comparison, 342–43, Fasti Barberiniani. Discussed by Carsten Hjort Lange, "Civil War and the (Almost) Forgotten Pact of Brundisium," in *The Triumviral Period: Civil War, Political Crisis, and Socioeconomic Transformations,* ed. Francisco Pina Polo (Zaragoza, Sp.: Prensas de la Universidad de Zaragoza), 139–41.

55 *Sextus could not approve so dishonorable a deed*: Plutarch, *Antony*, 32.5–8; Appian, *Civil Wars*, 5.73; Cassius Dio, *Roman History*, 48.38.1–3. See Pat Southern, *Mark Antony: A Life* (Stroud, UK: Tempus, 1998), loc. 2773 of 4044 (Kindle e-book).

57 *City of the Violet Crown*: Pindar, frag. 64.

57 *he headed east in the autumn of 39 BC and took his wife with him*: Gustavo García Vivas, *Octavia Contra Cleopatra. El Papel De La Mujer En La Propaganda Política Del Triunvirato. 44–30 A. C.* (Madrid: Liceus Ediciones, 2013), 71, citing Joyce Maire Reynolds and Kenan T. Erim, *Aphrodisias and Rome: Documents from the Excavation of the Theatre at Aphrodisias Conducted by Professor Kenan T. Erim, Together with Some Related Texts* (London: Society for the Promotion of Roman Studies, 1982), doc. 8 1.26, commentary, in the same location.

57 *"by nature excessively fond of women"*: Appian, *Civil Wars,* 5.76, trans. Horace White, in Appianus, Horace White, and E. Iliff Robson, *Appian's Roman History* (Cambridge, MA: Harvard University Press, 1912), 507.

58 *a small fortune as the "dowry"*: Cassius Dio, *Roman History*, 48.39.2; Seneca the Elder (Lucius Annaeus Seneca), *Suasoriae* 1.6. The charge might come from anti-Antony propaganda.

58 *The sources claim that Antony was jealous of Ventidius*: Cassius Dio, *Roman History*, 49.21; Plutarch, *Antony,* 34.4.

58 *Ventidius returned to Rome and celebrated a triumph*: Ibid.; ibid., 34.5.

58 *It would be 150 years before*: In 117/118 the Roman emperor Trajan (Marcus Ulpius Traianus) was permitted posthumously to celebrate a triumph over Parthia. See Plutarch, *Life of Antony,* ed. C. B. R. Pelling (Cambridge: Cambridge University Press, 1988), 212.

59 *Octavian now agreed to an informal meeting with Antony*: On the Tarentum conference, see Appian, *Civil Wars,* 5.92–95; Cassius Dio, *Roman History*, 48.54; Plutarch, *Antony,* 35; Plutarch, *Antony,* ed. comm., Pelling, 213–16.

60 *Skeptical historians*: See, for example, Ronald Syme, *The Roman Revolution* (Oxford: Oxford University Press, 2002 [Oxford: Clarendon Press,1939]), 225–26n2.

60 *Antony or his followers issued bronze coins around the time of Tarentum*: On the coins, see Susan Wood, *Imperial Women: A Study in Public Images, 40 B.C.– A.D. 68* (Boston: Brill, 1999), 41–51.

60 *the Roman historian Livy (Titus Livius) modeled the episode of the Sabine women*: Beth Severy, *Augustus and the Family at the Birth of the Roman Empire* (New York: Routledge, 2003), 42.

Chapter 4: Octavian's Victory, Antony's Defeat and Recovery

63 *"shattered in body and mind"*: Appian, *Civil Wars,* 5.111–12.

64 *the highest warship casualty rate*: See William M. Murray, *The Age of the Titans: The Rise and Fall of the Great Hellenistic Navies* (New York: Oxford University Press, 2012), 166–67.

64 *Octavian claimed that he captured thirty thousand runaway slaves*: Augustus, *Res Gestae,* 25.

64 *the hardest struggle that Octavian ever faced*: Suetonius, *Augustus,* 16.3.

66 *He scored a propaganda coup by recapturing several legionary standards*: Augustus, *Res Gestae,* 29.1.

66 *his publicists compared Octavian to Alexander the Great*: See Marjeta Šašel Kos, "Octavian's Illyrian War: Ambition and Strategy," in *The Century of the Brave: Roman Conquest and Indigenous Resistance in Illyricum During the Time of Augustus and His Heirs: Proceedings of the International Conference, Zagreb, 22.–26.9.2014,* ed. Marina Milecivic Bradač and Dino Demechili (Zagreb, Croatia: FF Press, 2018), 48–49.

67 *public relations staff*: see Scott, "Political Propaganda," 48–49.

68 *put on a mime mocking the twelve Olympian gods*: Suetonius, *Augustus*, 70; Suetonius, *Life of Augustus (Vita Divi Augusti),* ed., comm. D. Wardle, 443–46; Marleen Flory, *"Abducta Neroni Uxor:* The Historiographic Tradition on the Marriage of Octavian and Livia," *Transactions of the American Philological Association* 118 (1988): 343–59.

68 *criticized Octavian for the latter's weakness for playing dice*: Plutarch, *Antony,* 33.2.–4; Suetonius, *Augustus,* 70.2.

69 *In retrospect, Octavian might have looked like a giant, but, at the time, he was the underdog*: Christopher Pelling, "The Triumviral Period," in *The Cambridge Ancient History*, vol. 10, *The Augustan Empire, 43 B.C.–A.D. 69,* ed. Alan K. Bowman, Edward Champlin, and A. W. Lintott (Cambridge: Cambridge University Press, 1996), 49.

69   On His Drunkenness: Pliny, *Natural History,* 14.22. See Kenneth Scott, "Octavian's Propaganda and Antony's De Sua Ebrietate," *Classical Philology* 24, no. 2 (1929): 133–41.

69   *a litany of Octavian's alleged sexual misbehavior*: Suetonius, *Augustus*, 69.1–2.

70   *"Is she my wife?"*: Ibid., 69.2. That last sentence, "Is she my wife?" could also be translated as "She is my wife," because Latin has no question mark, and the word order could mean either a statement or an inquiry. But a statement would make little sense, since the point of Antony's laundry list of Octavian's affairs is that both men cheated on their wives—not that Antony was a bigamist (against Octavian's sister, no less). So, it was surely a question: "Is she my wife?"

73   *Antony had ninety thousand to a hundred thousand men*: Plutarch, *Antony*, 37.3–4, 38.1–2; A. S. Schieber, "Anthony and Parthia," *Rivista storica dell'Antichità* 9 (1979): 111.

73   *five miles long*: Plutarch, *Antony*, ed. comm., Pelling, 225.

73   *King Artavasdes of Armenia joined Antony along the way*: Plutarch, *Antony,* 37.3; Schieber, "Anthony and Parthia," 111.

74   *Octavia set sail from Italy on a mission to Athens*: Plutarch, *Antony*, 53.1–4.

75   *He sent Octavia a letter*: Ibid., 53.2; Cassius Dio, *Roman History,* 49.33.3–4; Plutarch, *Antony*, ed. comm., Pelling, 244–45.

76   *Octavian told her to divorce Antony*: Plutarch, *Antony*, 54.1; Plutarch, *Antony*, ed. comm., Pelling, 248, suggests that, in reality, perhaps Octavian only suggested in public that Octavia would have been justified in divorcing Antony had she wished.

76   *he reaffirmed his sister's dignity by having Octavia voted unprecedented honors*: Cassius Dio, *Roman History*, 49.38.1. It is unclear whether the vote came in the Senate or through a law of the people. See R. A. Bauman, "Tribunician Sacrosanctity in 44, 36 and 35 B. C.," *Rheinisches Museum Für Philologie* 124, no. 2 (1981): 174–78.

76   *An insult to Octavia was now equal to an insult to a public official*: Richard A. Bauman, *Women and Politics in Ancient Rome* (London: Routledge, 1992), 93.

76   *Octavian had the same honors voted as well to Livia*: Note that Cassius Dio, *Roman History*, 49.38.1, puts Octavia's name first before Livia's, in spite of Livia's greater importance overall in Rome's history.

77   *they would have made a sharp contrast to Cleopatra's eastern splendor*: As suggested by Marleen B. Flory, "Livia and the History of Public Honorific Statues for Women in Rome," *Transactions of the American Philological Association* 123 (1993): 295–96.

77   *The sources accuse Antony of hijacking a Roman triumph*: Plutarch, *Antony*, 50.6; Cassius Dio, *History of Rome*, 49.40.3–4.

78   *The procession supposedly climaxed at the feet of Cleopatra*: Cassius Dio, *History of Rome*, 49.40.3–4.

78   *a related story that appears in the sources*: Plutarch, *Antony*, 54.4–9; Cassius Dio, *History of Rome*, 49.41.

78 *the Gymnasium, a public building considered by some as the city's most beautiful*:
    Strabo, *Geography*, 17.795.

80 *Plutarch says that the ceremony in Alexandria showed that Antony hated Rome*:
    Plutarch, *Antony,* 54.5.

Chapter 5: The Coming of War

84 adulescentulus: *"a very young man"*: Tim G. Parkin, *Old Age in the Roman
    World: a Cultural and Social History* (Baltimore: Johns Hopkins University
    Press, 2003), 20–21.

85 *It was said that she had furnished a quarter of the warships*: Plutarch, *Antony*,
    56.2.

86 *They joined their voices with Ahenobarbus*: For example, Geminius, who came
    from Rome, on behalf of Antony's friends, to try to persuade him to send
    Cleopatra back to Egypt (ibid., 59.1–5).

86 *sponsored public buildings*: It is possible that Antony did so as well, an achieve-
    ment that later, hostile Augustan propaganda blotted out. See Duane W.
    Roller, "The Lost Building Program of Marcus Antonius," *L'Antiquité Clas-
    sique* 76 (2007): 87–98.

88 *A prophecy in Greek from around 33 BC*: W. W. Tarn, "Alexander Helios and
    the Golden Age," *Journal of Roman Studies* 22, no. 2 (1932): 135–60; Michael
    Grant, *Cleopatra* (New York: Simon & Schuster, 1972), 172–75.

89 *It was destiny*: Plutarch, *Antony*, 56.6.

90 *all the world around was filled with groans and lamentations*: Ibid., 56.7-10;
    Plutarch, *Plutarch's Lives*, vol. 9, trans. Perrin, 267.

91 *Now the Athenian Assembly voted divine honors to Cleopatra*: Plutarch, *Antony*,
    57.2–3.

91 *Octavia who attracted Antony's attention while he was in Athens*: Ibid., 57.4; Cas-
    sius Dio, *Roman History*, 50.3.2.

91 *"Take your things for yourself"*: Cassius Dio, *History of Rome,* 50.3.2; Seneca,
    Suasoriae 1.6.

92 *Antony's house in an upscale part of Rome*: Antony owned two houses in Rome:
    one on Palatine Hill (Cassius Dio, *Roman History*, 53.27.5) and the other—the
    former possession of Pompey the Great—across the valley of the Forum on
    a hill overlooking the later Colosseum. See Eva Margareta Steinby, *Lexicon
    Topographicum Urbis Romae*, vol. 2 (Roma: Quasar, 1993), 34, and Plutarch,
    Antony, 54.5. Both were fashionable addresses. It's not clear which house Oc-
    tavia lived in. For the date of May or June, see C. Suetonius Tranquillus, *Life
    of Augustus (Vita Divi Augusti),* trans., intro., comm. D. Wardle, 442.

92 *Octavia is said to have cried tears of distress*: Sarah Rey, "Les larmes romaines et
    leur portée : une question de genre?" *Clio: Women, Gender, History* 41, no. 1
    (2015): 243–64.

92 *it might seem as if she were one of the causes of the war*: Plutarch, *Antony*, 57.4.

92 *one almost wonders whether Octavian didn't somehow trick Antony into it*: Plutarch, *Antony*, ed. comm., Pelling, 259, suggests that Antony divorced Octavia in order to preempt her from divorcing him.

94 *signet ring and correspondence*: Appian, *Civil Wars*, 5.144.

94 *Plancus imitated a merman*: Velleius Paterculus, *History of Rome*, 2.83.2.

95 *Plancus got caught stealing and lost Antony's favor:* Ibid.

95 *Plancus and Titius broke with Antony over the divorce with Octavia*: Cassius Dio, *Roman History*, 50.3.2.

95 *Plancus and Titius had wanted Cleopatra back in Egypt*: Plutarch, *Antony*, 58.4.

95 *betrayal was a disease with Plancus*: Velleius Paterculus, *History of Rome*, 2.83.1. Another issue might have been the loss of Cleopatra's favor: Plutarch, *Antony*, 58.4.

95 *Octavian announced the contents of the document*: Plutarch, *Antony,* 58.4–6; Cassius Dio, *Roman History*, 50.3.3–5; Suetonius, *Augustus*, 17.

96 *there were still members left to criticize Octavian for his action*: Plutarch, *Antony*, 58.7.

96 *they offered to welcome those supporters to their side*: Cassius Dio, *Roman History*, 50.4.3–4.

96 *Octavian loved the theater*: Suetonius, *Augustus*, 99.1.

96 *Antony had supposedly once stood up at a well-attended banquet in order to rub Cleopatra's feet*: Plutarch, *Antony,* 58.10.

97 *After voting to declare war on Cleopatra*: Ibid., 60.1.

97 *Octavian carried out the official role of one of the priests known as* fetiales: Cassius Dio, *Roman History,* 50.4.5; see, for comparison, Augustus, *Res Gestae,* 7.3.

98 *"The whole of Italy voluntarily took oath of allegiance to me"*: Augustus, *Res Gestae,* 25, trans. Frederick W. Shipley, *Velleius Paterculus and Res Gestae Divi Augusti* (London: W. Heinemann, 1955), 385.

Chapter 6: The Invaders

107 *From time to time, ancient mariners sailed across open water*: see Tomislav Bilič, "The Myth of Alpheus and Arethusa and Open-Sea Voyages on the Mediterranean—Stellar Navigation in Antiquity," *International Journal of Nautical Archaeology* 38, no. 1 (2009): 116–32; James Morton, *The Role of the Physical Environment in Ancient Greek Sailing* (Leiden, Neth.: Brill, 2001),151, 153–54, 185–87.

109 *a two-day sail across the Ionian Sea*: William M. Murray, personal communication to author, September 2020.

110 *Antony was blockaded in Brundisium*: Julius Caesar, *Commentaries on the Civil War*, 3.23–28; Plutarch, *Antony*, 7.1–6; Appian, *Civil Wars*, 2.59; Cassius Dio, *Roman History*, 41.48.

110 *Brundisium had closed its gates to Antony twice*: Plutarch, *Antony,* 35.1; Appian, *Civil Wars,* 5.56–61, 66, 93–95.

111 *The sources report how unpopular those taxes were*: Plutarch, *Antony,* 58.1–2; Cassius Dio, *Roman History,* 50.10.3–6.

111 *Antony sent money to Italy*: Cassius Dio, *Roman History,* 50.7.3, 9.1; Servius, *Virgil's Aeneid,* 7.684; Grant, *Cleopatra*, 198.

112 *he gave money to his soldiers*: Cassius Dio, *Roman History,* 50.7.3.

112 *Octavian brought with him all of the senators and many Roman knights*: Ibid., 50.11.5; Syme, *Roman Revolution,* 292–93.

112 *"Antony intended to make war on the city of Rome and on Italy"*: Livy (Titus Livius), *Periochae,* 132.2.

112 *Antony decided to make war on his fatherland*: Velleius Paterculus, 2.82.4.

112 *Antony made a mistake in not forcing Octavian to fight before Octavian was ready*: Plutarch, *Antony,* 58.1–3; Plutarch, *Antony*, ed. comm., Pelling, 259–60.

112 *Antony set out to invade Italy unexpectedly*: Cassius Dio, *Roman History*, 50.9.2.

113 *one day she would dispense justice on the Capitoline Hill*: Ibid., 50.5.4; Propertius, *Elegies*, 3.11.45–46; *Latin Anthology*, 1.462.3; Ovid, *Metamorphoses*, 15.826–28; [Author Unknown,] *Elegy for Maecenas*, 1.53–54; Florus, *Epitome*, 2.21.2; Eutropius, *Abridgement of Roman History*, 7.7.1.

113 *The nature of Antony's ships tells the tale*: I am indebted to pioneering work by William Murray; see Murray, *Age of Titans,* 242–43.

114 *Finally, there were a few larger vessels*: The term of art for these largest ships is *polyreme,* or "many-oared" in Greek.

115 *Most of Antony's fleet, therefore, probably consisted of fives*: Murray and Petsas, *Octavian's Campsite Memorial*, 142–51; William M. Murray, "Reconsidering the Battle of Actium—Again," in *Oikistes: Studies in Constitutions, Colonies, and Military Power in the Ancient World. Offered in Honor of A. J. Graham,* ed. Vanessa B. Gorman and Eric W. Robinson (Leiden, Neth.: Brill, 2002), 342–43; Murray, *Age of Titans*, 235–38.

115 *Roman admirals tended to avoid naval sieges*: There were some examples of Roman naval sieges, such as the one conducted by Publius Cornelius Scipio Africanus at Utica (in today's Tunisia) in 204 BC, but they were exceptions.

116 *naval siege unit*: See Murray, *Age of Titans*, 95–100, 125–28, here and there.

116 *"terror-stricken at the magnitude of the fleet"*: Diodorus Siculus, *Library of History*, trans. Russel M. Geer (Cambridge, MA: Harvard University Press, 1954), vol. 10, bk. 20, p. 361, 20.83.2.

118 *Antony probed the possibility of invasion in late autumn*: Cassius Dio, *Roman History*, 50.9.2.

118 *Plutarch blasted Antony's delay*: Plutarch, *Antony,* 58.3; see Plutarch, *Antony,* ed., comm. Pelling, 260.

Chapter 7: The Naval Crown

120 *the naval crown*: Livy (Titus Livius), *Periochae,* 129; Cassius Dio, *Roman History*, 49.14.3; Seneca the Elder (Lucius Annaeus Seneca), *De Beneficiis,* 3.32.4;

Velleius Paterculus, *History of Rome,* 2.81.3; Virgil, *Aeneid* 8.683–84; Ovid (Publius Ovidius Naso), *Art of Love,* 3.392; Pliny, *Natural History,* 16.7–8. See the discussion in Meyer Reinhold, *From Republic to Principate: An Historical Commentary on Cassius Dio's Roman History Books 49–52 (36–29 B.C.)* (Atlanta: Scholars Press, 1987), 34; Lindsay Powell, *Marcus Agrippa: Right-Hand Man of Caesar Augustus* (Barnsley, UK: Pen & Sword Books, 2015), 63, 276nn124–27.

120 *"naval crown, that binds his manly brows"*: Virgil, *Aeneid*, trans. John Dryden, 8.683.

120 *Shown in profile on coins*: See, for example, "RIC I (Second Edition) Augustus 158" or "RIC I (Second Edition) Augustus 160," American Numismatic Society online, accessed April 12, 2021, http://numismatics.org/ocre/id/ric.1(2).aug.158 or http://numismatics.org/ocre/id/ric.1(2).aug.160, respectively.

121 *"eyes of the republic"*: Roger Crowley, *City of Fortune: How Venice Ruled the Seas*, (New York: Random House, 2011), 120.

121 *a logistical and supply chain stretching a thousand miles*: From Corcyra, it is a distance of 1,114 miles, or 968 nautical miles, or 1,793 kilometers to Alexandria, Egypt ("Orbis: The Stanford Geospatial Network of the Ancient World," Stanford University Libraries online, accessed April 12, 2021, http://orbis.stanford.edu).

122 *"A great strategy is to press the enemy more with famine"*: Vegetius, *De re militari*, 3.26, trans.; Paul Erdkamp, *Hunger and the Sword: Warfare and Food Supply in Roman Republican Wars (264–30 B.C.)* (Amsterdam: J. C. Gieben, 1998), 27.

122 *Roman commanders had employed such a strategy since the days of the Punic Wars*: Many examples in Jonathan P. Roth, *The Logistics of the Roman Army at War (264 B.C.–A.D. 235)* (Leiden: Brill, 1999), here and there.

122 *"by first capturing the towns that furnished them"*: Appian, *Civil Wars,* 5.118.

123 *"Infinite variety"*: Shakespeare, *Antony and Cleopatra*, act 2, scene 2, line 247.

123 *Methone was about 385 nautical miles from Brundisium*: Distances are based on calculations from "Orbis: Stanford Geospatial Network," http://orbis.stanford.edu.

The website does not include Methone, but it does include Cape Akitas, or Cape Akritas, today a sail of about ten nautical miles southeast of Methone ("Sailing Distance Calculator," Sail Greece, accessed April 12, 2021, https://www.sailgreeceyachts.com/sailing-distances-greece.html).

124 *the open-water route from Sicily to the Peloponnese*: See Tomislav Bilič, "The Myth of Alpheus and Arethusa and Open-Sea Voyages on the Mediterranean—Stellar Navigation in Antiquity," *International Journal of Nautical Archaeology* 38, no. 1 (2009): 116–32; Morton, *Role of Physical Environment in Ancient Greek Sailing*, 185–87.

124 *That route was roughly the same distance as the trip from southern Italy to Methone*: Distances based on calculations from "Sailing Distance Calculator," accessed April 12, 2021, https://www.sailgreeceyachts.com/sailing-distances

-greece.html. A distance of 751 kilometers, or about 395 nautical miles, comes from "Orbis: Stanford Geospatial Network," http://orbis.stanford.edu, but it follows a less direct route.

125 *Ancient navigators could look for mountains and other landmarks*: On ancient navigation, see Morton, *Role of Physical Environment in Ancient Greek Sailing*, 122–23, 185–94; James Beresford, *The Ancient Sailing Season* (Leiden, Neth.: Brill, 2013), 173–212; E. G. R. Taylor, *The Haven-Finding Art: A History of Navigation from Odysseus to Captain Cook* (New York: Abelard-Schuman, 1957), 3–64; Harold Augustin Callahan, *The Sky and the Sailor: A History of Celestial Navigation* (New York: Harper and Brothers, 1952), 10–18.

125 *In 200 BC a Roman fleet took the Macedonian stronghold of Chalcis*: Livy (Titus Livius), *History of Rome*, 31.23.

125 *Scholars have long surmised*: Beginning, it seems, with J. Kromayer, "Kleine Forschungen zur Geschichte des Zweiten Triumvirats. VII. Der Feldzug von Actium und der sogenannte Verrath der Cleopatra," *Hermes* 34, no. 1 (1899): 9. See also Giovanni Brizzi, "La Battaglia d'Azio," in *Cleopatra: Roma e l'Incantesimo Dell'Egitto,* ed. Giovanni Gentili (Milano, It.: Skira), 2013, 21–22.

126 *Agrippa probably attacked early in the sailing season, perhaps in March*: Kromayer, "Kleine Forschungen," 9; 25, n. 2, argues that Agrippa could not have started much later than March, if we are to fit in all his exploits in 31 BC before the Battle of Actium on September 2. On sailing in winter, see Beresford, *Ancient Sailing Season,* 269–70.

126 *other ways to travel light*: This point was made by Jean-Michel Roddaz, *Marcus Agrippa* (Rome: École française de Rome, 1984), 168–69.

126 *A Roman war fleet of forty quinqueremes or fives is known to have sailed in wintertime*: The commander was C. Lucretius Gallus, and the date was 171 BC; Livy (Titus Livius), *History of Rome,* 42.48.9.

126 *painted sea blue*: On the Romans' use of reconnaissance vessels and sea-blue camouflage, see Polybius, *Histories*, 3.95–96; Julius Caesar, *African War*, 26.3–4; Vegetius, *Epitome*, 4.37; N. J. E. Austin and N. B. Rankov, *Exploratio: Military and Political Intelligence in the Roman World* (New York: Routledge, 1995), 59–60, 62, 237.

126 *sailed from Naples to Cephalonia in five days during wintertime*: C. Lucretius Gallus, 171 BC; Livy, *History of Rome,* 42.48.9.

126 *At an average speed of four knots before a favorable wind—fast, but not unprecedented*: On the speed of Roman war fleets, see Lionel Casson, *Ships and Seamanship in the Ancient World* (Princeton, NJ: Princeton University Press, 1971), 292–96.

127 *defectors from Antony's camp*: Cassius Dio, *Roman History*, 50.9.4.

127 *Octavian caught a spy*: Ibid.

Chapter 8: The African King

128 *About Bogud*: On Bogud, see inter alia, G. Camps, "Bogud," *Encyclopédie Berbère* vol. 10 (Aix-en-Provence, France: EDISUD, 1991), 1557–58; Duane W. Roller, *The World of Juba II and Kleopatra Selene: Royal Scholarship on Rome's African Frontier* (London: Routledge, 2003), 55–58.

128 *He is supposed to have had an affair with Eunoe*: Suetonius, *Caesar*, 52.1; Sallust (Gaius Sallustius Crispus), *Jugurtha,* 80.6.

129 *Bogud's greatest battle came when he fought for Caesar at Munda*: Cassius Dio, *Roman History*, 43.36.1, 38.2–3.

129 *Moors were famously light, fast, and lethal horsemen*: On Moorish horsemen, see Michael Speidel, "Mauri Equites: The Tactics of Light Cavalry in Mauretania," *Antiquités africaines* 29 (1993): 121–26.

129 *this time he'd fought for his life*: Appian, *Civil Wars,* 2.104.

129 *Methone was highly defensible:* 431 BC: Thucydides, *Peloponnesian War,* 2.35.1–3; Illyrian raiders: Pausanias*, Description of Greece,* 4.35.6–7.

130 *In 1500 it would take a siege*: N. A. Bees, "Modon," in *Encyclopaedia of Islam,* 2nd ed., ed. P. Bearman et al., consulted online December 14, 2020, http://dx .doi.org.proxy.library.cornell.edu/10.1163/1573-3912_islam_SIM_5250.

130 *One source claims that Antony stationed a very strong garrison in Methone*: Orosius, *Historiae Adversus Paganos (History Against the Pagans),* 6.19.6.

131 *any barriers . . . and stockades*: See Murray, *Age of Titans*, 140, 290–91.

131 *Philippi in 42 BC*: Plutarch, *Brutus,* 47.1–4; Roth, *Logistics of the Roman Army at War*, 282.

131 *"Time is everything"*: Maev Kennedy, "Lord Nelson's Watch Expected to Fetch up to £450,000 at Sotheby's," *Guardian* (UK) online, June 22, 2018, https://www.theguardian.com/world/2018/jun/22/lord-nelson-watch-battle -of-trafalgar-auction-sothebys; William Clark Russell and Sérgio Antônio Sapucahy da Silva, *Horatio Nelson and the Naval Supremacy of England* (New York: G. P. Putnam's Sons, 1890), 203.

132 *night sailing along the coast is attested*: Morton, *Physical Environment in Ancient Greek Sailing*, 229–30.

132 *Successful ancient examples*: See the list of accounts of attack and defense in A. W. Lawrence, *Greek Aims in Fortification* (Oxford: Clarendon Press, 1979), 53–66. See also Philip de Souza, "Naval Forces," in *The Cambridge History of Greek and Roman Warfare,* vol. 1, *Greece, the Hellenistic World, and the Rise of Rome,* ed. Philip Sabin, Hans van Wees, and Michael Whitby (Cambridge: Cambridge University Press, 2007): 450–51.

132 *Philo of Byzantium . . . advised attacking a city*: Philo (Philo Mechanicus), *Poliorketika,* 4.1.1–4; Lawrence, *Aims in Fortification*, 99, 101.

132 *Philo also recommended the use of special climbing equipment*: Ibid., 4.3.72–75; 107.

133 *Agrippa came back and finally took Tyndaris*: Appian, *Civil Wars*, 5.109, 116.

133 *Agrippa and Octavian seized the city of Siscia*: Appian, *The Illyrian Wars*, 22–24 (where the city is called Segesta); Cassius Dio, *Roman History*, 49.37.

133 *Methone was walled*: Venetian-Ottoman fortress: See Kevin Andrews, *Castles of the Morea*, rev. ed., foreword by Glenn R. Bugh (Princeton, NJ: American School of Classical Studies at Athens, 2006), 58–83. Hellenistic revetments: Lawrence, 473–74. Roman walls: John C. Kraft and Stanley E. Aschenbrenner, "Paleogeographic Reconstructions in the Methoni Embayment in Greece," *Journal of Field Archaeology* 4, no. 1 (Spring 1977): 22; Pausanias, *Description of Greece*, 4.35.1–2.

133 *mentioned in four separate sources*: Agrippa took Methone by storm and killed King Bogud in it (Strabo, *Geography*, 359 8.4.3; Cassius Dio, *Roman History*, 50.11.3; Porphyry of Tyre, *On Abstinence from Animal Food*, 1.25). Agrippa's attack came from the sea (Strabo, *Geography*, 359 8.4.3). Although the city of Methone was supposedly defended by a very strong garrison of Antony's supporters, Agrippa launched a successful assault. (*Mothonam urbem ualidissimo Antoniano praesidio munitam expugnauit*, Orosius, *Against the Pagans*, 6.19.6.)

134 *the best way to capture the city of Syracuse was to sail right in and attack*: The general Lamachus, 415 BC, as noted in Thucydides, *Peloponnesian War*, 6.49.

134 *"by an attack from the sea"* (ex epiplou): Strabo, *Geography*, 359 8.4.3.

134 *Sapientza, one of the Oenussae islands*: Sapientza is the modern name of the island; the ancient name is unknown. The sailing distance between Prote and Sapientza is about twenty nautical miles, according to "Sailing Distances Calculator," Sail Greece, accessed April 12, 2020, https://www.sailgreeceyachts.com/sailing-distances-greece.html.

134 *prelude to the Battle of Mylae*: Appian, *Civil Wars*, 5.106. On launching a surprise naval attack at night, see Polybius, *Histories*, 1.49.6–50.64, and Philip de Souza, "Naval Battles and Sieges," in The *Cambridge History of Greek and Roman Warfare*, vol. 1, *Greece, the Hellenistic World, and the Rise of Rome*, ed. Philip Sabin, Hans Van Wees, and Michael Whitby (Cambridge: Cambridge University Press, 2007): 444.

134 *Rome's successful attack on the Greek city of Chalcis in 200 BC*: Livy, *History of Rome*, 31.23.

135 *Perhaps it was either March 14 or March 29*: Fred Espenak, "Phases of the Moon: -0099 to 0000 (0100 to 0001 BCE," AstroPixels.com, last modified December 21, 2014, http://astropixels.com/ephemeris/phasescat/phases-0099.html.

135 *The Romans timed their attack on Chalcis for just that hour*: Livy, *History of Rome*, 31.23.

135 *In 259 BC a Roman general captured Sardinian towns*: Sextus Julius Frontinus, *Stratagems*, 3.9.4. Frontinus refers to the general as Lucius Cornelius Rufinus, which may refer to Lucius Cornelius Scipio.

135 *The consequences of the seizure of Methone*: I am indebted to Michael Grant, *Cleopatra*, 204–5, for his discussion of the strategic consequences of the fall of Methone.

136 *Like some ancient Sir Francis Drake*: Drake's raid took place in Cádiz, Spain, in 1587.

136 *"was now watching for the merchant vessels"*: Cassius Dio, *Roman History*, 50.11.3. Translated: Cassius Dio Cocceianus, Earnest Cary, and Herbert Baldwin Foster, *Dio's Roman History*, vol. 5 (New York: G. P. Putnam's Sons, 1917), 459.

136 *Agrippa's attacks can be considered a form of swarming*: On swarming, see John Arquilla and David Ronfeldt, *Swarming & the Future of Conflict* (Santa Monica, CA: Rand, 2000).

137 *"At any rate, my great-grandfather Nicarchus used to tell"*: Plutarch, *Antony*, 68.4; Plutarch, *Plutarch's Lives*, vol. 9, trans. Perrin, 295.

137 *complaining that they had to drink sour wine*: Plutarch, *Antony*, 59.8.

137 *changing the name honored on their coins*: Grant, *Cleopatra*, 204.

138 *"was a certainty long before the battle"*: Velleius Paterculus, *Roman History*, 2.84.1.

138 *"the capture of Methone in itself meant that the war was half lost already"*: Grant, *Cleopatra*, 205.

Chapter 9: Sitting on a Ladle

141 *Omens were weapons*: Plutarch, *Antony*, 60.2–7; Cassius Dio, *Roman History*, 50.8.1-6, 10.2.3.

141 *Antony left Italy because he kept losing to Octavian in games*: Plutarch, *Antony*, 33.2–4; *On the Fortune of the Romans*, 319–20.

141 *Trash talk*: Plutarch, *Antony*, 62.2–4; Cassius Dio, *Roman History*, 50.9.5–6.

145 *Agrippa had already captured Corcyra*: Cassius Dio, *Roman History*, 50.11.1; Orosius, *Against the Pagans*, 6.19.7. Reinhold, *From Republic to Principate*, 102, argues convincingly against Dio's claims that Octavian first tried to capture Corcyra in the winter but was turned back by a storm, and that he finally captured the island in the spring. Agrippa deserves the credit.

146 *Dio claims that they were too confident to accept*: Cassius Dio, *Roman History*, 50.12.1.

146 *"What's so terrible," she said, "if Caesar [that is, Octavian] is sitting on a ladle?"*: Plutarch, *Antony*, 62.6.

146 ladle *was, it seems, obscene, if obscure slang for "penis"*: Plutarch, *Antony*, ed., comm. Pelling, 62.6, 272, citing J. N. Adams, *The Latin Sexual Vocabulary* (London: Duckworth, 1982), 23; Amy Coker, "How Filthy was Cleopatra? Looking for Dysphemistic Words in Ancient Greek," *Journal of Historical Pragmatics* 202 (2019): 186–203.

147 *Antony had already accused Octavian of having been Julius Caesar's passive partner in bed*: Suetonius, *Augustus*, 68.1.

148 *nearly fifty years later, it was still possible to visit its remains*: Tacitus, *Annals,* 2.53.

149 *reaching more than five hundred feet at the highest peak*: Google Earth; William M. Murray, personal communication to author, September 11, 2020.

149 *at an elevation of about three hundred feet*: 83 meters (equals 272 feet), according to Vergos Kostas, authorized lecturer and guide, Ioannina, Greece, personal communication to author, September 14, 2020.

149 *a modern mole there*: It is located at a place called Mytikas.

150 *As surface inspection shows*: Murray, personal communication to author, September 2020.

150 *but Antony was prepared for him*: Plutarch, *Antony*, 63.1; Plutarch, *Antony*, ed. comm., Pelling, 273.

151 *This camp lay around two miles south of Octavian's camp at Michalitsi*: T. Rice Holmes, *The Architect of the Roman Empire* (Oxford: Clarendon Press, 1928), 1:149.

151 *"before the eyes of Antony and his fleet"*: Velleius Paterculus, *Roman History*, 2.84.2.

152 *Quintus Nasidius*: Appian, *Civil Wars*, 5.139; Cassius Dio, *Roman History*, 50.13.5; Velleius Paterculus, *Roman History*, 2.84.1.

152 *Antony's men saluted him as imperator*: Southern, *Antony*, loc. 3528 of 4044 (Kindle e-book); "RRC 545/1," American Numismatic Society online, accessed April 12, 2021, http://numismatics.org/crro/id/rrc-545.1.

153 *defection of King Deiotarus Philadelphus of Paphlagonia*: Cassius Dio, *Roman History*, 50.13.5.

153 *Rhoemetalces of Thrace*: Reinhold, *From Republic to Principate*, 103.

153 *Octavian's agents there talked two legions into defecting to the young heir of Caesar*: Appian, *Civil Wars*, 3.40; Cassius Dio, *Roman History*, 45.12.1–2.

153 *he was almost captured*: Plutarch, *Antony*, 63.9–11. See Plutarch, *Antony*, ed. comm., Pelling, 276.

154 *the poet Horace wrote of two thousand Gallic cavalrymen*: Horace, *Epodes*, 9.17–20.

Chapter 10: Apollo's Revenge

157 *some with malaria, others with dysentery*: These are the most probable diseases to have stricken Antony's men.

157 *"The fleet in view, he twanged his deadly bow"*: Homer, *The Iliad*, , trans. Alexander Pope, bk. 1, ll. 67–72.

158 *Antony's agents fanned the Greek countryside*: Plutarch, *Antony*, 62.1.

158 *as long as there was a man in Greece*: Orosius, *Against the Pagans*, 6.19.4.

158 *his agents had to whip free men in central Greece*: Plutarch, *Antony*, 68.4.

159 *"Why leave we not the fatal Trojan Shore"*: Homer, *Iliad*, trans. Pope, bk. 1, ll. 79–82.

159 *Antony had gone from besieger to besieged*: W. W. Tarn, "The Battle of Actium," *Journal of Roman Studies* 21 (1931): 188.

159 *Agrippa sailed boldly into the Corinthian Gulf and briefly captured its crown jewel*: Cassius Dio, *Roman History,* 50.13.6; Velleius Paterculus, *Roman History*, 2.84.2.

160 *Ahenobarbus had had enough*: Plutarch, *Antony*, 63.3–4; Velleius Paterculus, *Roman History*, 2.84.2; Suetonius, *Nero*, 3.1; Cassius Dio, *Roman History*, 50.13.6. We don't know Ahenobarbus's route to Octavian's camp, but the sea is usually too rough in the Bay of Gomaros for him to have been rowed there in a small boat (Vergos, personal communication to author, September 18, 2020).

160 *Caesar, who had done the same*: Plutarch, *Caesar*, 34.5. See Plutarch, *Antony*, ed., comm. Pelling, 63.3–4, 274.

161 *Iamblichus, the Syrian king, and Quintus Postumius*: Cassius Dio, *Roman History*, 50.13.7.

161 *there were daily desertions*: Velleius Paterculus, *Roman History*, 2.84.1.

161 *Marcus Junius Silanus*: Plutarch, *Antony*, 59.6; for the chronology, see Syme, *Roman Revolution*, 295.

161 *Lucius Gellius Publicola*: See "Publicola," in Hubert Cancik et al., *Brill's New Pauly: Encyclopaedia of the Ancient World*, English ed. (Leiden, Neth.: Brill, 2002–2010). Adoption among Roman nobles usually involved adults. Like marriage, it was meant to forge political alliances.

161 *Marcus Valerius Messalla Corvinus*: See "Corvinus," in Cancik et al., *Brill's New Pauly*.

162 *Antony sent Dellius and Amyntas into Macedonia and Thrace*: Cassius Dio, *Roman History*, 50.13.8.

162 *His name appears on coins struck on the island between 39 and 32 BC*: Michael Grant, *From Imperium to Auctoritas: A Historical Study of Aes Coinage in the Roman Empire, 49 B.C.–A.D. 14* (Cambridge: University Press, 1946), 39–41.

163 *It was probably at this point that Antony decided to withdraw his legions*: Cassius Dio, *Roman History*, 50.14.1–3.

166 *Even Canidius Crassus*: Plutarch, *Antony*, 63.6.

167 *He called a council of war*: Ibid., 63.6–8; Cassius Dio, *Roman History*, 50.14.4.

167 *Pompey's camp at Pharsalus*: Julius Caesar, *Civil War*, 3.96.1.

168 *"Trick Rider of the Civil Wars"*: Seneca, *Suasoriae* 1.7.

168 *gossip said that Dellius wrote smutty letters to Cleopatra*: Seneca, *Suasoriae* 1.7; Holmes, *Architect,* 1:149.

168 *King Dicomes of the Getae*: Plutarch, *Antony*, 63.4; Cassius Dio, *Roman History*, 51.22.8.

169 *dividing and wasting his strength among ships*: Plutarch, *Antony*, 63.7; *Plutarch, Antony*, ed. comm., Pelling, 275.

170 *The sources claim that it was Cleopatra*: Plutarch, *Antony*, 63.8; Cassius Dio, *Roman History*, 50.15.1–3.

170 *Cleopatra might have made an additional case to Antony in private*: Si Sheppard, *Actium 31 BC: Downfall of Antony and Cleopatra* (Oxford: Osprey, 2009), 62. Indeed, Octavian had to face a near mutiny of demobilized veterans in Italy

in the winter after the battle, but these didn't include Antony's men: Cassius Dio, *Roman History*, 51.4–5.

170 *Antony and Cleopatra might have hoped to be lucky enough*: Plutarch, *Antony*, 64.1; Cassius Dio, *Roman History*, 50.15.3; Orosius, *Against the Pagans*, 6.19.8.

171 *Antony, says Plutarch, was a mere appendage to Cleopatra*: Plutarch, *Antony*, 62.1.

171 *Cleopatra was supposedly just a frightened female who gave in to bad omens*: Cassius Dio, *Roman History*, 50.15.2–3.

171 *nor was she selfishly thinking only of her escape*: Plutarch, *Antony*, 63.8.

171 *one last high-profile defection: Dellius*: Ibid., *Antony*, 59.6; Cassius Dio, *Roman History*, 50.23.1; Velleius Paterculus, *Roman History*, 2.84.2; Seneca, *Suasoriae* 1.7.

172 *Octavian and Agrippa had a debate*: Cassius Dio, *Roman History*, 50.31.1–2.

172 *Agrippa, however, put it otherwise*: Cassius Dio, *Roman History*, 50.31.1–3. Dio's statement that Antony's fleet had suffered from a gale the morning of the battle is surely mistaken (Reinhold, *From Republic to Principate*, 113–14), as is his suggestion that Octavian and Agrippa waited until the morning of the battle to come up with a plan.

Chapter 11: The Clash

176 *Meanwhile, underwater archaeology has discovered about thirty ancient warship rams*: Murray, "The Rostrate Façade of the Victory Monument," pp. 5–6 n.9.

176 *especially by the archaeologist William M. Murray*: Murray and Petsas, *Octavian's Campsite Memorial*, 55–56; Murray, *Age of Titans*, 38–47.

176 *the so-called* dekanaia, *or "ten-ship monument"*: Strabo, *Geography*, 7.7.6.

177 *burn some of their ships*: Plutarch, *Antony*, 64.1; Cassius Dio, *Roman History*, 50.15.4. See Plutarch, *Antony*, ed. comm., Pelling, 276.

177 *170 ships or less than 200 ships*: Florus, *Epitome*, 2.21.5; Orosius, *Against the Pagans*, 6.19.6.

177 *Yet the psychological impact of burning his tens would have been devastating*: I am indebted to Peter Yao for this argument.

177 *Perhaps Antony found it impossible to admit to himself as well that his cause was lost*: Murray, *Age of Titans*, 243.

177 *Antony and Cleopatra had their considerable war chest loaded*: Cassius Dio, *Roman History*, 50.16.3, 30.4; see, for comparison, commentary by Reinhold, *From Republic to Principate*, 106.

178 *They are supposed to have carried out the operation as secretly*: Cassius Dio, *Roman History*, 50.15.4.

178 *"Not one fugitive of the enemy should be allowed to make his escape"*: Plutarch, *Antony*, 64.4, Plutarch, *Plutarch's Lives*, vol. 9, trans. Perrin, 283, modified.

178 *Plutarch reports that a centurion approached Antony*: Plutarch, *Antony*, 64.2–4; Shakespeare, *Antony and Cleopatra*, act 3, scene 7, lines 61–66.

179 *"miserable logs of wood?"*: Plutarch, *Antony*, 64.3.

179 *it was particularly important to have combat veterans when choosing marines*: Philo, *Poliorketika* 21[98.24], cited in Murray, *Age of Titans*, 296.

180 *Dawn broke at Actium at 6:07 a.m.*: I refer to navigational twilight, "Preveza, Greece—Sunrise, Sunset, and Daylength, September 2020," Time and Date AS, accessed April 12, 2021, https://www.timeanddate.com/sun/greece /preveza?month=9&year=2020.

180 *Plutarch records that Antony made the rounds of his ships*: Plutarch, *Antony*, 65.4.

181 *Dio has Antony tout his experience and impressive record*: For Antony's speech, see Cassius Dio, *Roman History*, 50.16–23.

182 *Eutuchēs ("Prosper") and his mule, Nikon ("Victory")*: Plutarch, *Antony*, 65.5, with the ultimate source presumably being the now-lost *Memoirs* of Augustus.

183 *As the second-century AD historian Florus put it*: Florus, *Epitome*, 2.21. See in a similar vein, Livy, *Periochae,* 133; Velleius Paterculus, *Roman History*, 2.84.1; Cassius Dio, *Roman History*, 50.18.5; 23.2–3; 29.1–4.

183 *Based on the evidence of the Actium Victory Monument, a reasonable estimate*: Murray, *Age of Titans*, 236.

183 *The sources describe this fleet as "heavy"*: Appian, *Civil Wars,* 5.11.98–99; see, for comparison, Cassius Dio, *Roman History*, 50.19.3.

184 *short of rowing manpower, especially fit and healthy manpower*: Velleius Paterculus, *Roman History*, 2.84.1.

185 *Antony might have done well to mass his forces*: See the suggestion of Murray, "Reconsidering the Battle of Actium," 348–49.

185 *"Young Caesar [Octavian], on the stern"*: Virgil, *Aeneid*, trans. Dryden, 8.679–84.

186 *Agrippa kept his fleet about a mile away*: Plutarch, *Antony*, 65.6; John Carter, *The Battle of Actium* (London: Hamish Hamilton, 1970), 215–20; Murray, "Reconsidering the Battle of Actium," 350–51.

187 *eight legions and five praetorian cohorts on his ships*: Orosius, *Against the Pagans*, 6.19.8.

187 *Antony boarded twenty thousand legionaries and two thousand archers*: Plutarch, *Antony,* 64.1.

187 *the average number of deck soldiers on each side's ships*: Carter, *Battle of Actium*, 217, estimates that Antony's ships averaged about 110 to 120 deck soldiers, and Octavian's, about 90; William M. Murray, "The Ship Class of the Egadi Rams and Polybius's Account of the First Punic War," in Jeffrey G. Royal and Sebastiano Tusa, eds., *The Site of the Battle of the Aegates Islands at the End of the First Punic War: Fieldwork, Analyses and Perspectives 2005–2015* (Rome: "L'Erma" di Bretschneider, 2019), 29, estimates that Antony had 95 men per ship.

187 *Antony has left us his coin hoard of forty-one denarii*: "Actium (Greece; ACT)," American Numismatic Society online, accessed April 12, 2021,

http://numismatics.org/chrr/id/ACT; Irène Varoucha-Christodoulopoulou, "Acquistions du Musée d'Athènes," *Bulletin de Correspondance Hellénique* 84 (1960): 495–96.

187 *We might guess that the soldier buried them before the battle*: To be sure, the coins might have belonged to another of Antony's soldiers than one who fought aboard ship.

188 *Five gravestones from northeastern Italy state that the deceased was an Actium veteran*: L. J. F. Keppie, "A Note on the Title 'Actiacus,'" in *Legions and Veterans: Roman Army Papers, 1971–2000* (Stuttgart, Ger.: Franz Steiner Verlag, 2000), 97–98.

188 *the only battle in Roman history to give its name to its veterans*: Octavian and his propagandists might have had in mind Marathon, the Greek battle whose veterans proudly bore the label "Marathon Fighters" (*marathonomachoi*).

189 *recalls a Gaius Billienus*: See "Billienus, C.," in Cancik et al., *Brill's New Pauly*.

189 *One of them, Lucius Sempronius Atratinus, actually served Antony as an officer*: See "Sempronius," ibid.

189 *he shares it with a Latin grammarian of the era*: G. Funaioli, ed., *Grammaticae Romanae fragmenta* (Leipzig, Ger.: Teubner, 1907), 491–92.

189 *Judging from a mosaic illustration*: Nile mosaic, Palestrina, Italy.

190 *around noon, the sea breeze began to blow*: Plutarch, *Antony*, 65.5.

191 *"Moving they fight"*: Virgil, *Aeneid*, trans. Dryden, 8.689–90.

191 *An account of the battles of the Sicilian War*: Appian, *Civil Wars*, 5.106–8, 118–21.

192 *The men on shore at Actium shouted out orders*: Cassius Dio, *Roman History*, 50.32.1.

192 *Antony's men were too weak, tired, and few in number to deliver much of a blow*: As suggested by Murray, "Reconsidering the Battle of Actium," 342, and *Age of Titans*, 241.

192 *a tactic of deception*: Sheppard, *Actium 31 BC*, 78.

192 *"iron hand"*: Cassius Dio, *Roman History*, 50.32.5.

Chapter 12: The Golden Ship with Purple Sails

194 *The queen waited for just the right moment*: Murray, "Reconsidering the Battle of Actium," 353.

195 *"She called to the winds"*: Virgil, *Aeneid*, 8.707–8.

195 *The time was between two and three in the afternoon*: Carter, *Battle of Actium*, 224.

195 *raising the purple sail on her golden ship*: Florus, *Epitome*, 2.21.11.8; see, for comparison, Pliny, *Natural History*, 19.5.22, and Plutarch, *Antony*, 60.3.

195 *The sources agree that she led the breakout*: Plutarch, *Antony*, 66.5; Cassius Dio, *Roman History*, 50.32.1–3; Velleius Paterculus, *Roman History*, 2.85.3; Florus, *Epitome*, 2.21.11.8.

195 *Josephus, writing a little more than a century after the battle*: Josephus, *Against Apion*, 2.59.

195 *Cassius Dio, writing more than a century after Josephus*: Cassius Dio, *Roman History*, 50.32.1–3.

195 *"Yon ribrauded nag of Egypt"*: Shakespeare, *Antony and Cleopatra*, act 4, scene 10, lines 13–18.

196 *Plutarch says that they were too amazed*: Plutarch, *Antony*, 66.6.

196 *Josephus implies that by treacherously deserting Antony*: Josephus, *Against Apion*, 2.59.

196 *Velleius Paterculus, by contrast, puts the blame squarely on Antony*: Velleius Paterculus, *History of Rome*, 2.85.3.

196 *Plutarch has it both ways*: Plutarch, *Antony*, 66.7–8.

197 *Cassius Dio, on the other hand, gives Antony a break*: Cassius Dio, *Roman History*, 50.33.3.

197 *Antony, like Cleopatra, moved with a precision and decisiveness*: Plutarch, *Antony*, 66.8–67.1.

197 *she recognized him and raised a signal*: Plutarch, *Antony*, 67.1.

197 *the* echeneïs, *or "ship detainer"*: Pliny, *Natural History*, 32.2–4; Aristotle, *History of Animals*, 2.14.

198 *they raised their sails and threw their towers into the sea*: Cassius Dio, *Roman History*, 50.33.4.

198 *Naval history has known more successful breakouts*: For example, the escape of most of the Swedish fleet from the "Vyborg Gauntlet" (1790) or most of the allied fleet from the siege of Toulon (1793). In both cases, the successful escapees suffered heavy losses.

198 *arguably left Greece with, at most, about ninety warships*: Murray, "Reconsidering the Battle of Actium," 346–47.

198 *Eurycles of Sparta*: Plutarch, *Antony*, 68.2–4; *Plutarch, Antony*, ed. comm., Pelling, in the same location. See, for comparison, Cassius Dio, *Roman History*, 51.1.4.

199 *Eurycles's story of avenging his murdered father, Lachares, sounds suspiciously like Octavian's story*: I am indebted to Philip de Souza for this suggestion, personal communication to author, November 22, 2019.

199 *it continued for what seemed like a long time*: Plutarch, *Antony*, 68.1; Velleius Paterculus, *History of Rome*, 2.85.4; Suetonius, *Augustus*, 17.2.

199 *practical considerations tend to confirm that the fight continued*: For the argument, see Jacqueline Leroux, "Les Problèmes stratégiques de la bataille d'Actium," *Recherches de philologie et de linguistique* 2 (1968) 52–55; Murray, "Reconsidering the Battle of Actium," 346–47, 353–54.

199 *most of Antony's men didn't even know that their leader had fled*: Plutarch, *Antony*, 68.3.

200 *Velleius adds that Octavian repeatedly shouted out the truth*: Velleius Paterculus, *History of Rome*, 2.85.4.

200 *Agrippa and Octavian had not yet won the battle*: Cassius Dio, *Roman History*, 50.34.1.

200 *not unprecedented for Romans to use fire as a weapon at sea*: Flaming projectiles had been used successfully in the Philippi campaign of 42 BC. Appian, *Civil Wars,* 4.115; William Ledyard Rodgers, *Greek and Roman Naval Warfare: A Study of Strategy, Tactics, and Ship Design from Salamis (480 B.C.) to Actium (31 B.C.)* (Annapolis, MD: United States Naval Institute, 1937), 494.

200 *the use of fire at Actium*: Cassius Dio, *Roman History*, 50.34–35; Horace, *Odes*, 1.37.13; Florus, *Epitome*, 2.21.6; Servius (Maurus Servius Honoratus), *Commentary on Virgil's Aeneid*, 8.682; Virgil, *Aeneid*, 8.694; see, for comparison, Appian, *Civil Wars,* 5.121.

201 *Dio notes an interesting vignette*: Cassius Dio, *Roman History*, 50.34.4. I am indebted to Adrienne Mayor, research scholar, Classics and History and Philosophy of Science, Stanford University, and to Dr. Simon Cotton, Department of Chemistry, University of Birmingham, email of July 17, 2020.

202 *Sharks are no longer common in the Mediterranean, but*: See Joshua Rapp Learn, "Historical Art Paints a Picture of Past Shark Abundance," Hakai, last modified May 22, 2018, https://www.hakaimagazine.com/features/historical-art -paints-picture-past-shark-abundance/.

202 *Antony's men began to surrender around four in the afternoon*: Plutarch, *Antony,* 68.1; Cassius Dio, *Roman History*, 50.34.5.

202 *They did so reluctantly*: Plutarch, *Antony,* 68.1; Velleius Paterculus, *History of Rome*, 2.85.5.

202 *Octavian spent the night on his liburnian*: Suetonius, *Augustus*, 17.

203 *Octavian claimed later to have captured 300 warships*: Plutarch, *Antony*, 68.1.

203 *Plutarch reports five thousand deaths in Antony's fleet*: Ibid.

203 *Orosius puts the number of deaths at twelve thousand*: Orosius, *Against the Pagans*, 6.19.12.

203 *Roman corpses floating in the sea at Actium*: Propertius, *Elegies,* 2.15.41, trans. Jasper Griffin, "Propertius and Antony," *Journal of Roman Studies* 67 (1977): 19.

203 *"continually yielded up the purple and gold-bespangled spoils"*: Florus, *Epitome*, 2.21.11.7, in Florus, *Epitome of Roman History*, trans. E. S. Forster (Cambridge, MA: Harvard University Press, 1929), 327.

203 *Octavian's men hailed him as imperator*: Orosius, *Against the Pagans*, 6.19.14; *Inscriptiones Latinae Selectae* 79.

204 *"They wanted this"* (hoc voluerunt): Suetonius, *Caesar*, 30.

204 *Octavian is supposed to have addressed the men on Antony's ships energetically*: Velleius Paterculus, *Roman History*, 2.85.3–5.

204 *"Apollo, from his Actian height"*: Virgil, *Aeneid*, trans. Dryden, 8.704–6.

207 *Antony sat depressed alone on the prow of the* Antonias: Plutarch, *Antony,* 67.1, 5.

207 *Virgil imagines her leaving Actium pale*: Virgil, *Aeneid*, 8.709.

207 *The commander and the queen were reconciled, the story goes*: Plutarch, *Antony,* 67.6.

207 *Cleopatra's maids patched up the quarrel between the imperator and the queen*:
     Ibid.
208 *Antony wrote a letter to Theophilus*: Ibid., 68.9.
208 *Theophilus's son, Hipparchus*: Ibid., 68.10; Pliny, *Natural History,* 35.200.
208 *Not everyone around the defeated couple at Taenarum was trustworthy*: Cassius
     Dio, *Roman History*, 51.5.3.
209 *According to the pro-Octavian tradition*: Ibid., 51.1.5; Plutarch, *Antony,* 68.5;
     Velleius Paterculus, *Roman History*, 2.85.6.
209 *Octavian proposed a generous settlement*: Keppie, "Antony's Legions," 81–83;
     L. J. F. Keppie, *The Making of the Roman Army: From Republic to Empire*
     (Totowa, NJ: Barnes & Noble Books, 1984): 134–36.

Chapter 13: "I Preferred to Save Rather Than to Destroy"

212 *"Wars, both civil and foreign"*: Res Gestae Divi Augusti 3, trans. Frederick W.
     Shipley, *Velleius Paterculus and Res Gestae Divi Augusti* (London: W. Heine-
     man, 1955), 349.
212 *Octavian's "sole possession of all power"*: Cassius Dio, *Roman History*, 51.1.1;
     trans. M. Reinhold, *From Republic to Principate*, 118.
212 *the audacious vow that he had sworn at the age of nineteen*: Cicero, *Letters to At-*
     ticus, 16.15.3.
213 *Romans were more spirited in defeat than in victory*: For the sources, see Carlin
     A. Barton, *Roman Honor: The Fire in the Bones* (Berkeley: University of Cal-
     ifornia Press, 2001), 50.
214 *There was talk of Antony and Cleopatra going to Hispania*: Cassius Dio, *Roman*
     History, 51.6.3.
214 *Octavian fortified positions on the coast of Hispania*: Osgood, *Caesar's Legacy*,
     387–88, plus Dessau, *Inscriptiones Latinae Selectae*, 2672; Adrian Keith Golds-
     worthy, *Antony and Cleopatra* (New Haven, CT: Yale University Press, 2010),
     loc. 6076 + 6076n7 of 8957, Kindle e-book.
214 *either to deceive Octavian or to murder him*: Cassius Dio, *Roman History*, 51.6.4.
216 *"Let it be recorded in the* fasti *[official records] that Caesar turned down the*
     crown": Cicero, *Philippics,* 2.85–87.
217 Speuda bradēos, *Greek for "make haste slowly"*: Suetonius, *Augustus*, 25.4.
217 *Octavian claimed to have offered pardon to Roman citizens*: Augustus, *Res Ges-*
     tae, 3.
218 "Victoria vero fuit clementissima": Velleius Paterculus, *Roman History,* 2.86.2.
218 *Dio, writing two centuries later*: Cassius Dio, *Roman History*, 51.2.4, 51.16.1.
218 *The names of seven high-profile victims have survived*: Ibid., 51.2.4–6; Velleius
     Paterculus, *Roman History,* 2.87.3; Reinhold, *From Republic to Principate*, 124,
     for the sources.
218 *among the executed is Gaius Scribonius Curio*: Cassius Dio, *Roman History*,
     51.2.5; Syme, *Roman Revolution*, 299.

219 *In spring 30 BC he sailed to the island of Rhodes*: Flavius Josephus, *The Jewish War*, 1.391–92, and *Jewish Antiquities*, 15.187–195.

220 *Arruntius had fled Rome disguised as a centurion*: Appian, *Civil Wars,* 4.46; Velleius Paterculus, *Roman History,* 2.77.2.

220 *a man of old-fashioned gravitas*: Velleius Paterculus, *Roman History,* 2.86.2.

220 *Surely it also occurred to Octavian*: There is no evidence for the delicious theory of Syme, *Roman Revolution*, 297, that the pardon was a reward for Sosius's having betrayed Antony's fleet in the battle.

220 *A few years earlier*: Josephus, *Jewish War*, 1. 1.353, 357; Barton, *Roman Honor*, 144.

220 *he held a prestigious if relatively powerless priesthood*: In 17 BC. *Corpus Inscriptionum Latinarum* (Berlin: Berlin-Brandenburgische Akademie der Wissenschaften, 1863–) vol. 6: 32323. See "Sosius," in Cancik et al., *New Pauly*.

220 *Another of Octavian's pardons*: The people's tribune was one Gaius Furnius. See Reinhold, *From Republic to Principate*, 124.

221 *Octavian "made friends with the Greeks"*: Plutarch, *Antony,* 68.6.

221 *but most received generous treatment*: Ibid.; Dio Chrysostom, *Orations,* 31.66; G. W. Bowersock, *Augustus and the Greek World* (Oxford: Clarendon Press, 1965), 85n4; Osgood, *Caesar's Legacy*, 385–86.

221 *initiating him into the cult of the Mysteries*: Cassius Dio, *Roman History*, 51.4.1, 54.9.10; Suetonius, *Augustus*, 93; Plutarch, *Antony,* 23.2; *Plutarch, Antony,* ed. comm., Pelling, 176.

222 *One lucky city was Rhosus*: On Rhosus, Seleucus, and Octavian, see Osgood, *Caesar's Legacy*, 375–77, 386, with references.

222 *In early 30 BC Octavian had to hurry back to Italy*: Plutarch, *Antony*, 73.2; Suetonius, *Augustus*, 17.3; Cassius Dio, *Roman History*, 51.3–5.1.

223 *The trip would take an estimated eight days*: "Orbis: Stanford Geospatial Network," http://orbis.stanford.edu.

223 *"the greater part of the populace and still others"*: Cassius Dio, *Roman History*, 51.4.4, translated by Cassius Dio Cocceianus, Earnest Cary, and Herbert Baldwin Foster, *Dio's Roman History*, vol. 6 (London: W. Heinemann, 1914): 13.

224 *He put up his own property for auction*: Cassius Dio, *Roman History*, 51.5.2.

224 *Antony and Cleopatra learned of Octavian's departure and return at the same time*: Ibid., 51.4.7–8.

224 *Lepidus the Younger, was accused of conspiring to assassinate Octavian*: Velleius Paterculus, *History of Rome*, 2.88.

Chapter 14: Passage to India

230 *Pinarius had issued coins*: "Filters," American Numismatic Society online, accessed April 12, 2021, http://numismatics.org/search/results?q=issuer_facet:%22L.%20Pinarius%20Scarpus%22&lang=en.

230 *Marcus Antonius Aristocrates*: Jean-Sébastien Balzat and Benjamin W. Mills, "M. Antonius Aristocrates: Provincial Involvement with Roman Power in the Late 1st Century B.C.," *Hesperia: The Journal of the American School of Classical Studies at Athens* 82.4 (2013): 651–72.

230 *Plutarch is full of talk of Antony's depression*: Plutarch, *Antony*, 67.1, 5–6.

231 *Antony built himself a refuge on a jetty*: Ibid., 69.6-70.8; Plutarch, *Antony*, ed. comm., Pelling, 291.

231 *she sailed into the harbor with the prows of her ships garlanded*: Cassius Dio, *Roman History*, 51.5.4.

233 *"Big book, big bad"*: Callimachus, in Rudolf Pfeiffer, *Callimachus*, vol. 1: *Fragmenta* (Oxford: Clarendon Press, 1949), frag. 465, p. 353.

234 *A carved sandstone stele*: Walker and Higgs, *Cleopatra*, cat. no. 173, pp. 174–75.

234 *Cleopatra had a new fleet built*: Plutarch, *Antony*, 69.3–5; Cassius Dio, *Roman History*, 51.7.1.

235 *We know of three ancient accounts*: See Plutarch, *Antony*, ed. comm., Pelling, 26, 28–29, 294, 296.

236 *Plutarch and Cassius Dio are largely in agreement*: Cassius Dio, *Roman History*, 51.6.4–6, 7.1, 8.1–6, 9.5–6; Plutarch, *Antony*, 72–73.

237 *Cleopatra had gathered it in a new structure*: Plutarch, *Antony*, 74.2; Cassius Dio, *Roman History*, 51.6.5–6.

238 *Thyrsus*: Ibid., 73.1–5; ibid., 51.8.6–7, 9.5.

240 *Augustan poets claim that he took it by storm*: Propertius, *Elegies*, 3.9.55; *Carmen de bello actiaco*, col. ii., 14–19.

240 *Dio is more persuasive when he writes*: Cassius Dio, *Roman History*, 51.9.5–6.

240 *Plutarch refers more circumspectly to a report*: Plutarch, *Antony*, 74.1.

241 *there were many ways to die*: Ibid., 75.1.

242 *his goal was a glorious death*: Ibid., 75.4.

242 *Caesar attended a dinner party in Rome*: See Barry Strauss, *The Death of Caesar: History's Most Famous Assassination* (New York: Simon & Schuster, 2015), 105–6.

242 *The next scene is one of Plutarch's finest touches*: Plutarch, *Antony*, 75.4–6.

243 *"The God Abandons Antony"*: *"Apoleipein O Theos Antonion,"* Constantine Cavafy and Geōrgios P. Savvidēs, *Poiēmata* (Athēnai: Ikaros, 1984), 24; first published, 1911. Trans. Barry Strauss.

Chapter 15: The Bite of the Asp

244 *Dio states that she had, while Plutarch notes*: Cassius Dio, *Roman History*, 51.10.4; Plutarch, *Antony*, 76.3.

245 *had bodyguards and a taster*: Pliny, *Natural History*, 21.9.12, claims that Antony distrusted Cleopatra enough that he insisted on having a taster whenever they ate and drank together.

245 *flee the palace to her nearby mausoleum*: Plutarch, *Antony*, 76.4; Cassius Dio,

Roman History, 51.10.6. The site of Cleopatra's mausoleum is not known, but many scholars believe that it was near the palace; see, for example, Owen Jarus, "Where Is Cleopatra's Tomb?," Live Science, last modified July 27, 2020, https://www.livescience.com/where-is-cleopatra-tomb.html.

245 *and prepared to die*: For the sources on Antony's suicide, see Plutarch, *Antony*, 76.3; Cassius Dio, *Roman History*, 51.10.4; Livy, *Periochae*, 133.

245 *the freedman who had done his duty by killing his patron Cassius*: Plutarch, *Brutus*, 43.8. The freedman's name was Pindarus.

246 *Dio thought that she heard an uproar*: Cassius Dio, *Roman History*, 51.10.8.

246 *Plutarch describes the bizarre scene*: See, for comparison, ibid., 51.8–9; Plutarch, *Antony*, 76.2–3.

249 *Octavian personally viewed Antony's corpse*: Suetonius, *Augustus*, 17.4.

249 *Requests are supposed to have come in from many kings and generals*: Plutarch, *Antony*, 82.1; Roller, *Cleopatra*, 146.

249 *According to one source, Antony's corpse was embalmed*: Cassius Dio, *Roman History*, 51.15.1; Plutarch, *Antony*, 84.3, refers to burial.

250 *Octavian entrusted the mission to Gaius Proculeius*: I follow the more detailed version of Plutarch, *Antony,* 78.5–79.6. For a different and more compressed version, see Cassius Dio, *Roman History*, 51.11.4–5.

250 *Octavian had turned to Proculeius and asked him to take Octavian's life*: Pliny, *Natural History,* 7.46; Suetonius, *Augustus*, 16.3.

250 *she made him speak to her through the bars of the gate*: Whether they spoke in Greek, Latin, or through an interpreter is unknown.

253 *"her beauty was unable to prevail over his self-control"*: Florus, *Epitome*, 2.21.11.9; Florus, *Epitome*, trans. Forster, 327.

253 *jewelry for his sister, Octavia, and his wife, Livia*: Dio has Cleopatra send the gifts for Livia to Octavian after the meeting, in order to lull him into complacency about the danger of suicide. Cassius Dio, *Roman History*, 51.13.3.

254 *"I will not be shown in a triumph"*: Livy, *Fragment* 54, plus notes of Acron and Porphryion.

256 *"No one knows the truth"*: Plutarch, *Antony,* 86.4.

256 *"No one knows for certain"*: Cassius Dio, *Roman History*, 51.14.1.

257 *"A fine deed, this, Charmion!"*: Plutarch, *Antony*, 85.7; Plutarch, *Plutarch's Lives*, vol. 9 trans. Perrin, 329, translation modified.

257 *The earliest sources speak of two snakes*: Virgil, *Aeneid*, 8.697; Horace, *Odes*, 1.37.27; see, for example, Florus, *Epitome*, 2.21.11, and Propertius, *Elegies*, 3.11.53.

258 *A baby Egyptian cobra*: Regarding size, see "Cobra," San Diego Zoo Wildlife Alliance online, accessed April 12, 2021, https://animals.sandiegozoo.org /animals/cobra.

258 *to kill an adult human*: On this and other matters involving a cobra bite, I rely on a personal communication from Harry W. Greene, author of *Snakes: The Evolution of Mystery in Nature* (Berkeley: University of California Press,

1997) and emeritus professor, Department of Ecology and Evolutionary Biology, Cornell University, September 13, 2020. I am also grateful to Adrienne Mayor, research scholar, Classics and History and Philosophy of Science, Stanford University.

258 *in order to experiment with various deadly poisons*: Plutarch, *Antony*, 6–8; Cassius Dio, *Roman History*, 51.11.2; Aelian, *On the Nature of Animals*, 9.11; Galen 14.235–36; *Carmen de Bello Actiaco* col. v 36–43; Plutarch, *Antony*, ed. comm., Pelling, 296–97.

260 *"Amid her ruin'd halls she stood"*: Horace, *Odes*, 1.37; John Conington, trans. *The Odes and Carmen Saeculare of Horace*, 3rd ed. (London: Bell and Daldy, 1865), 38.

Chapter 16: "I Wanted to See a King"

261 *"The people," writes Plutarch, "were beside themselves with fear"*: Plutarch, *Antony,* 80.2.

262 *He said that he would spare the people of Alexandria*: Ibid., 80.1; Cassius Dio, *Roman History,* 51.16.3–4; Themistius, *Orations*, 8.108b–c, 173b–c; Julian, *To Themistius*, 265c; *Caesar*, 21.326b; *Epistles*, 51.433d–34a.

262 *Philostratus made such a public spectacle*: Plutarch, *Antony,* 80.30–4; Plutarch, *Antony*, ed. comm., Pelling, 311–12.

262 *"In history, only a few lines are found about you"*: C. P. Cavafy, "Caesarion," ll.16–17, trans. Barry Strauss.

262 *Two statues in the Greco-Egyptian style*: Walker and Higgs, *Cleopatra*, cat. nos. 171–72, pp. 172–74.

263 *traditional, pharaonic-style reliefs*: See the granite stele of Cleopatra and Caesarion from Karnak, now in the Museo delle Antichità Egizie, cat. 1764, in Turin, Italy, in Giovanni Gentili, ed., *Cleopatra: Roma e l'incantesimo dell'Egitto* (Milan, It.: Skira, 2013), cat. no. 17, 100–102, 251–52.

263 *"several of the Greeks relate"*: Suetonius, *Caesar*, 52.2.

263 *The sources agree that Caesar was tall*: On Caesar's features, see Jeremy Paterson, "Caesar the Man," in *A Companion to Julius Caesar*, ed. Miriam Griffin (Chichester, UK: John Wiley & Sons, 2015), 126–27.

264 *he gave her permission to call the child by his name*: Suetonius, *Caesar*, 52.1.

264 *"Heir of the God that saves"*: Michael Gray-Fow, "What to Do with Caesarion?," *Greece & Rome* 61, no. 1 (2014): 38n3.

265 *Nicolaus of Damascus, for instance, who taught his half siblings*: Nicolaus, *Life of Augustus and Autobiography,* ed. Toher , 3–6, 288.

265 *Cleopatra had him enrolled in the ephebate*: Plutarch, *Antony,* 71.3; Cassius Dio, *Roman History,* 51.6.1.

268 *Antyllus, like Caesarion, was betrayed*: For the details of the end of Antyllus, see Plutarch, *Antony,* 81; Cassius Dio, *Roman History,* 51.6.2, 15.5; Suetonius, *Augustus*, 17.5.

268 *and who did so with an elegant irony*: Plutarch, *Antony,* 81.5.

269 *For eighteen days, if an ancient source can be believed*: Clement of Alexandria, *Stromateis,* 21.129.1–2.

270 *Octavian showed his respect to Alexander's mummy*: Cassius Dio, *Roman History,* 51.16.5; Suetonius, *Augustus*, 18.1.

270 *"I wanted to see a king, not corpses"*: Ibid.

271 *It began, on the very first day*: Dates in this paragraph are based on the Roman calendar *in use at the time*, not the one later revised by Augustus, beginning in 8 BC. For the details, see T. C. Skeat, "The Last Days of Cleopatra: A Chronological Problem," *Journal of Roman Studies* 43 (1953): 98, 100.

271 *"delivered the republic from a most severe danger"*: *Corpus Inscriptionum Latinarum,* 2nd edn., vol. 1: p.323 and 244 = *IIt.* 13.2.191 (Fasti Amiternini); Cassius Dio, *Roman History*, 51.19.4–6; Reinhold, *From Republic to Principate*, 148–49.

Chapter 17: The Triumph of Augustus

274 *by displaying booty from Alexandria on all three days*: Cassius Dio, *Roman History* 51.21.7–8.

274 *The frieze decorated the altar at Augustus's Victory Monument in Nicopolis*: Konstantinos Zachos, *An Archaeological Guide to Nicopolis. Rambling Through the Historical, Sacred, and Civic Landscape*, Monuments of Nicopolis 10 (Athens: DIPCA–Scientific Committee of Nicopolis, 2015), 60, 66–68; Zachos, "The Tropaeum of the Sea-battle of Actium at Nikopolis: An Interim Report," *Journal of Roman Archaeology* 16 (2003): 90–92; Zachos, "The Triumph of Augustus on the Actium Monument at Nicopolis" (lecture, September 24, 2013), https://www.youtube.com/watch?v=LmaOgpXJHMA.

274 *Another sculpted relief from this era*: A frieze from the Temple of Apollo Sosianus, today on display in the Centrale Montemartini, Rome.

275 *Octavian was accompanied by two young men*: Suetonius, *Tiberius,* 6.4.

275 *Two younger children stood beside Octavian*: Mary Beard, *The Roman Triumph* (Cambridge, MA: Harvard University Press, 2009), 224–25.

275 *Although it was customary for the consul and the magistrates to lead the procession*: Cassius Dio, *Roman History,* 51.21.9.

275 *Adiatorix, the ruler of a small kingdom*: Strabo, *Geography,* 12.3.6, 35; Robert Alan Gurval, *Actium and Augustus: The Politics and Emotions of Civil War* (Ann Arbor: University of Michigan Press, 1995), 28–29.

276 *Alexander of Emesa*: Cassius Dio, *Roman History*, 51.2.2; Gurval, *Actium*, 29.

276 *A Roman poet claims that captured ships' beaks:* Propertius, *Elegies*, 2.1.31–34.

276 *the beaks were attached to the front of the Temple of the Deified Julius*: Cassius Dio, *Roman History*, 51.19.2.

276 *"The victor to the gods his thanks express'd"*: Virgil, *Aeneid,* trans. Dryden, 8.714–720.

277 *The two older children of Antony and Cleopatra appeared*: Cassius Dio, *Roman History*, 51.21.9.

278 *Octavian had received his political authority from a military victory*: Ibid., 51.22.1–2.

280 *he was stepping down from power*: Ibid., 53.2–12.

282 *"a cunning fox imitating a noble lion"*: Horace, *Satires*, 2.3.185–86.

283 *"empire without end"*: Virgil, *Aeneid* 1.279.

285 *they chose to name a month after him*: Cassius Dio, *Roman History*, 55.6.6–7; Suetonius, *Augustus*, 31; Macrobius (Macrobius Ambrosius Theodosius), *Saturnalia*, 1.12.35.

286 *Since Imperator Caesar Augustus entered into his first consulship*: Macrobius, *Saturnalia*, my translation, 1.12.35.

286 *Sextus Pacubius, a tribune of the people*: Otherwise unknown. Ibid.

287 *a man whose virtues everyone acknowledged*: P. Köln, 4701, lines 12–14, in Köln et al., *Kölner Papyri* (Wiesbaden: VS Verlag für Sozialwissenschaften, 1987), 113–14.

288 *Cleopatra Selene died probably in 5 BC*: Roller, *World of Juba II and Kleopatra Selene*, 251.

288 *Octavia C F Soror Augusti*: "Académie des inscriptions & belles-lettres," *L'Année Épigraphique,* Année 1928 (Paris: Presses Universitaires de France, 1929): 26, number 88.

289 *reminders of Augustus's conquest of Egypt*: See M. E. J. J. van Aerde, *Egypt and the Augustan Cultural Revolution, An Interpretative Archaeological Overview,* Babesch Supplements, 38 (Leuven, Belg.: Peeters, 2019).

290 *it began to be known as the Eternal City*: Stephanie Malia Hom, "Consuming the View: Tourism, Rome, and the Topos of the Eternal City," *Annali d'Italianistica*, "Capital City: Rome 1870–2010," 28 (2010): 91–116.

290 *"I found a Rome of bricks"*: Cassius Dio, *Roman History*, 56.30.3.

Illustration Credits

1. bpk Bildagentur / Muenzkabinett, Staatliche Museen, Berlin, Germany/ Reinhard Saczewski/ Art Resource, NY

2. Metropolitan Museum of Art

3. Metropolitan Museum of Art

4. bpk Bildagentur / Antikensammlung, Staatliche Museen, Berlin, Germany/ Christoph Gerigk/ Art Resource, NY

5. Katherine K. Adler Memorial Fund/The Art Institute of Chicago

6. bpk Bildagentur / Muenzkabinett, Staatliche Museen, Berlin, Germany/ Dirk Sonnewald/ Art Resource, NY

7. Rowan/Wikimedia Commons

8. Metropolitan Museum of Art

9. Metropolitan Museum of Art

10. Photo by Matthew Sears

11. Photo by Barry Strauss

12. Scala / Art Resource, NY

13. Rijksmuseum, Amsterdam

14. Image courtesy of Konstantinos L. Zachos

15. Photo by Barry Strauss

16. Illustration by Richard Scott. Image courtesy of William M. Murray

17. Metropolitan Museum of Art

18. Metropolitan Museum of Art

Index

Page numbers in *italics* refer to maps.

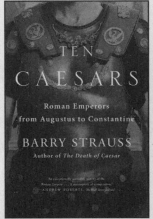
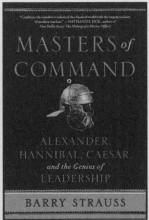
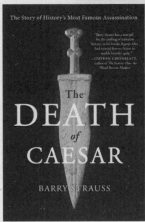
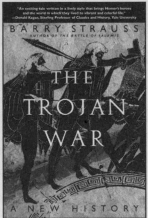
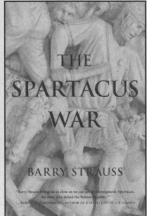